Daylighting Performance and Design

Gregg D. Ander, AIA

VAN NOSTRAND REINHOLD

I⫯P™ A Division of International Thomson Publishing Inc.

New York ∎ Albany ∎ Bonn ∎ Boston ∎ Detroit ∎ London ∎ Madrid ∎ Melbourne
Mexico City ∎ Paris ∎ San Francisco ∎ Singapore ∎ Tokyo ∎ Toronto

Cover photo courtesy of Timothy Hursley
Cover design: Paul Costello

Copyright © 1995 by Van Nostrand Reinhold
I(T)P ™   A division of International Thomson Publishing Inc.
           The ITP logo is a trademark under license

Printed in the United States of America
For more information, contact:

Van Nostrand Reinhold
115 Fifth Avenue
New York, NY 10003

International Thomson Publishing GmbH
Königswinterer Strasse 418
53227 Bonn
Germany

International Thomson Publishing Europe
Berkshire House 168-173
High Holborn
London WCIV 7AA
England

International Thomson Publishing Asia
221 Henderson Road #05-10
Henderson Building
Singapore 0315

Thomas Nelson Australia
102 Dodds Street
South Melbourne, 3205
Victoria, Australia

International Thomson Publishing Japan
Hirakawacho Kyowa Building, 3F
2-2-1 Hirakawacho
Chiyoda-ku, 102 Tokyo
Japan

Nelson Canada
1120 Birchmount Road
Scarborough, Ontario
Canada M1K 5G4

International Thomson Editores
Campos Eliseos 385, Piso 7
Col. Polanco
11560 Mexico D.F. Mexico

2   3   4   5   6   7   8   9   10   BBR   01   00   99   98   97   96   95

Library of Congress Cataloging-in-Publication Data
Ander, Gregg D.
      Daylighting performance and design / by Gregg D. Ander.
            p.   cm.
      Includes bibliographical references and index.
      ISBN 0-442-01921-1
      1. Daylighting.   2. Architectural design.   3. Light in
      architecture.   I. Title.
NA2794.A53   1995   94-45674
729′.28-dc20   CIP

To Lisa, Jason, Jesse, and Erik

FOREWORD

The ebb and flow of professional interest in daylight over the last 50 years mimics the diurnal cycle of the sun. The 1990s are witnessing a resurgence of interest in daylighted buildings, driven in part by a renewed interest in the welfare of occupants within buildings and by longer term, broader concerns encompassed within the "Green Buildings" and sustainable design movements.

The creation of well-daylighted buildings remains a challenge that is surprisingly difficult to meet. Flooding a building with daylight requires no particular architectural skill. A more appropriate response must balance the needs of owners, occupants, and society by integrating concerns for aesthetics, amenity, comfort, energy efficiency, and cost effectiveness. Great architectural designs have not always been environmentally friendly and elegantly engineered solutions sometimes fail to meet basic human needs. Design teams need better and more relevant information to address this problem.

Daylighting Performance and Design should prove useful to design professionals who are striving to satisfy the human preference for view and daylight while meeting our responsibilities to energy efficiency and sustainable development. It establishes performance potentials for good daylighting designs, balanced with a sense of what has been accomplished to date. The useful data and guidelines provided within the document are complemented with recommendations for seeking additional assistance elsewhere. It should be a valuable resource for architects, engineers, lighting designers, and energy consultants.

Daylighting Performance and Design will stimulate the uninitiated to explore the potentials of daylighting, guide the novice to tools and techniques that will help explore alternative design options, and assist the experienced designer in stretching the boundaries of past design solutions.

Stephen Selkowitz
Lawrence Berkeley Laboratory

Architecture connects us to daily life, clarifies our relationships with one another and to the realities of place and time. We would do the opposite—obscure and isolate—only out of neglect or indifference or error.

Among other things, architecture is about fit, revelation, and prediction. It should fit with what is there and what transpires, and it should reveal what is there and how events change. And the fit and revelation are not just *now*, at the start of design, but over time, in the future; thus, prediction.

Nothing is more important to architecture in this process than daylight. Daylight does much more than merely allow us to carry on the tasks and activities we built the building for; it reveals the passage of the day and tells us something about the quality of the day outside the building. It informs and connects.

Traditionally, architects have dealt with daylight in buildings qualitatively, intuitively, and instinctively—simply because the tools were not available to deal with it quantitatively. It is not a question of one or the other, of the quantitative or the qualitative, but of both; we can now, thanks to research and experimental application, approach daylighting qualitatively and quantitatively at the same time.

Daylighting Performance and Design balances elegantly and straightforwardly that essential pair, the qualitative and quantitative.

Joseph Esherick, FAIA
AIA Gold Medal Winner

ACKNOWLEDGMENTS

The following individuals are recognized for their support in preparing this book: Jean Aleman, Kelly J. Andereck, Bill Anton, James E. Craddock, Greg Cunningham, Stephen Dent, Donald Mauritz, Fuller Moore, Steve Selkowitz, Jonathan Starr, Barry Wasserman, Joe Wilcox, and Michael Wilde.

PREFACE

The relationship between people, daylight, and architectural form is intimate. Daylight introduces life, variation, and drama into otherwise banal spaces. Throughout the history of civilization our buildings have articulated this relationship. Daylight as a design variable, can profoundly influence building orientation, form, scale, the character of interior spaces, and the way that interior space is perceived.

This manual has been designed and assembled to address the more pragmatic issues of daylighting, such as how daylighting strategies impact a building's electric lighting system as well as the total connected electrical load. Although the potential for improved efficiency and energy savings is significant, effective daylighting design requires that time and effort be expended to solve the series of problems and issues which currently act as obstacles to the widespread use of daylighting. The building designer can add to the design palette, technical information about daylight with which the client may make cost-effective decisions.

Gregg D. Ander, AIA

CONTENTS

I use light abundantly, as you may have suspected; Light for me is the fundamental basis of architecture. I compose with light.

—Le Corbusier

Without a glass palace Life becomes a burden. Glass opens up a new age Brick building only does harm.

—Scheerbart

A room is not a room without natural light. Natural light gives the time of day and the mood of the seasons to enter.

—L. Kahn

CHAPTER 1

FUNDAMENTALS OF DAYLIGHTING

As a design feature, the use of daylighting within a building creates a more pleasing and productive atmosphere for the people within. This occurs not only because daylight provides a direct link to the outdoor environment but also because natural light supplies a perpetually evolving pattern of space illumination. Fluctuations in light levels are gradual and usually unnoticed, but the effect is one of visual interest, creating a comfortable and more stimulating environment.

However, daylighting is more than simply installing a few skylights. It is a dynamic lighting technology that involves consideration of heat gain, glare, variations in light availability, and sunlight penetration into a building. A successful design will address details such as shading devices, aperture size and spacing, glazing materials, and surface reflectance characteristics. In large measure the art and science of daylighting is not so much how to provide enough daylight as how to do so without its possible undesirable effects.

As an efficiency measure, daylighting is most effective during bright sunny afternoons when it can supplant the need for electric lighting entirely. Because an electric utility must provide enough generating capacity to serve the highest demand predicted for its service territory, daylighting has the potential not only to reduce the building's overall energy consumption but also to lower the peak demand.

Electric lighting directly accounts for approximately 20% to 25% of the total electrical energy used in the United States. In the commercial sector, lighting accounts for 37% (34% interior, 3% exterior) of electrical energy consumption (see Figure 1.1). Lighting also has an indirect impact on the total energy use because the heat generated by electric fixtures alters the loads imposed on the mechanical cooling equipment. As a rule of thumb, each unit of electric lighting contributes to an additional one-half unit of electricity for space conditioning because of the contributions from the heat generated by electric lighting. The energy savings from reduced lighting loads can directly reduce air-conditioning energy usage by an additional 10% to 20%.

There seems to be a strong interest in efficiency issues not only from a technical standpoint but also as they relate to social

Architecture is the masterly, correct and magnificent play of volumes brought together in light. Our eyes are made to see forms in light . . . cubes, cones, spheres, cylinders or pyramids are the great primary forms that light reveals to advantage. . . . It is of the very nature of the plastic arts.
LE CORBUSIER

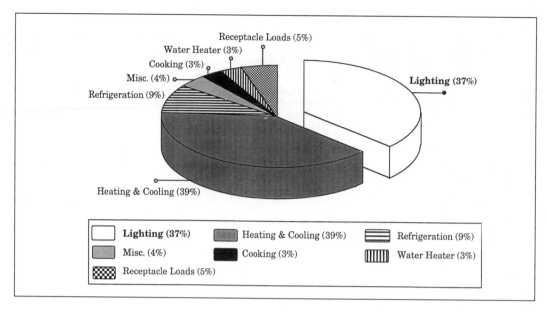

FIGURE 1.1
Commercial electricity use in the United States. (Courtesy of the Electric Power Research Institute of Palo Alto, California.)

and behavioral issues. These issues often involve enhanced comfort, satisfaction, and productivity and may even have a relationship to the number of worker's compensation claims filed against an employer. Although there is great interest in this area, there appears to be mostly anecdotal evidence in the area with few exceptions. The Center for Building Performance and Diagnostics (CBPD) at Carnegie Mellon has conducted many building surveys and postoccupancy evaluations to better understand the effect of design features on occupants. Appendix F contains a survey form developed to access the impacts of perceived comfort for a series of postoccupancy evaluations conducted at the College of Environmental Design at California Polytechnic State University at Pomona.

Daylighting may potentially play a key role in supporting "sustainable" development. As clients begin to demand sustainable solutions and the design community embraces these challenges to produce buildings that reduce environmental impacts, daylighting solutions have the opportunity to play a significant role through pollution avoidance. By virtue of improving a building's efficiency, you would expect to see a reduction in annual kilowatt hours so the amount of pollutants emitted at a utility generating station will reduce the amount of airborne pollutants including nitrogen oxide (NO_x), carbon dioxide (CO_2), and sulfur dioxide (SO_2), all of which contribute to reductions in air quality. The Environmental Protection Agency and most utilities have data on the relationship between kilowatt hours and pollution avoidance values. Table 1.1 represents the latest conversion values for the United States.

A key concern the design team confronts is visualizing various design solutions and quantifying the impacts of fenestration-related decisions. Some design firms regularly perform this type of service as a "basic service," whereas other firms consider it an additional service and obtain additional compensation to cover any added design and analysis time and sell the client based on anticipated reductions in operating

Table 1.1
Emission Factors

STATES	CO_2 (LB/KWH)	SO_2 (G/KWH)	NO_X (G/KWH)
CT, ME, MA, NH, RI, VT	1.1	4.0	1.4
NJ, NY	1.1	3.4	1.3
DE, DC, MD, PA, VA, WV	1.6	8.2	2.6
AL, FL, GA, KY, MS, NC, SC, TN	1.5	6.9	2.5
IL, IN, MI, MN, OH, WI	1.8	10.4	3.5
AR, LA, NM, OK, TX	1.7	2.2	2.5
IA, KS, MO, NE	2.0	8.5	3.9
CO, MT, ND, SD, UT, WY	2.2	3.3	3.2
AZ, CA, HI, NV	1.0	1.1	1.5
AK, ID, OR, WA	0.1	0.5	0.3
National average	1.5	5.8	2.5

costs. Many utilities offer design assistance or incentives to optimize buildings, and these may include assistance to solve for daylighting-related issues. It is important to remember that the daylighting design process involves the ideas of many disciplines, including architectural, mechanical, electrical, and lighting (see Figure 1.2). These design team members need to be brought into the process early to ensure that the concepts and ideas are carried through the entire design, construction, and operating process (see Figure 1.3). Ample opportunity exists for miscommunication throughout the daylighting system design process. The way a building is designed versus how it is built versus how it is operated is important to integrate. Building commissioning is often a critical function to ensure a building performs as designed.

Design Issues

Architects and designers who are sensitive to basic daylighting fundamentals can

FIGURE 1.2
Standard design process.

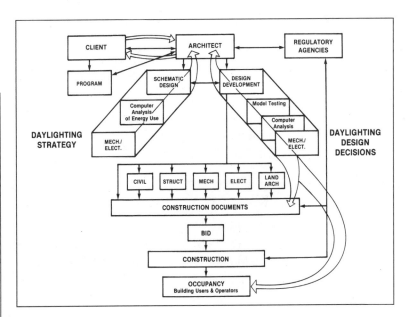

FIGURE 1.3
Integrated daylighting design process. (Courtesy of Scott Ellinwood, FAIA.)

FIGURE 1.4
Plan showing room-specific illumination requirements.

achieve an aesthetically pleasing space without sacrificing cost or creativity. An awareness of certain issues that can occur when daylighting is employed will assist in the success of an effective design.

Veiling Reflections

Veiling reflections obscure the details seen by reducing the contrast. Thus, avoid creating conditions within the building where disabling veiling reflections may occur, particularly in spaces where there are critical tasks.

There are many types of visual tasks with various degrees of criticality (see Figure 1.4). A receptionist may not require the same level of illumination as a graphic designer. Many spaces in a building can be lighted that do not require a high degree of illuminance.

Quantity

Introduce as much controlled daylight as possible, and as deeply as possible, into the building interior. Appendix B lists recommended illuminance categories and illuminance values for lighting design.

Generally the human eye can adjust to high levels of luminance without producing dis-

comfort. In fact, the more light available, the better people can see. Veiling reflections, and excessive brightness differences should be addressed.

Glare

The aim of an efficient daylighting design is not only to provide illuminance levels sufficient for good visual performance but also to maintain a comfortable and pleasing atmosphere that is appropriate to its purpose. Glare, or excessive brightness contrast within the field of view, is one aspect of lighting that can cause discomfort to the occupants of a space (see Figure 1.5).

FIGURE 1.5
Typical office glare.

Although brightness and brightness contrast are important in providing a stimulating visual environment, excessive contrast between foreground and background may disrupt the eye's ability to distinguish objects from their background and to perceive detail. The human eye can function quite well over a wide range of luminous environments, but it cannot function well if extreme levels of brightness are present in the field of view at the same time.

Some contrast in brightness levels may not be undesirable. Dull uniformity in lighting, although never harmful, can lead to tiredness and lack of attention—neither of which is compatible with a productive environment. However, it is necessary to ensure that glare is kept under control and that extreme levels of brightness are not present in the field of view at the same time.

Glare is not a design issue most of the time; it is critical only when certain viewing conditions occur. In this regard, understanding the conditions that might cause glare is the first step toward finding a design solution to deal with it or to avoid the problem altogether.

Glare is a subjective phenomenon and as such is difficult to quantify. Nonetheless, a generalized form of glare quantification can be derived by studying changes in contrast ratio. The study quantifies the average response of a large number of people to the same glare situation. This type of analysis is used to determine a glare constant for individual apertures and a glare index for all light sources in the field of view.

However, assessments of the physical factors can be correlated to the magnitude of the described sensation so that glare discomfort can be estimated. Studies of these factors have resulted in the development of glare indices, which can be utilized at the design stage to address glare discomfort

and are integral to many computer-based design tools.

Design Variables

Site Elements

Sky conditions vary the nature and quantity of the light entering a building. Three types of sky conditions are utilized to estimate illumination levels within a space.

The *overcast sky* is the most uniform type of sky condition and generally tends to change more slowly than the other types. It is defined as being a sky in which at least 80% of the sky dome is obscured by clouds. The overcast sky has a general luminance distribution that is about three times brighter at the zenith than at the horizon. The illumination produced by the overcast sky on the earth's surface may vary from several hundred footcandles to several thousand, depending on the density of the clouds (see Figure 1.6).

The *clear sky* is less bright than the overcast sky and tends to be brighter at the horizon than at the zenith. It tends to be fairly stable in luminance except for the area surrounding the sun, which changes as the sun moves. The clear sky is defined as being a sky in which no more than 30% of the sky dome is obscured by clouds. The total level of illumination produced by a clear sky varies constantly but slowly throughout the day. The illumination levels produced can range from 5,000 to 12,000 footcandles.

The *cloudy sky* has a cloud cover that may range from quite heavy to very light. The cloudy sky is defined as being a sky in which 30% to 80% of the sky dome is obscured by clouds. It usually includes widely varying luminance from one area of

The choice of a structure is synonymous with the light which gives image to that space....A plan of a building should read like a harmony of spaces in light.

L. KAHN

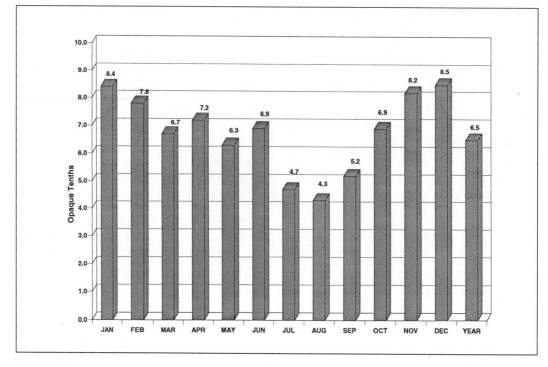

FIGURE 1.6
Typical bar graph indicating cloud cover measured in tenths. (Additional climatic data are provided in Appendix C.)

FIGURE 1.7
External obstruction that may impact available illuminance and solar heat gain.

the sky to another and tends to change quite rapidly. The cloudy sky may provide periods when direct sun reaches the building site and some periods when, for all practical purposes, the sky appears overcast.

Appendix C gives weather data for a variety of climate zones, including average clear-cloudy conditions. It is quite valuable to perform a climatic analysis to formulate proper design responses.

External obstructions surrounding a window will affect the amount of daylighting entering a space. Many of these conditions, such as cloud cover and sun position, are purely a function of the climate. External obstructions on the other hand, such as trees and other buildings can permanently alter the amount of daylight allowed to enter a window opening (see Figure 1.7). The patterns of obstruction will normally vary for each window. They can have different shapes, different positions relative to the window, and different light-blocking or reflecting characteristics.

Design Strategies

Increase Perimeter Daylight Zones

Extending the perimeter form of a building may improve the building's performance by increasing the total daylighting area. The trade-offs between an increased perimeter exposure and a compact building form are shown in Figure 1.8. The thermal impact of electric lights and the increased linear footage of window wall should be given

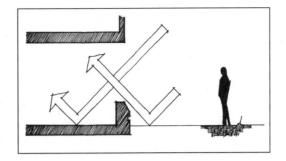

FIGURE 1.9
Section showing uncontrolled fenestration.

careful attention when these strategies are considered.

Allow Daylight Penetration High in a Space

With the location of an aperture high in a wall, deeper penetration will result. There will be less likelihood of excessive brightness in the field of view by reflecting and scattering light before it gets to task level.

Use the Idea of "Effective Aperture" for Initial Estimates of the Optimum Glazing Area

When the effective aperture, the product of the window-to-wall ratio and the visible transmittance of the glazing, is around 0.18, daylighting saturation will be achieved. Additional glazing area or light will be

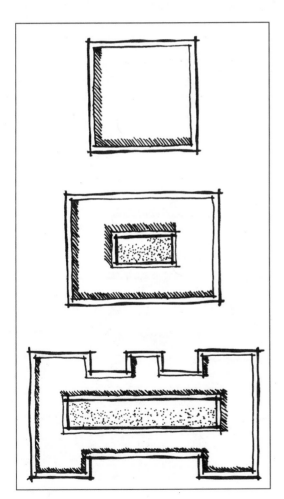

FIGURE 1.8
Articulated plans showing increased daylighting zones.

FIGURE 1.10
Section showing overhang to control direct beam.

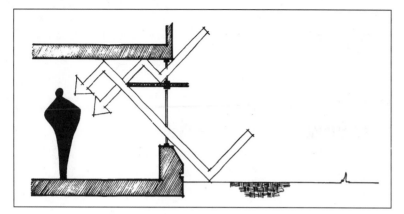

FIGURE 1.11
Section through typical light shelf.

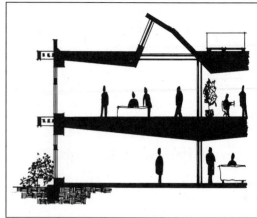

FIGURE 1.12
Building section showing sloped ceiling treatment.

counterproductive because it will increase the cooling loads more than it will reduce the lighting loads.

Reflect Daylight Within a Space to Increase Room Brightness

Although the source of daylight is the sun, surfaces and objects within a space reflect and scatter daylight. An increase in visibility and comfort can be achieved through increasing room brightness by spreading and evening out brightness patterns. A reduction in intensity occurs from reflecting and partially absorbing light throughout a space. A light shelf, if properly designed, has the potential to increase room brightness and decrease window brightness (see Figure 1.11).

Slope Ceilings to Direct More Light into a Space

Sloping the ceiling away from the fenestration area will help increase the brightness of the ceiling further into a space (see Figure 1.12).

Avoid Direct Beam Daylight on Critical Visual Tasks

Poor visibility and discomfort will result if excessive brightness differences occur in

the vicinity of critical visual tasks. It is a fallacy to believe that good daylighting design entails merely adding large apertures of glazing to a building design. Fenestration controls should be considered if direct beam illumination is undesirable (see Figure 1.13).

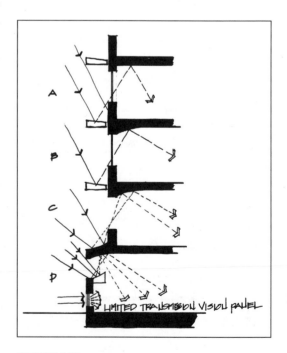

FIGURE 1.13
Building section showing fenestration treatments to control direct beam.

FIGURE 1.14
Section showing vegetation and lattice to filter daylight.

FIGURE 1.15
Exterior facade with lattice system.

Use Direct Sun Cautiously in Areas Where Noncritical Tasks Occur

Patterns of light and shadows from the sun tracking across the sky can add an exciting and dynamic feature to a space. A feeling of well-being and a sense of time and orientation often impact the occupants of such a space. However, if they are integrated poorly, the occupants may have difficulty in seeing, and, in addition, unwanted heat gain may result.

Filter Daylight

When harshness of direct light is a potential problem, filtering can be accomplished by vegetation, curtains, or louvers. This will help soften and distribute light more uniformly (see Figures 1.14 and 1.15).

Consider Other Environmental Control Systems

Fenestration systems can potentially allow light, heat, air, and sounds into a space. Ventilation; acoustics; views; electric lighting systems; and heating, ventilating, and air-conditioning (HVAC) systems all need to be considered during the design process (see Figure 1.16).

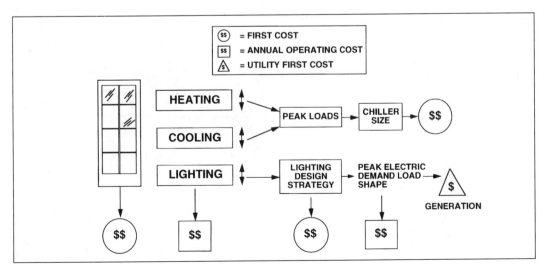

FIGURE 1.16
Glazing-related decision point diagram.

Design Elements

Several design considerations impacting light affect a building in terms of form and shape. Probably the most significant design determinant when implementing daylighting strategies is the geometry of a building's walls, ceiling, floors, windows, and how each relates to the other. An understanding of the effects of the various building elements will provide the basis for manipulating form to achieve adequate lighting levels. It is also important to understand geometric relationships in terms of lighting functions, as well as to comprehend the quantitative relationships that accompany various geometric forms. A review of measured or calculated illumination levels for various design functions will be helpful, as will the experience. Designers need to manipulate the configurations and measure the results before they can properly understand the quantitative relationships. This can be accomplished through physical model tests, computer simulations, or both.

Exterior Elements

Overhangs can be useful controls for fenestration. In addition to blocking the direct beam from the sun, they will also reduce the amount of sky seen from within a room, thus reducing the amount of diffuse skylight admitted through the opening.

Reflected light from the ground or other surfaces can also be caught by an overhang and directed back into the interior of a room (see Figure 1.17). The result will be a slightly higher illuminance level and a more even distribution of light in the space.

Light shelves are fixed reflective devices, located at or near a window, that reflect and disperse sunlight onto ceilings and walls. They are used to minimize bright incoming natural light near the window and to maximize the light penetrating the interior spaces. As a design feature, light shelves typically create a strong horizontality on the exterior of the building (see Figure 1.18).

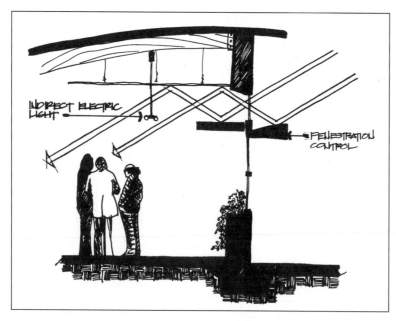

FIGURE 1.17
Wall section showing light shelf.

FIGURE 1.18
Elevation showing light shelf.

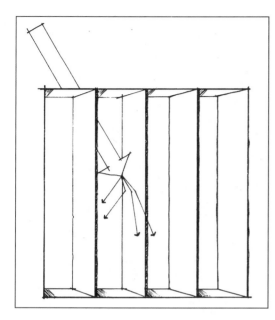

FIGURE 1.19
East/west window control scheme.

Horizontal louvers are an effective method of blocking direct beam light during the summer when sun angles are high while allowing some sunlight penetration during the milder seasons. Movable louvers can be controlled electronically or mechanically to respond to changing sky and weather conditions.

Vertical louvers or *fins* are advantageous for east and west orientations to block direct beam and to reflect light into the interior (see Figure 1.19). The louvers or fins can be fixed or movable (see Figure 1.20).

FIGURE 1.20
Movable louver system.

Daylight tracking and *reflecting systems* are designed to enhance the daylighting potential of skylights by tracking and reflecting sunlight through the aperture and into the open spaces below. This type of equipment can be either dynamically controlled to follow the path of the sun or completely stationary, using strategically placed mirrors to capture the direct beam daylight.

Because low-angle daylight can be better utilized, the use of this equipment is able to extend the hours within a day, as well as the months within a year, that natural light can effectively replace or complement electric lighting.

In-Wall and Roof Elements
Glazing Materials

Historically, the simplest method to maximize the amount of available daylight within a building was to increase the total amount of glazing present in the building envelope. In many cooling dominated climates, admitting more light has, until recently, meant admitting unwanted heat gain as well. However, recent advancements in glazing technology have specifically reduced this liability.

Three characteristics of glazing need to be understood to properly understand the performance properties of fenestration.

The *visible transmittance* (VT) of a glazing is the fraction of visible light energy transmitted through a glazing. Clear, double-strength single glass typically transmits 89% of the light that strikes it and thus has a VT of 0.89.

The *shading coefficient* (SC) of a glazing is the ratio of solar heat gain through a given glazing system compared with the solar heat gain through a clear, double-strength single glass.

The *U-value* represents the rate of heat transfer each hour through 1 ft^2 of a material per degree of temperature difference between the two sides of that material.

Appendix D lists some common glazings and their associated characteristics.

The performance properties of clear, single glass can easily be altered using any four methods. Combinations of these modifications can expand even further the effectiveness of the resultant glazing units.

Tinted glazings use heat-absorbing materials dispersed throughout the glass to reduce the amount of solar radiation passing through the glass but at the same time will reduce the amount of visible light passing through the material.

The color of the tint, however, will affect the relationship between the two characteristics. Gray glasses will reduce both the light and the heat, which are transmitted at a fairly consistent rate. Bronze glasses will reduce more light energy than heat energy. Blue-green glasses will reduce heat energy while still maintaining a fairly high visible light transmittance. Therefore, the blue-green tints will produce the highest performance in daylighting applications.

Metallic coatings of various types can be applied to glazings to modify their characteristics.

Reflective metallic coatings will dramatically reduce both the light and heat transmittance through direct reflection and are thus not recommended for daylighting applications.

Low-emissivity, or "low-e," coatings are transparent to the visible light range of the electromagnetic spectrum but are reflective to most long-wave infrared heat radiation (see Figure 1.21).

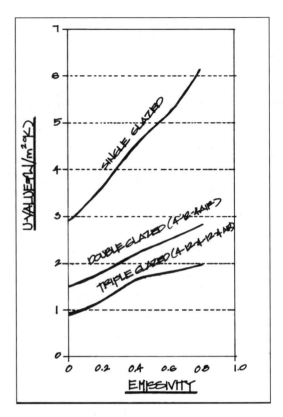

FIGURE 1.21
Graph illustrating emissivity as a function of U-value.

Sputtered, or "soft-coat," low-e coatings can be manipulated to transmit or reflect selective ranges of the electromagnetic radiation spectrum and, as a result, can be adjusted for optimum performance in any given climate. One disadvantage of the coating is that it must be applied to one of the inner surfaces of a dual-paned glazing unit to protect the thin layer of metallic particles.

Soft low-e coatings, in all their variations, can also be applied to a thin plastic film, which is then suspended between two panes of glass. The extra gas space formed by the suspended film will additionally decrease the conductivity of the glazing unit.

Pyrolitic, or "hard-coat," low-e coatings are fused to the glass while it is still hot to create an integral film that is extremely resistant to abrasion and corrosion. The coat-

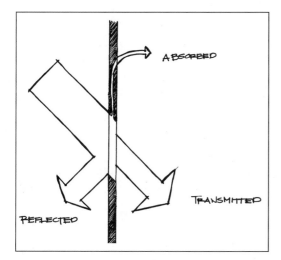

FIGURE 1.22
Characteristics of glazing.

ings can be used for single-pane application, but they offer inherently less variety in thermal and optical characteristics, because the deposition process allows less control than the sputtering process.

Multipaned glazing units trap a layer of still air between panes of glass to increase the thermal resistance of the window. As the number of air layers increases, so does the thermal resistance of a product. Dou-

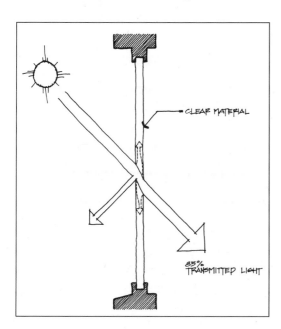

FIGURE 1.23
Typical diffuse transmission.

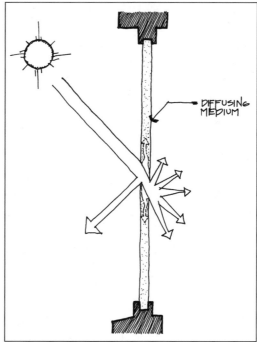

FIGURE 1.24
Nondiffuse transmission.

ble-paned units have essentially become the design standard in many climates. The demand for triple-paned units has been replaced by units using the suspended low-e films, because the thickness, weight, and cost of the units are much lower.

Gas fills are commonly used to replace the air between two panes of glass because inert gases such as argon, krypton, and sulfur hexafluoride (SF_6) are less conductive than air. As a result, they can reduce the amount of heat transfer between the glazing surfaces.

Effective Aperture

In the simplest of terms, as the area of an aperture increases, the amount of daylight received in a space also increases. However, as explained earlier, the glazing material within that aperture can effectively reduce the amount of visible light that is allowed to enter. Therefore, aperture size alone is not an effective determinant to measure illumination levels. If the glazing in an opening is a perfectly transparent material, the "effective aperture" size would be equal to the area of the opening (because the VT of the glazing would be 1.0). If, however, the glazing has a VT of 0.50, the opening will transmit only half of the light striking it, and the "effective aperture" will be half of the actual size of the opening.

The "effective aperture," or light-admitting potential of a glazing system, is determined by multiplying the visible transmittance (VT) by the window-to-wall ratio (WWR). The window-wall ratio is the ratio of the net window glazing area to the gross exterior wall area.

$$EA = WWR \times VT$$

This attribute can be useful in evaluating the cost-effectiveness and the daylighting potential of a schematic building configuration.

Aperture Location

The location of an aperture will affect the distribution of the light admitted through the aperture.

The height of a window from the finished floor will dictate the depth of penetration. The higher the window, the deeper the daylight will penetrate. One rule of thumb states that the depth of daylight penetration is about 2½ times the distance between the top of a window and the windowsill (see Figure 1.25).

Interior Elements
Room Geometry

The depth that daylight will penetrate is dependent on the ceiling height relative to the top of the window. A high window height will allow entering daylight to strike the ceiling plane and be reflected into the interior of the space.

The depth of the room has a direct effect on the intensity of illumination as well. If a space is modeled, keeping the floor-to-ceiling height and the area and location of the window constant, changing the room depth will cause a change in light intensity. With deeper rooms, the same quantity of incoming light is distributed over a larger area (see Figure 1.26).

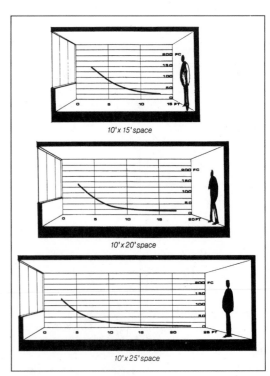

10' x 15' space

10' x 20' space

10' x 25' space

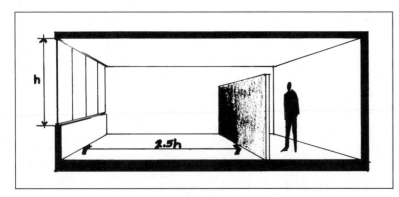

FIGURE 1.25
Rule of thumb for window configuration.

FIGURE 1.26
Light intensity as a function of room depth.

Reflectances of Room Surfaces

The reflectance values of room surfaces will greatly impact the performance of a daylit space. The ceiling is the most important surface in reflecting the daylight coming into a space onto the work plane. The next most important surface is the back wall, followed by the side walls, and finally, the floor.

As the designer, keep the ceiling as light as possible and use only the floor for patterns or deep colors. Dark colors on a floor will have the least impact on the daylit space.

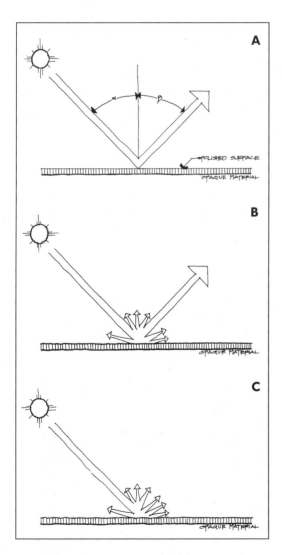

FIGURE 1.27
Reflectance properties. Specular reflection (**A**), combined specular and diffuse reflection (**B**), and diffuse reflection (**C**).

Interior Shading Controls

Several types of manual interior control devices can be used to eliminate excessive bright spots and also get daylight where it is needed.

Venetian blinds are effective because they can be fixed to block direct beam sunshine or can be partially closed to reflect in the space while still allowing a view to the outdoors. Blinds offer versatility and tend to increase the ratio of ground-reflected light to direct sky contribution.

Draperies are often used as control devices because they can add texture, color, and flexibility to a space. Fabrics are available in a range of weaves with varying shading coefficients. An appropriate weave pattern can soften the light to necessary levels.

Roller shades of various degrees of opaqueness can be an effective control device for reducing glare and direct beam penetration. One benefit of the interior controls is that they can be easily and completely retracted during those times that sunlight and daylight are desirable.

Design Options
Sidelighting

Sidelighting concepts use the walls of a building as the location of apertures to admit daylight (see Figure 1.28). The apertures can also serve by incorporating view and ventilation as a design dynamic.

Sidelighting provides illumination with a strong directionality due to the diminishing light levels as the distance from the aperture increases. Daylight admitted through wall apertures is ideal for illuminating horizontal surfaces and work planes.

As a disadvantage, sidelighting may cause glare because of the high contrast between

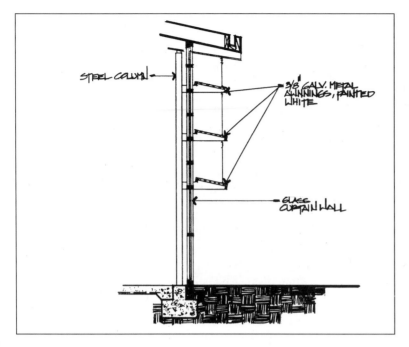

FIGURE 1.28
Sidelighting with direct beam control. (Detail courtesy of IBI Group, Irvine, California.)

the aperture and the surrounding wall surfaces. Proper shading devices, either exterior or interior, can largely mitigate this liability.

Vertical windows have been used for centuries by architects and designers for natural lighting, amenity, and comfort.

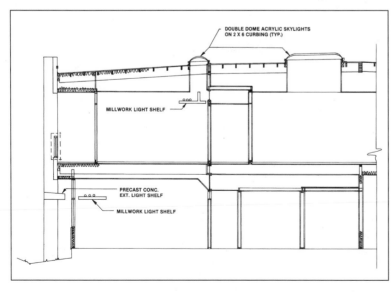

FIGURE 1.29
Bilateral daylight contribution.

Window size and height are important variables in sidelighting design. A basic understanding of some of the relationships between these factors will help the designer direct ample amounts of light where it is desired.

- As the window area increases, the amount of daylight received in a space increases.
- The height of the window above the finished floor will dictate the depth of penetration. The higher the window, the deeper the area that can effectively use the natural light.
- As the height of the window sill increases, the point of maximum illumination moves away from the window.

The contribution of light from the ground and other exterior reflecting surfaces can be a significant component of the total penetration of illumination on clear days.

Spaces can be daylit with windows unilaterally, bilaterally, and multilaterally with varying effects. Unilaterally lit rooms receive light entering through windows in one wall only. Bilaterally lit spaces are illuminated by light entering through apertures in opposing walls, and multilaterally lit areas receive light entering through fenestration in at least two nonopposing walls.

Clerestories are vertical windows whose sill height is above eye level but below ceiling height (see Figure 1.30). They are therefore not necessarily view apertures and so may easily incorporate glazings that are not transparent.

The principal advantage of clerestories is that the elevated vertical glazings introduce daylight high into a space, resulting in less likelihood of excessive brightness in the field of vision. In addition, because they open onto the bright part of the sky dome

FIGURE 1.30
Clerestory aperture.

close to the zenith, they can allow brighter and deeper daylight penetration into a building than can a window.

Clerestories provide excellent lighting for horizontal work planes, as well as vertical display surfaces. Daylight entering through a sufficiently high clerestory will typically reach a vertical surface without striking intermediate objects, thus avoiding shadows on these areas (see Figure 1.31). Light admitted through clerestories also exhibits less variation between maximum and minimum illuminances compared with a window and thus produces relatively even illumination.

The only major drawback to clerestories is that they require tall floor-to-ceiling heights if they are to function properly. Gymnasiums, libraries, galleries, museums, and circulation spaces all are excellent spaces in which to admit natural light through clerestories.

Toplighting

Toplighting concepts allow daylight to penetrate a space from apertures that are located above the ceiling line and usually constitute part of the roof of the building (see Figure 1.32).

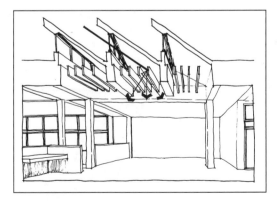

FIGURE 1.31
Clerestory aperture detail by Edward Mazria. (From Moore, Fuller, *Concepts and Practice of Architectural Daylighting*, VNR, New York, 1986. Used by permission.)

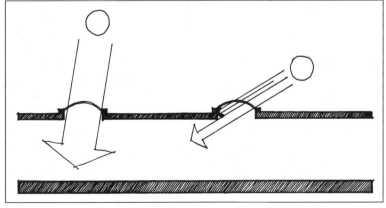

FIGURE 1.32
Toplighting aperture. Skylight performance under sunny conditions is dependent on solar altitude.

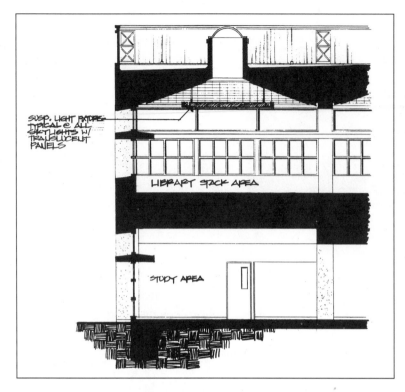

FIGURE 1.33
Bilateral strategy of Antelope Valley Library.
(Courtesy of Spencer Hoskins Architects.)

All toplighting concepts provide interior light with distribution patterns and character significantly different from those provided by sidelighting. Placement and frequency of the roof apertures can produce lighting effects extending from a fairly uniform level of ambient light to dramatic accent lighting in strategic areas (see Figure 1.33).

Toplighting often restricts natural light to the upper level of the building. Another drawback of toplighting is that the penetration of direct beam sunlight into a space must always be carefully controlled to prevent occupant discomfort (see Figure 1.34).

Skylights are defined simply as horizontal glazed roof apertures that are parallel to the roof. Skylighting is an excellent toplighting strategy because large quantities of light can be admitted to all areas of single-story buildings or into the top floor of multistory buildings, with relatively small openings (see Figure 1.35).

The layout and spacing of skylights in a roof determine the light distribution characteristics of the area below the skylights. While maintaining a constant aperture area, the arrangement can vary from a single large

FIGURE 1.34
Toplighting through deep lightwell. (Illustrated by Moshe Safdie. Courtesy of the Canadian National Gallery.)

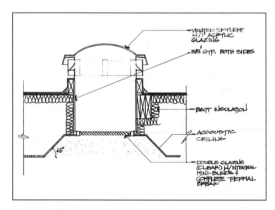

FIGURE 1.35
Typical skylight construction detail showing splayed ceiling treatment through plenum.

skylight to many small skylights distributed uniformly across the roof with varying effects.

Large, widely spaced skylights are usually the most economical to install but may result in uneven light distribution, reduced energy savings, and possible glare problems. Small, closely spaced skylights, on the other hand, will provide more uniform lighting conditions and greater energy savings but may be more costly to install.

The general rule of thumb is to space skylights at 1.0 to 1.5 times the ceiling height. Variations will inevitably occur because skylight placement must also be coordinated with the structural, mechanical, and lighting systems.

Diverse glazing options provide opportunities for the designer to select from diffuse light, direct beam sunlight, or any combination of the two that may be appropriate to a space. Glazing characteristics are discussed in more depth in a later section.

Roof monitors are raised sections of a roof with vertical or sloped apertures on one or more sides. Although these devices require architectural coordination, proper orientation, and special drainage details, they allow the top floor of a building to benefit from daylight with less heat gain than is normally associated with toplighting.

Core Daylighting

Core daylighting refers to a strategy that implements optical systems to light spaces of a building with sunlight that may receive both electric lighting and cooling loads. This is not a new concept because simple forms of this strategy existed in early Egyptian cultures that used mirror strategies to light deep spaces within the tombs of the Pharaohs.

There are generally three elements to core daylighting systems: the light collection system, the light transportation system, and the light distribution system.

Collection system The core daylighting collection system captures daylight and redirects it. Collection systems may be located on the exterior of a building on the roof or at exterior walls. Two types of core daylighting light collection systems exist: active optical systems and passive optical systems.

Active optic systems use a tracking system that follows the sun as it moves across the sky and redirects the direct beam solar into the interior of a building (see Figure 1.36). The direct beam radiation that strikes the active mirror or lens is then directed to an input aperture of the light transportation system. This type of system is significantly

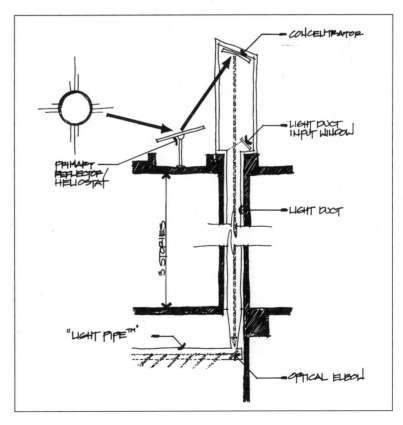

FIGURE 1.36
Beam daylighting system.

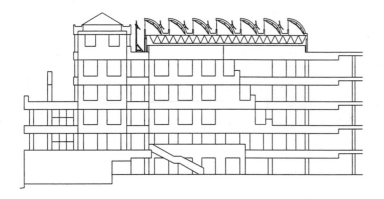

FIGURE 1.37
3M building section.

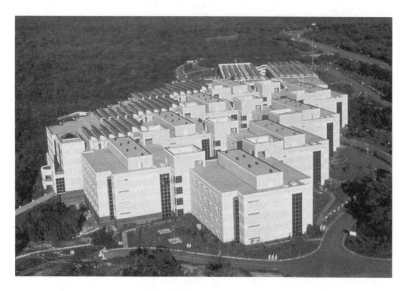

FIGURE 1.38
3M building complex showing roof layout.

disadvantaged in partly cloudy or overcast sky conditions because there is very little light input. An advantage of these types of active systems is that the visible radiation collected can be closely controlled and redirected with a high degree of certainty. On the other hand, this system can be a very complex mechanical device with fairly high associated first costs.

Passive optical systems implement fixed elements to view the most favorable or brightest portion of the sky dome and redirect the light into the light transportation

system. The positioning of these types of collector systems must be tuned for a specific latitude to assure optimal performance. With no moving parts, this type of system is less costly for both first cost and maintenance-related expenses. A drawback is the reduced control of the directionality of the collected daylight.

Transportation system The core daylighting system moves the collected daylight from the collection system to the light distribution system where the light requirement exists. New materials have been developed to overcome some of the limitations associated with transporting light any significant distance. The most common types of transportation systems are either fiber optic or light ducts lined with a highly reflective material.

Distribution system The core daylighting distribution system receives its light input from the transportation system and distributes light onto a target area or a space. This element of the system then carries light from the transportation system and emits light within the building. The devices used to accomplish this once again include both optical fibers or optical light pipes or light guides.

An example of this type of strategy has been incorporated into the design of a commercial building in Austin, Texas, for the 3M Company, which manufactured many films used in the design (see Figures 1.37 to 1.40).

The daylighting system designed and installed at 3M Company's Austin facility marks the third generation of the passive optic system pioneered at the Civil and Mineral Engineering (C/ME) building, a joint venture between BRW Architects and 3M, at the University of Minnesota. This system, designed in conjunction with the engineers at 3M to use their spreading film

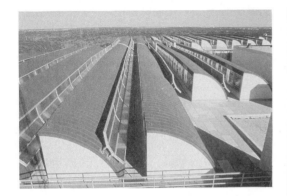

FIGURE 1.39
3M building roof detail.

FIGURE 1.40
3M building atrium.

in the collector system, is used to light a five-story, 65-ft tall, 50,000-ft^2 atrium connecting multiple office blocks. 3M's expertise was teamed with CRSS Architects, Inc., Houston, Texas, for the building's design. One of the major objectives for the Austin Center was to provide an integrated building campus that brought together all functions of the 3M business (laboratory, administrative, marketing, sales, etc.) into one single structure where people could move freely between locations and interact with each other on a daily basis. It was also important that interior offices have windows with access to natural daylight. Thus, the solution incorporated an enclosed atrium, located between the separate buildings, that was equipped with a daylighting system that could provide natural lighting while reducing the building's energy load.

Three Fresnel panels were used to make up the exterior primary collector and consisted of a daylighting film laminated to polystyrene panels having an acrylic exterior surface. Three similar panels were fabricated for the interior secondary reflector. The film's Fresnel grooves run horizontally on the primary collectors, spreading the light ± 5 degrees in the north-south direction, whereas the grooves run vertically on the secondary collectors, spreading the light ± 5 degrees in the east-west direction. The primary reflector spreads the light 10

degrees in the north-south (vertical direction), and the secondary reflectors spread the light 10 degrees in the east-west (horizontal) direction. With this film orientation, the harsh solar images would not be cast on the atrium floor 65 ft below. The finished panels were mounted on a metal frame fastened to the adjacent roof structure or dormer. The exterior collectors and vertical glazings between the primary and secondary collectors are easily accessible from the building's roof. The total fenestration of glazed area, consisting of the north-facing vertical windows, is approximately 28% of the atrium's total floor space. The system also performs well on cloudy days; for the average overcast day, unusually high light levels are produced within the atrium space. Occupants have reportedly said that they feel that the atrium is brighter on these days than the outside appears to be. The 3M system also significantly reduces the solar heat gains that would normally be associated with a glazed atrium daylighting system. This heat reduction results from the fact that the lenses are made of a material that is an excellent reflector of the visible spectrum but is much less reflective of the infrared wavelengths. With this Austin daylighting system, nearly 58% of the infrared radiation is removed from the light entering the space.

Atrium

The atrium building finds its origins from the ancient Greek and Roman courtyard house where the courtyard performed as the social center of the house. Today, the atrium behaves in a similar fashion (see Figure 1.41). Typically, the centroidial placement of the atrium allows it to serve as both an element for circulation and an element for spatial order. An atrium enjoys numerous functions that can effectively provide pleasant and comfortable environments while allowing opportunities for significant energy savings. Recent changes in glazing and system technologies have allowed large-scale atrium spaces to func-

FIGURE 1.41
Atrium of Brown Derby Hotel. (Photograph courtesy of Susan Ryan Colletta, Denver.)

tion with more reliability, less water leaks, less maintenance, and fewer other related problems displayed in the past.

Just as the ancient Roman and Greek courtyard house benefited from shade, thermal heat storage and transfer, ventilation, and evaporative cooling, the atrium performs similarly. An atrium designed for maximum energy savings and efficiency should incorporate daylighting, ventilation, and passive heating and cooling techniques as design features. Because the atrium is a centroidially located space protected by glazing, it effectively creates a second perimeter zone within a building. Daylight is able to penetrate into the large interior space while the intervening surfaces reflect the light to adjacent spaces on lower floors. Aspect ratios determine the quantity and location of solar radiation on and within the atrium.

Section Aspect Ratio

The section aspect ratio (SAR) affects daylighting, passive heating, and cooling factors within the atrium. A high SAR effectively reduces or eliminates the amount of solar radiation that will reach the lower portions of the space. However, a high SAR does contribute to passive cooling process by thermal convective means. A low SAR is ideal for daylighting, passive heating, and radiative cooling.

The orientation size and geometry of the space, size, and placement of apertures, in addition to facade reflection properties, play important roles in the ability of daylight to penetrate into the interior spaces of a building. However, among the numerous issues considered during the design process, climate presents the greatest potential influence. Local climate conditions affect heating, cooling, and daylighting design strategies. In daylighting, design strategies need to address predominant sky conditions to maximize daylight. For example, predominantly cloudy sky conditions will maximize its daylighting potential with a stepped atrium section. In general, an overhead daylighting source enables the most daylight to penetrate the space because the sky dome is brightest at the zenith. Vertically glazed atrium spaces may enhance exterior views, but the quantity of daylight is not ideal under cloudy sky conditions, and the quality can prove to be too severe if fenestration controls are not used. In hot climate zones where solar heat gain is prohibitive, clerestories are effective, especially with exterior fenestration controls.

An atrium design can allow the intervening floors to be open to it. However, this approach brings with it a number of acoustic and fire safety considerations to which the designer must be responsive.

An atrium can also be thermally separated from the rest of the building by transparent or translucent materials. This allows the total amount of glazing area on partition surfaces to be increased because the atrium effectively serves as a buffer zone between the conditioned spaces and the outside environment.

CHAPTER 2

INTEGRATION WITH ELECTRIC LIGHTING

A complete daylighting system not only involves the various architectural features to capture and disperse natural light but also incorporates automatic photosensitive controls to adjust the level of the electric lighting when sufficient daylight is available. These controls are essential to an energy saving daylighting system (see Figure 2.1).

An automatic control device generally consists of two components: a sensing device to measure the available daylight (see Figure 2.2) and a controller that either switches or dims the electric lights.

Switching Controls

Switching controls, sometimes referred to as on/off controls, simply turn the electric lights off when there is ample daylight (see Figure 2.3). Conversely, when the illuminance drops below the required design levels, the lights turn on.

Although switching controls are typically the most economical, the least amount of energy savings can be realized because the luminaires remain on at any time that the available daylight is below the specified design level.

Switching controls create large differences in illumination levels that can be quite disconcerting to the occupants of a space because the sudden variations in light are easily detectable.

Stepped Controls

Stepped controls, on the other hand, provide intermediate levels of electric lighting control and further integration with daylighting. Stepped controls provide a simple method to achieve transitional levels of illumination. They control the individual lamps within a luminaire to allow different combinations of lamps to operate at appropriate times. Thus, with a three-lamp fixture, the intermediate steps would consist of one lamp on, two lamps on, and all lamps on.

As a result, the building occupants are much less aware of the turning on and off of lights because the incremental levels are

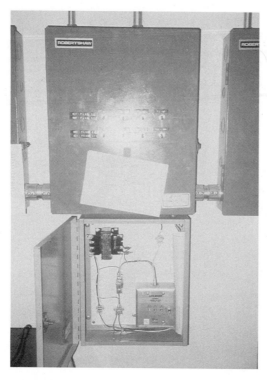

FIGURE 2.1
Control system with relays.

less perceptible, and therefore stepped controls are less distracting.

In addition, stepped controls can provide more comfortably lit spaces because at least one lamp can be allowed to remain on at all times. This will avoid a darkened ceiling, which creates an uncomfortable cave-like environment for the occupants.

FIGURE 2.2
Ceiling-mounted light sensor.

Dimming Controls

Dimming controls continuously adjust electric lighting by modulating the power input to the lamps to complement the level of illumination provided by daylight (see Figure 2.4). This type of controller can achieve the highest degree of energy savings because it will provide only the amount of light required to meet a predetermined level of illumination.

Not all lamps and ballasts will function properly with dimming controllers, so care must be taken by the designer to provide equipment that is compatible with this type of control device.

Selection Considerations

Selection considerations for daylighting controls will vary according to the characteristics of the space. The designer should include:

- Type of space (industrial, office, retail)
- Types of lamps, ballasts, or both
- Layout of fixtures
- Size and shape of the room

The optimal control system will adjust the electric lighting without adversely affecting the illumination quality of the space. Time delays are recommended to reduce rapid responses to varying light intensity changes, particularly on partly cloudy days.

The photo relay should also incorporate a deadband for the lighting to be switched off when the daylight illuminance on the photocell exceeds some level. However, it will not be restored until the daylight drops considerably below the switch-off threshold.

Many lighting control systems can also be interfaced with existing energy management systems (EMSs) to provide additional con-

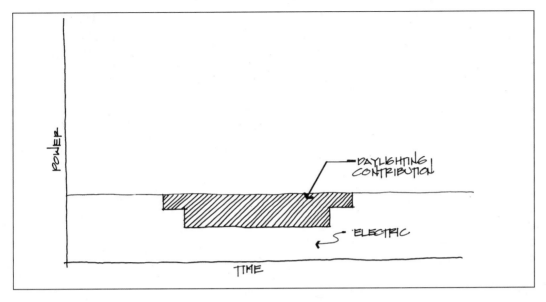

FIGURE 2.3
Typical on/off profile with a stepped function.

trol possibilities. An energy management system can, for example, schedule the operation of the lights to conform to building occupancy. In addition, the extra intelligence available in an EMS may allow the building operator to prevent the control system from reacting in an undesirable manner.

Integration with the EMS

The EMS industry has advanced rapidly over the past decade. Today's EMSs are intelligent, microprocessor-based building monitoring and control systems that are an integral part of most commercial buildings.

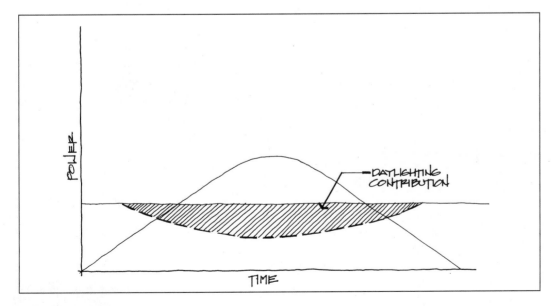

FIGURE 2.4
Typical dimming control profile.

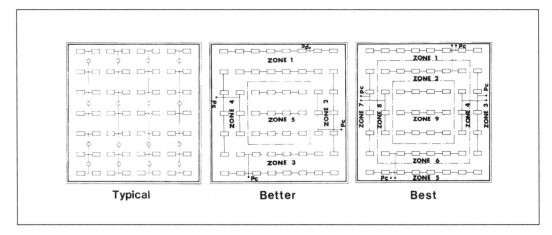

FIGURE 2.5
Control zoning schemes.

This EMS technology and market penetration provide building owners and designers with a tremendous opportunity for innovation and operational flexibility.

EMSs are generally building and site-wide installations composed of numerous controllers residing on a distributed local area network (LAN). This distribution of EMS "processor power" permits a wide range of control options for both *stand-alone* functions (i.e., simple thermostatic operations) and building-wide *supervisory* applications (i.e., demand limiting). In either situation, the LAN provides the additional benefit of centralized information access from any operator workstation. Figure 2.6 presents a simplified schematic of a typical EMS architecture.

Integrating the EMS and Lighting Controls

Today, it is common for an EMS to be used for scheduling both interior and exterior lighting systems. The EMS is typically implemented at the circuit breaker level. For example, a large office area may include several dozen individual lighting zones (i.e., light switches), even though electrical power is supplied via only a few circuits of an electrical panel. In this situation, the EMS will typically be used as a master schedule for the overall building's lighting, whereas zone level control remains dependent on the manual occupant actions. In addition, several override switches may be incorporated into the EMS to permit occupant-initiated "after hours" lighting (e.g., a corridor located push button that signals the EMS to activate a particular lighting circuit for a prescribed period).

Over the past several years, more extensive occupancy- and daylighting-based controls have been incorporated into building designs. The controls increase energy savings by respectively tailoring lighting schedules to a building's zone level occupancy and by using ambient light. These new types of lighting controls can be implemented in either a *stand-alone* (EMS-independent) or *supervised* manner. A schematic representation of the various lighting controls is presented in Figure 2.7.

EMS-based daylighting controls tend to be more macro than zone level. In larger (open area) daylit portions of a building, the EMS may include light sensors that convert measured footcandles into a proportional volt-

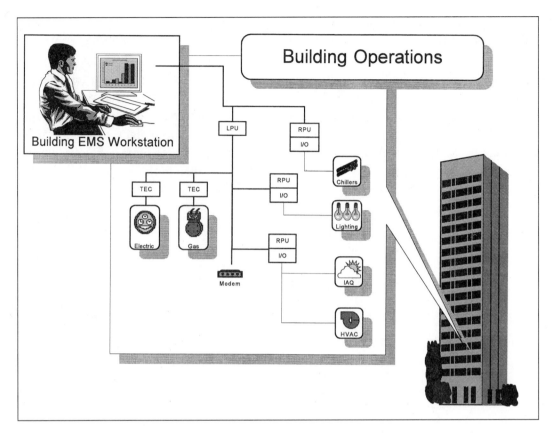

FIGURE 2.6
Energy management system control diagram. (Courtesy of the Energy Simulation Specialists, Inc.)

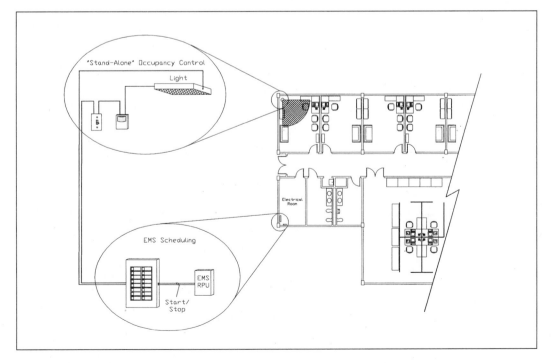

FIGURE 2.7
Lighting control system. (Courtesy of the Energy Simulation Specialists, Inc.)

age or amperage signal monitored by the EMS. The EMS then acts on the input signals to control the area's electric lighting sources. This may include discrete stage control (for multilevel lighting systems) or true proportional control through continuously adjustable light fixtures (dimmable electronic ballasts). In such situations, the EMS-based control permits easy reset or even scheduling of light-level set points.

At the smaller zone level (e.g., a perimeter office), direct EMS daylighting control is typically not economical. In this case, any zone level daylighting control will likely be integral to the zone's occupancy sensor. Such devices are available for either discrete or continuous lighting level control that are appropriate for the specific lighting system installed in the zone.

CHAPTER 3

DAYLIGHTING DESIGN TOOLS

During the last half of the nineteenth century, methods for calculating illumination from natural sources first became available. Since then, the literature on daylight calculation methods has become extensive. The following section provides an introduction to daylighting calculation methods. The methodologies will help reinforce the intuitive feeling the designer has for natural illumination. The calculation tools are most useful during the design process to help resolve both the quantitative and qualitative issues.

3.1 HAND CALCULATION METHODS

Lumen Method

The lumen method closely parallels the methods used in electric lighting calculations, both of which require the "coefficient of utilization." The coefficient of utilization is defined as the ratio of light incident on a reference point to the light entering a space. This approach was first taken in the late 1920s when an empirically based method was initiated to determine the coefficient of utilization. In this method, rooms were measured with varying dimensions, window sizes, and interior surface reflectances. The results found that coefficients of utilization varied within a moderate range; however, to avoid complexity, a single value of 0.4 was adopted that limited the accuracy. Much of the complexity associated with empirically based data was eliminated in the early 1950s by Bill Griffith and his colleagues who developed coefficient of utilization tables from a series of measurements conducted in both experimental rooms and physical models. Funding for Griffith's work, as well as the publication of his results, was provided by the Libbey-Owens-Ford Company, which is the reason Griffith's method is referred as the LOF method. The lumen method, as refined by

Coefficient of Utilization from Window Without Blinds.
Sky component E_{xvsky}/E_{xhsky} = 0.75.

ROOM DEPTH/WINDOW HEIGHT		PERCENT				WINDOW WIDTH/WINDOW HEIGHT			
	D	0.5	1	2	3	4	6	8	INFINITE
	10	0.824	0.864	0.870	0.873	0.875	0.879	0.880	0.883
	30	0.547	0.711	0.777	0.789	0.793	0.798	0.799	0.801
1	50	0.355	0.526	0.635	0.659	0.666	0.669	0.670	0.672
	70	0.243	0.386	0.505	0.538	0.548	0.544	0.545	0.547
	90	0.185	0.304	0.418	0.451	0.464	0.444	0.446	0.447
	10	0.667	0.781	0.809	0.812	0.813	0.815	0.816	0.824
	30	0.269	0.416	0.519	0.544	0.551	0.556	0.557	0.563
2	50	0.122	0.204	0.287	0.319	0.331	0.339	0.341	0.345
	70	0.068	0.116	0.173	0.201	0.214	0.223	0.226	0.229
	90	0.050	0.084	0.127	0.151	0.164	0.167	0.171	0.172
	10	0.522	0.681	0.739	0.746	0.747	0.749	0.747	0.766
	30	0.139	0.232	0.320	0.350	0.360	0.366	0.364	0.373
3	50	0.053	0.092	0.139	0.163	0.174	0.183	0.182	0.187
	70	0.031	0.053	0.081	0.097	0.106	0.116	0.116	0.119
	90	0.025	0.041	0.061	0.074	0.082	0.089	0.090	0.092
	10	0.405	0.576	0.658	0.670	0.673	0.675	0.674	0.707
	30	0.075	0.134	0.197	0.224	0.235	0.243	0.243	0.255
4	50	0.028	0.050	0.078	0.094	0.104	0.112	0.114	0.119
	70	0.018	0.031	0.048	0.059	0.065	0.073	0.074	0.078
	90	0.016	0.026	0.040	0.048	0.053	0.059	0.061	0.064
	10	0.242	0.392	0.494	0.516	0.521	0.524	0.523	0.588
	30	0.027	0.054	0.086	0.102	0.111	0.119	0.120	0.135
6	50	0.011	0.023	0.036	0.044	0.049	0.055	0.056	0.063
	70	0.009	0.018	0.027	0.032	0.035	0.040	0.041	0.046
	90	0.008	0.016	0.023	0.028	0.031	0.034	0.035	0.040
	10	0.147	0.257	0.352	0.380	0.387	0.391	0.392	0.482
	30	0.012	0.026	0.043	0.054	0.060	0.067	0.070	0.086
8	50	0.006	0.013	0.021	0.026	0.029	0.033	0.035	0.043
	70	0.005	0.011	0.017	0.021	0.023	0.026	0.027	0.034
	90	0.004	0.010	0.015	0.019	0.021	0.023	0.025	0.030
	10	0.092	0.168	0.248	0.275	0.284	0.290	0.291	0.395
	30	0.006	0.014	0.026	0.032	0.036	0.041	0.044	0.059
10	50	0.003	0.008	0.014	0.017	0.019	0.022	0.024	0.032
	70	0.003	0.007	0.012	0.014	0.016	0.018	0.019	0.026
	90	0.003	0.006	0.011	0.013	0.015	0.016	0.017	0.024

(Source: IESNA Lighting Handbook. Published with permission by the Illuminating Engineering Society of North America, 120 Wall Street, New York, NY 10005.)

Griffith, has also been adopted by the Illuminating Engineering Society (IES) of North America as part of their Recommended Practice of Daylighting. The following calculation process best summarizes the lumen method and is described in greater detail in the IES's most recent Recommended Practice of Daylighting.

When developing a preliminary building design, the architect must first establish a variety of interior visual criteria and basic lighting performance requirements for each project. Then the designer must determine the parameters of the available daylight for the particular location and select the appropriate daylight data utilized as a basis for the design purposes. He or she is ready to calculate daylight contributions for various design schemes.

Due to varying sky conditions, the amount of available daylight is extremely variable for almost all localities. From sunrise to sunset, from winter to summer, and from day to day, the amount of available light from the sun and sky is constantly changing.

Except in a few isolated instances, very few instrumented data on daylight are available. Thus, it is impossible to establish a single set of conditions that can be established as an "absolute" design base.

Generally the designer will find the maximum and minimum sky conditions or the conditions considered most prevalent or typical as the most advantageous for calculating accurate measurements. If the particular locality in question has a high percentage of overcast days, the designer might choose to give more weight to the advantages and disadvantages of his or her proposed design under the overcast sky. If the locality has a high percentage of clear days, he or she might choose to ignore the overcast sky condition and design for clear sky and sun.

Figure 3.1.1 shows a typical lumen method illuminance curve as a function of solar altitude used to provide an indication of the illumination that may be expected for a particular sky, solar altitude, and building orientation. It should be kept in mind that these charts provide only very approximate illumination levels, and their use should be replaced in the event that more accurate local data are available.

For a cloudy or overcast sky scenario, the illumination of the unobstructed horizontal plane of the ground (or roof plane) will be needed for determining the daylight contri-

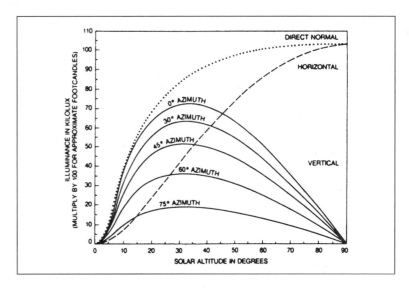

Figure 3.1.1
Illuminance from the sun under clear sky conditions as a function of solar altitude and azimuth. (Source: *IESNA Lighting Handbook*. Published with permission by the Illuminating Engineering Society of North America, 120 Wall Street, New York, NY 10005.)

bution to the interior from toplight openings and for determining reflected light from the ground. The illumination on the vertical plane of the fenestration will be needed for determining sidelighting contributions.

The illumination from a clear sky condition will be needed only for determining the daylight contribution from sidelighting where direct sun is not falling incident on that wall. The illumination from both clear sky and direct sun is required for determining the daylight contributions from toplight openings, for side wall lighting where the wall is exposed to direct sun, and for determining reflected ground light.

After the designer has determined the illumination on the horizontal or vertical surface from the sky selected, the illumination contribution from sun can be determined on the illuminance curve and added to the illumination contribution from the sky.

The percentage of time that any sky condition is likely to occur is another factor used in selecting design sky conditions. The National Oceanic and Atmospheric Administration (NOAA) or simulation weather files may provide a basis for estimating the number of hours per month when illumination levels or solar radiation will be above or below certain thresholds.

The data in the lumen method charts are taken from these types of sources citing measurements at numerous weather stations throughout the country. Data are based on hourly observations of the "percent cloud cover," that is, the degree of cloudiness, in tenths of the entire sky, zero to $\frac{3}{10}$ being considered clear, $\frac{4}{10}$ to $\frac{7}{10}$ partly cloudy, and $\frac{8}{10}$ to $\frac{10}{10}$ overcast.

A completely overcast sky might be thin and bright or dense and dark, resulting in different illumination levels on the ground. Although the illuminance data are derived from weather bureau instrumentation, extensive local information may not be available and may be a limiting factor for this methodology.

Predicting Interior Daylighting

Interior illumination is determined for each of several conditions and then added together for final results. For instance, illumination from windows and skylights can be determined separately and then added together for final results.

The calculation process used for the lumen method for determining interior daylighting is based on a process of interpolation of test data from actual testing. There are inherent limitations to the general type of room, fenestration, openings, and controls tested. However, with the use of a little common sense, these parameters can be expanded to fit a wide variety of building and fenestration designs.

BRS Daylighting Protractors

The BRS Daylight Protractors were devised primarily to simplify the calculation of the sky factor and sky component and to enable daylight measurements to be made from the delineation of a design of buildings.

In this respect, they are not design methods but merely an aid to design and are used to test the adequacy of a design at the stage at which scale drawings are available. This type of procedure is very suitable in the early stages of a design to determine the approximate dimensions and positions of fenestration as it relates to the daylight factor.

The components of the daylight factor in a building consist not only of the light that reaches the point directly from the sky but also the light reaching the point after reflection from external surfaces and from surfaces within the room—the ceiling, walls, floor, and furnishings. The daylight factor can therefore be considered to comprise three distinct components: the sky component, the externally reflected component, and the internally reflected component.

All three components are functions of the fenestration area, but the relative values of each vary with the particular conditions to which each is subject. In other words, the distance from the fenestration, degree of external obstruction, reflectances of external and internal surfaces all will impact this value. Building codes exist in certain parts of the world that require a minimum daylight factor within spaces.

The distinction between the components of the daylight factor is made primarily to facilitate the calculation of interior daylight and to enable methods best suited to the calculation of direct and reflected light to be used where appropriate, but it has advantages when the relative amounts of direct and diffused light are required, as in the determination of modeling effects.

The daylight factor and its components are defined by the Commission Internationale de l'Eclairage (CIE) as follows:

> The daylight factor is the ratio of the daylight illumination at a point on a given plane due to the light received directly or indirectly from a sky of assumed or known luminance distribution, to the illumination on a horizontal plane due to an unobstructed hemisphere of this sky. Direct sunlight is excluded for both values of illumination [see Figure 3.1.2].

The BRS Daylight Protractors are composed of a set of circular protractors that resemble in appearance and mode of operation the ordinary angular protractor (see Figure 3.1.3). The use of the Protractors in elementary daylight situations is simple and straightforward, although refinements in technique are possible that allow the Protractors to be used in the determination of direct daylight in more complex situations. The complete set of BRS Daylight Protractors is composed of two sets of five, corresponding to uniform sky and CIE overcast sky conditions. Each Protractor within each set applies to a particular slope of glazing and, in one case, to unglazed openings.

The Protractors are designed to be used with designer-scaled drawings, but any other drawings to scale that show the glazing in section and plan can be employed if detailed drawings are not available. Care should be taken so that the drawings show the thicknesses of window walls and

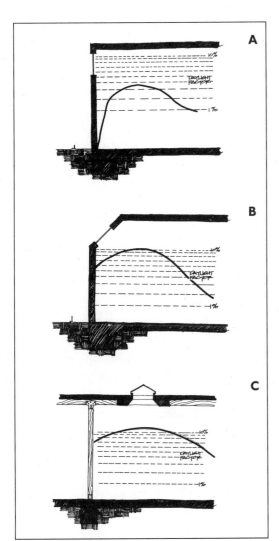

Figure 3.1.2
Daylight factor for various apertures.

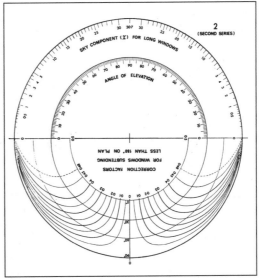

Figure 3.1.3
B.R.S. Sky Component Protractor for vertical glazing (CIE overcast sky). (Source: Building Research Establishment, *B.R.S. Daylight Protractors*, Department of the Environment, United Kingdom.)

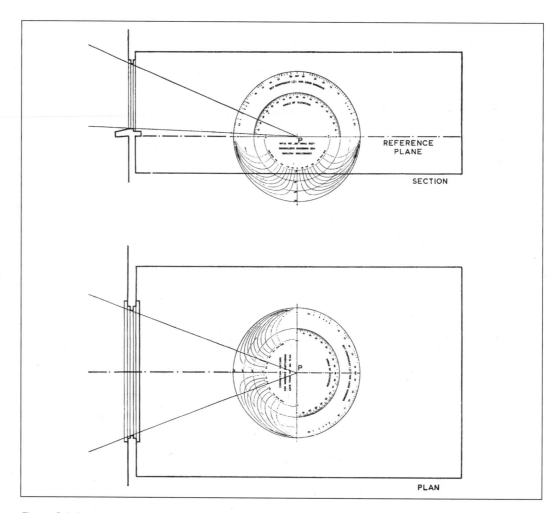

Figure 3.1.4
Typical B.R.S. Protractor to determine the sky component from a vertically glazed window. (Source: Building Research Establishment, *B.R.S. Daylight Protractors*, Department of the Environment, United Kingdom.)

include internal and external projections such as sills, blind boxes, and overhangs, and external obstructions and other details such as louvers known to interfere with the admission of daylight to the interior.

In most cases the scaled drawings prepared in standard production of architectural design work will work for determining sky components. Although the scale of the drawings is not critical, the Protractor can be laid conveniently over the section or plan, sight lines drawn accurately, and the intercepts read off without difficulty. A large scale helps in the accurate location of sight lines to the operative edges of window openings and is essential when accurate readings must be made for the detailing of a window, for example, in allowing for the reduction in daylight caused by the window frame and bars, columns, baffles, and louvers. In some cases it is possible to use a small-scale drawing of the entire room or building from which to obtain a first estimate of the probable daylighting levels and a large-scale drawing of the window itself from which to assess the effective area of the glazing.

The process of taking the sight line from the edges of the fenestration to the point in the interior is shown in Figure 3.1.4.

Skylight Calculations*

This discussion presents the Skylight Worksheets, a set of simple analysis procedures for focusing on some of the specifics of your skylight design. It assumes familiarity with many of the basic concepts and terms of daylighting and skylights. These should be understood before attempting to quantify skylight energy savings.

The Skylight Worksheets are used for optimizing the basic physical parameters of the skylight system:

- Skylight size and shape
- Glazing material
- Light well size and shape

The overall goal of this analysis is to maximize lighting energy and cost savings. Saving energy is not the only, or even primary, reason for using skylights, but controlling energy costs is a real concern for building owners, and reducing energy consumption is an increasing concern in building codes and regulations. The Skylight Worksheets provide an easy way to address this complex issue. They are based on years of research, practical experience and computer analysis, and are useful for establishing the basic parameters of your skylight design. . . .

The basic sequence of the Worksheets is illustrated on the flowchart [shown in Figure 3.1.5]. The Worksheets assume that you are starting early in the design sequence, and know very little as yet about the specifics of your skylight design. They help you answer basic questions

about the skylight design likely to be best for your situation.

There are other ways the Worksheets can be used, depending on your style as a designer and the nature of the problem you are addressing. As you become familiar with their structure, you will adapt them to your needs, as you would with any tool.

There are five Skylight Worksheets that guide you step-by-step through the analysis. You will need to provide some basic information about your building design. . . . If you are not far enough along in your design process to provide all the information required, the Worksheets will suggest default values that can be used in the interim. As the Worksheets are presented, there are sample Worksheets, filled in with an example to illustrate the process.

The Worksheets are organized into "Steps." As you get further along, you will notice

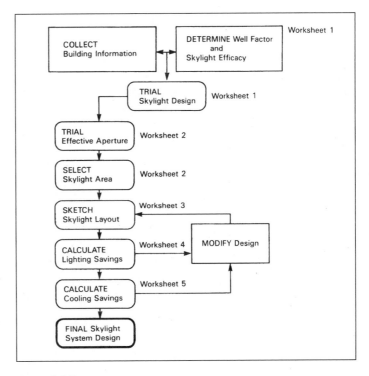

Figure 3.1.5
Worksheet flowchart.

---

*Excerpted with permission from the *American Architectural Manufacturers Association Skylight Handbook—Design Guidelines* (SHDB-1) with P.C. disk. Available: $100.00 (book only $50.00). Write to AAMA, 1540 East Dundee Road, Palatine, IL 60067. Call (708) 202–1350.

references to numbers developed in earlier steps. For example, when you are asked for the Gross Floor Area, you will be referred to Step 2, where that information is recorded. There are five Worksheets, but the numbering of steps is continuous from beginning to end; there is only one Step 4, and it is found on Worksheet 1.

The following sections explain in detail what is required for each Step of each Worksheet. It is recommended that you read through this discussion step-by-step the first time you go through the Worksheets, and refer back to it if you have questions later on.

Skylighting design is an iterative process. After you have the basic parameters of your design, you can refine that information in the context of your building and your design goals, and you can repeat some of the calculations. This will yield a more accurate picture of the energy and cost performance of your design.

WORKSHEET 1
Trial Design Worksheet

As with many design analyses, you need a trial design to begin. This includes information about the size and configuration of your skylighting system, and provides a basis for the initial analysis. It is used as a starting point in further developing and refining the system. Your trial design should be based on some reasonable assumptions about the kind of skylight system you might use in your building. You do not need to spend a great deal of effort in choosing a trial design, however, because the analysis is quick and simple enough that you can easily start over with a different trial design at a later time.

If you wish, you can use the trial skylight design represented by the default values on the Worksheets and illustrated in the examples. This is an ordinary square, 4' × 4' skylight with tinted glazing and a simple, rectangular light well.

Instructions

STEP 1: Choose Representative Location

There are six skylighting zones, and seven representative cities used in the Worksheets. Worksheet 1 shows the zones and the names of these cities. Each zone represents approximately constant daylight availability.

Choose the zone that includes your own location. Check off the representative city for that zone.

STEP 2: Find Basic Building Information

This information will be used in various parts of the Worksheets. It applies to the portion of your building that is skylit and had daylighting controls. If only part of the building has skylights, treat it as a discrete building throughout this analysis and ignore the nondaylit parts. If there are different daylit areas containing different occupancies, for example separate office and warehouse areas, you should analyze them separately.

List the Occupancy type; this is primarily for reference.

List the Desired Average Illuminance, which should correspond to the control setting of the daylighting system; e.g., if the control system is designed to maintain 50 footcandles, that would be the Desired Average Illuminance. This should also correspond to the illuminance required for the visual task to be performed. [See Appendix B for a more complete listing of illuminance requirements, as recommended by the Illuminance Engineering Society of North America.]

List the Gross Floor Area, in square feet, for the daylit area in question. This should include only the floor area of building with skylighting and daylight controls for the electric lights. Gross floor area means that you should ignore the floor area taken up by partitions and other obstructions, and use the overall area of the space.

List the Lighting Power Density (LPD), in Watts/square foot (W/sf). . . . This calculation basically involves summing the lamp and ballast wattage for all luminaires, and dividing by the gross floor area. Refer to the IES Handbook for a more detailed description of the calculation.

Check off the applicable daylighting control system type. If you are using a step control system with more than two steps, use the continuous dimming choice. See [Chapter 2] for a discussion of daylighting controls.

STEP 3: Select Trial Skylight

Consult manufacturers' literature for skylight sizes and glazing options. Select a skylight unit that is close to what you will want in your design, to use on a trial basis. As mentioned above, the default value is for an ordinary, 4′ × 4′ skylight.

List skylight opening area, in square feet, for a single skylight unit. This number will be used later to derive the number of skylights.

List glazing characteristics: visible transmittance and shading coefficient. These are decimal fractions, such as 0.82. They are discussed more fully in [Chapter 1, and Appendix D] contains a table of representative values for typical glazing materials. Refer to manufacturer's literature, when available, for actual numbers. The shading coefficient should be for glazing in a horizontal position, if available.

STEP 4: Determine Trial Well Factor

If there will be a light well, you should sketch a trial configuration for it. It should be consistent with the trial skylight and with what you know about ceiling thickness and other building design characteristics. . . . If none of the typical well configurations apply to your design, calculate the well factor using the defaults.

List the well height, as measured from the bottom of the glazing to the ceiling plane, in inches. If it is not a constant value, use the maximum height.

List the well length, in feet. If there are splayed walls to the well, calculate the maximum length of the well at the ceiling plane.

List the well width, in feet. Again, use the maximum width.

	VISIBLE TRANSMITTANCE* (VT)	SHADING COEFFICIENT* (SC)	SKYLIGHT EFFICACY* (SE)
Single Glazing			
clear glass (colorless)	0.88	0.94	0.94
clear acrylic (colorless)	0.92	0.98	0.94
clear polycarbonate (colorless)	0.83	0.99	0.84
diffusing acrylic	0.17–0.72	0.20–0.87	0.80–0.85
diffusing polycarbonate	0.43	0.72	0.60
tinted glass (¼″ bronze)	0.49	0.67	0.73
tinted glass (¼″ blue/green)	0.75	0.67	1.12
tinted glass (bronze)	0.49	0.75	0.65
Double Glazing			
polycarbonate			
clear/clear	0.69	0.93	0.74
diffusing/clear	0.36	0.66	0.55
bronze/clear	0.43	0.72	0.60
bronze/diffusing	0.22	0.56	0.39
acrylic			
clear/clear	0.85	0.89	0.96
diffusing/clear	0.48	0.58	0.83
bronze/clear	0.25	0.43	0.58
bronze/diffusing	0.17	0.32	0.53

All numbers are average and will vary with material thickness, degree of tint, and skylight design.

List the reflectance of the well walls, as a decimal fraction. [Manufacturers' literature may have these values for many products.]

Calculate the Well Index (WI), as shown on the worksheet.

Use the graph to find the Well Factor (WF), based on reflectance and WI. Start with the Well Index you just calculated. Draw a vertical up to the sloped line corresponding to the well wall reflectance (interpolate as necessary). From that intersection, draw a horizontal line to find the Efficiency of Well, or Well Factor (WF).

STEP 5: Determine Skylight Efficacy

[Refer to the table on page 40 for representative values.]

Calculate SE, using the visible transmittance (VT) and shading coefficient (SC) from Step 3, and the well factor (WF) from Step 4, above.

WORKSHEET I

(Note: See [Trial Design Worksheet, pages 39–41] for more information and an example of the use of the form.)

STEP 1: Choose Representative Location

The map shows zones of roughly equal daylight availability. Each has a representative city. Choose the zone that contains your own location. Note: For Zone 2, data is provided for both Madison, WI and Washington, DC. Choose the location whose climate, especially for cooling, is most similar to that of your location.

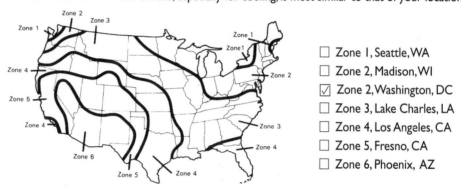

☐ Zone 1, Seattle, WA
☐ Zone 2, Madison, WI
☑ Zone 2, Washington, DC
☐ Zone 3, Lake Charles, LA
☐ Zone 4, Los Angeles, CA
☐ Zone 5, Fresno, CA
☐ Zone 6, Phoenix, AZ

STEP 2: Find Basic Building Information

Occupancy

office

(office, retail, etc.)

Desired Average Illuminance (default: 50 fc)

50	fc

Gross Floor Area

10,000	sf

(with daylighting)

Lighting Power Density (default: 1.5)

1.5	W/sf

Daylighting Control System: (Continuous Dimming) ☐   1-Step ☐   2-Step ☑
(Note: Ceiling height does not enter into this calculation. It is assumed that skylight spacing is less than or equal to 1.5 times ceiling height. . . .)

STEP 3: Select Trial Skylight

If possible, list the following details for a trial skylight. If not, enter the default values and skip to end of Step 4.

Area of typical skylight opening (individual unit)

16	sf

(default: 16)

Visible transmittance, VT =

0.50

(default: .50)

Shading coefficient, SC =

0.44

(default: .44)

STEP 4: Determine Trial Well Factor (WF)

If possible, perform this analysis with a trial light well design. If not, use [the following] default well factor. . . .

Sketch trial design below:

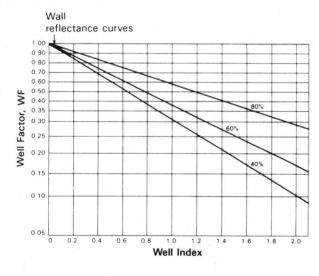

List the well dimensions:

Well Height (in.), H = $\boxed{18''}$
(default: 18)

Maximum Well Width (ft.), W = $\boxed{5'}$
(default: 5)

Maximum Well Length (ft.), L = $\boxed{5'}$
(default: 5)

Well Wall Reflectance $\boxed{0.80}$
(default: .80)

Calculate Well Index, using well dimensions listed above:

$$\text{Well Index} = \frac{H \times (L + W)}{24 \times W \times L} = \frac{\boxed{18''} \times \boxed{5'} + \boxed{5'}}{24 \times \boxed{5'} \times \boxed{5'}} = \boxed{0.30}$$
(default: .3)

Use the graph to find Well Factor, using values listed above. Start at Well Index. Draw up to appropriate wall reflectance curve, and across to find Well Factor; enter result below.

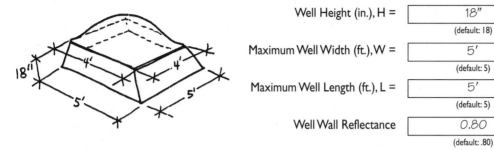

Well Factor, WF = $\boxed{0.90}$
(default: .90)

STEP 5: Determine Skylight Efficacy (SE)

Use values listed above in Steps 3 and 4 to calculate SE. . . .

$$\text{Skylight Efficacy} = \frac{WF \times VT}{SC} = \frac{\boxed{0.90} \times \boxed{0.50}}{\boxed{0.44}} = \boxed{1.02}$$
(default: 1.02)

WORKSHEET 2
Skylight Area Worksheet

Once the basic skylight parameters are determined on Worksheet 1, you are ready to find the target skylight area for your building. The numbering of steps continues on Worksheet 2 from where it left off on Worksheet 1.

Step 6 presents a method for determining a target range of Effective Apertures (EA) to use in initial skylight system sizing. The target ranges are based on optimum EAs which produce minimum peak electricity demands for the building. This usually means the skylighting system is not causing increases in the cooling system size, and that peak demand charges from the electric utility will be reduced. . . .

If your design is far enough along that you know the number of skylights, the well factor, and the visible transmittance of your skylight system, you should skip directly to Steps 10–12, and work out the actual EA.

You can then compare this to the Trial EA that is found in Step 6 for your location. If your actual EA is larger than the maximum EA or smaller than the minimum EA, you should consider adjusting your design. You can also proceed to Worksheets 4 and 5 to explore the cost savings of your design.

Instructions
STEP 6: Target the Effective Aperture (EA)

[The figures shown after Step 12 contain] seven sets of graphs, one for each of the representative locations. Within each set there are three graphs, corresponding to three different levels of required illuminance. The graphs indicate bands of EAs that yield maximum savings from skylighting. The graphs are used to find the range of EAs to target in your design. In general,

the ranges are broad, because there is not a sharp optimum point on skylight performance curves. There are many design options within the range of EAs, which allows you flexibility in designing your skylight system.

Choose the [Effective Aperture (EA) graph] that matches your Representative Location (Step 1), and Desired Average Illuminance (Step 2). There are solid line curves for maximum EA, and dashed line curves for minimum EA. Follow the directions on the form for finding the maximum and minimum values of EA. These should be entered in the appropriate blanks under Step 7 below.

STEP 7: Determine Skylight-to-Floor Ratio (SFR)

There are two calculations here, one for the maximum and one for the minimum SFR. They use the maximum and minimum EAs found in the previous step.

For each calculation, use the glazing visible transmittance (VT, from Step 3) and the well factor (WF, from Step 4).

Calculate SFR as shown on the form.

STEP 8: Determine Skylight Area

For both maximum SFR and minimum SFR, multiply by Gross Floor Area (from Step 2), to find skylight area in square feet.

STEP 9: Determine Number of Skylights

For the minimum and maximum skylight areas, divide by the size of the trial skylight (from Step 3) and round up to arrive at the number of skylights that correspond to each case. These numbers set upper and lower limits for your trial skylight design. The Trial Design Worksheet helps you to relate these numbers to your building design.

At this point, skip to the beginning of Worksheet 3. Steps 10–12 are only to be used when you are working with a known skylight design.

STEP 10: Determine Total Skylight Area

This calculation starts with the number and size of skylights, and gives the total skylight area (in square feet). The Unit Area is the opening area of a single skylight unit, and is taken from Step 3.

STEP 11: Determine Skylight-to-Floor Ratio (SFR)

This calculation finds the SFR. Again, the calculation should only include the floor area of building with skylighting and daylight controls for the electric lights. Gross floor area means that you should ignore the floor area taken up by partitions and use the overall area of the space.

STEP 12: Determine Effective Aperture (EA)

...The EA that results may be used in other parts of the Worksheets. It may be compared to the EAs for your location found in Step 7, and it may be used in the lighting and cooling savings worksheets (Worksheets 4 and 5) that follow.

Optimum Effective Area Graphs Based on Peak Demand

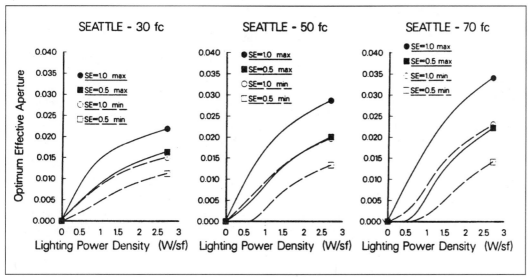

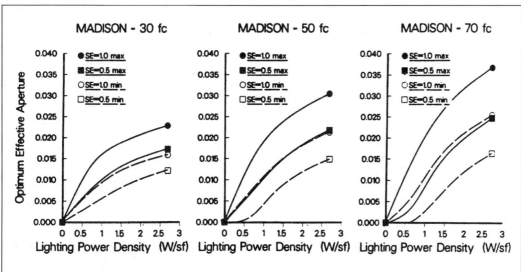

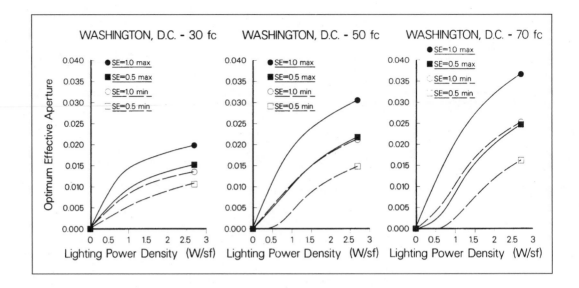

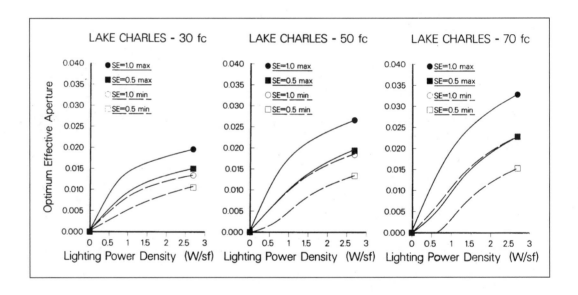

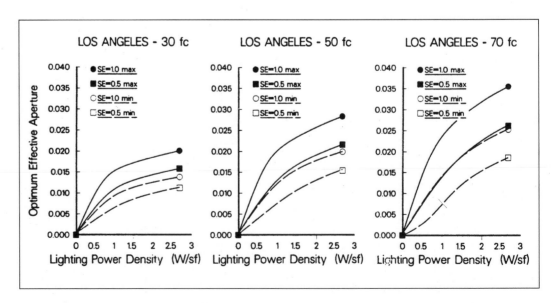

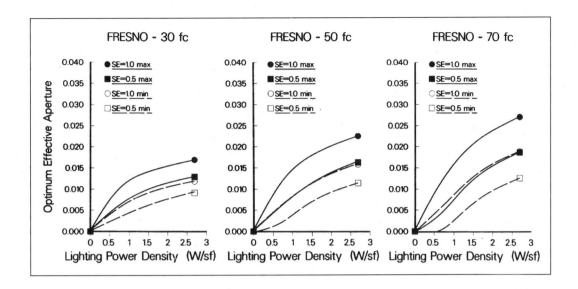

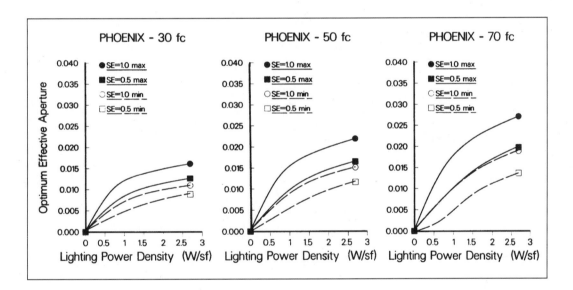

WORKSHEET 2

Note: Use [page 48] of this form (Steps 6–9) for first cut estimates of skylight area; use [page 49] (Steps 10–12) for subsequent analysis, when actual skylight sizes are known. See [Skylight Area Worksheet, pages 44–47] for more information and an example of the use of this form. Some "Step" numbers refer to Form 1 information.

STEP 6: Find Trial Effective Aperture (EA)

Choose the graph from [pages 45–47 that] corresponds to your Representative Location (Step 1) and to your Desired Average Illuminance (Step 2). Enter the graph at the LPD for your design (Step 2). Draw up to the dashed line curve that is closest to your SE (Step 5); mark the intersection points (you may interpolate between dashed curves). Repeat this step for the solid line curves. Draw horizontal lines from these points to find minimum and maximum Effective Apertures (EA). Enter these numbers in Step 7 below.

STEP 7: Determine Trial Skylight-to-Floor Ratio (SFR)

Minimum EA = $\boxed{0.015}$ Maximum EA = $\boxed{0.024}$

$$\text{SFR} = \frac{\text{Min EA}}{\text{VT} \times \text{WF}} = \frac{\boxed{0.015}}{\boxed{0.50} \times \boxed{0.90}} \qquad \text{SFR} = \frac{\text{Max EA}}{\text{VT} \times \text{WF}} = \frac{\boxed{0.024}}{\boxed{0.50} \times \boxed{0.90}}$$

    (Step 3) (Step 4)   (Step 3) (Step 4)

Minimum SFR = $\boxed{0.033}$ Maximum SFR = $\boxed{0.053}$

STEP 8: Determine Trial Skylight Area

Minimum Total Skylight Area:
Min. Area = Min. SFR × Gross Area = $\boxed{0.033}$ × $\boxed{10,000}$
          (Step 7)   (Step 2)   sf

Minimum Area = $\boxed{330}$ sf

Maximum Total Skylight Area:
Max. Area = Max. SFR × Gross Area = $\boxed{0.053}$ × $\boxed{10,000}$
          (Step 7)   (Step 2)   sf

Maximum Area = $\boxed{530}$ sf

STEP 9: Determine Trial Number of Skylights

Minimum Number of Skylights:
Min. Nmbr = Min. Area ÷ Unit Area = $\boxed{330}$ ÷ $\boxed{16}$
           (Step 8)   (Step 3)   sf

Minimum Number = $\boxed{21}$
              (round up)

Maximum Number of Skylights:
Max. Nmbr = Max. Area ÷ Unit Area = $\boxed{530}$ ÷ $\boxed{16}$
           (Step 8)   (Step 3)   sf

Maximum Number = $\boxed{34}$
              (round up)

Note: The following three steps are used to calculate Effective Aperture (EA) when the number of skylights, the well factor, and the visible transmittance of the skylight are known. . . .

STEP 10: Determine Total Skylight Area

Number of Skylights $\times$ Unit Area = $\boxed{30}$ $\times$ $\boxed{16}$ $\times$ $\boxed{480}$ Total Skylight Area
     (#)   (sf each)   # sf each   sf
               (Step 3)

STEP 11: Determine Skylight-to-Floor Ratio (SFR)

Total Skylight Area $\div$ Gross Floor Area = $\boxed{480}$ $\div$ $\boxed{10,000}$ = $\boxed{0.048}$ Skylight-to-Floor Ratio (SFR)
  (Step 10)   (Step 2)   sf   sf

STEP 12: Determine Effective Aperture (EA)

$\boxed{0.048}$ $\times$ $\boxed{0.50}$ $\times$ $\boxed{0.90}$ = $\boxed{0.022}$ Effective Aperture
 SFR   VT   WF   EA
(Step 11) (Step 3) (Step 4)

WORKSHEET 3
Trial Layout Worksheets

The Trial Layout Worksheet provides two sketch areas of grids for you to do a quick layout of the maximum and minimum numbers of skylights determined on the previous worksheet.

At this point, you should go back to your building plans and look at how these trial designs relate to your other design goals. Check the following details:

- Coordination with the structural system and interior layout
- Skylight spacing
- Spacing-to-ceiling height ratio
- Lighting quality considerations
- Appropriateness of the trial skylight size and well design in light of other design considerations

Based on this analysis, you can decide if your trial skylight and well designs are acceptable, or you can modify them. Any of the parameters could be changed. For example, you may decide that you want to use a larger skylight with a lower transmittance glazing and a deeper well for reasons of lighting quality.

If you do choose a different skylight or well design, return to Step 3 on Worksheet 1 and go through the analysis again, this time using the new parameters. The major difference this time through is that you would use Steps 10–12, along with Step 6 to learn if your new design still falls within the optimum range. If it has moved out of the optimum, you should consider modifying it again to get back within that range.

WORKSHEET 3

Note: See [Trial Layout Worksheets, page 50] for more information and an example of the use of this form.

Use the following sketch areas to lay out trial skylight areas on your floor plan. Alternatively, do trial layouts on building design drawings.

If this analysis leads to a different skylight or well design, return to Step 3, Form 1, and recalculate to refine the worksheet calculations.

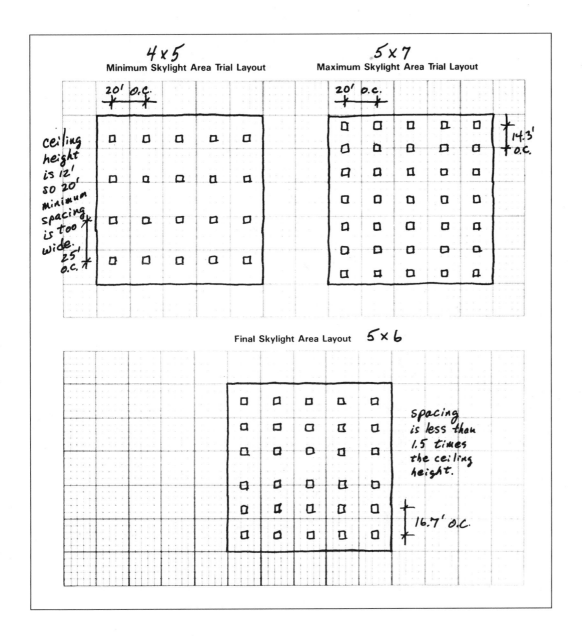

WORKSHEET 4
Lighting Savings Worksheet

This Worksheet helps you to estimate the actual lighting energy and cost savings from the daylight system.

Instructions

STEP 13: Find Full Load Lighting Hours

This is the number of hours of full load, or undimmed, lighting operation in a year that your building would require without the daylighting system operating (no dimming). The default value corresponds to typical office working hours, as shown in [the figure below]. This schedule was used as the basis for the savings calculations in these Guidelines. The calculations are valid as long as the occupancy schedule for your building is similar to this schedule. If, on the other hand, your building's schedule is substantially different, refer to Appendix E

for a procedure to adjust the calculations to your actual schedule.

For example, if the building is a school that finishes operation during the afternoon and is closed on weekends, then the daylighting system will turn off lights for a larger fraction of the time than it would in an office, and the lighting energy savings would be different. Likewise, if the building is a restaurant that operates only in the afternoon and nighttime hours, its energy savings would also be different.

The default lighting schedule is shown in [the figure below]. For most hours, not all of the lights are turned on. For instance, at 10 a.m. on a weekday, 90% of the lights are turned on, while at 5:30 p.m. only 50% of the lights are on. This is because some of the occupants have left for the day and turned off lights. On Saturdays, only some of the lights are on during the morning, and fewer during the afternoon.

Default Lighting Schedule

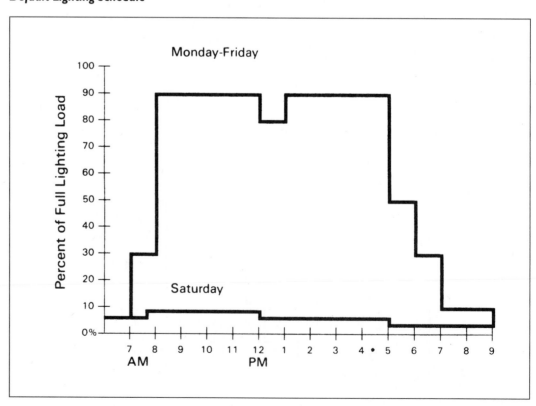

STEP 14: Find Fraction of Lighting Energy Saved

[From the eighteen Lighting Energy Savings] graphs: choose the graph for the Representative City you selected (Step 1) and for your Desired Average Illuminance (Step 2). Use the curve that corresponds to your control system type (Step 2). Interpolate as necessary. Follow the directions on the form to find the Fraction of Lighting Energy Saved.

STEP 15: Calculate Lighting Energy Saved

This calculation yields the total number of kilowatt-hours of electricity saved per year by the daylighting system. Multiply the Lighting Power Density, by the gross floor area, and by the number of full load lighting hours and the fraction of lighting energy saved. Division by 1000 converts to kilowatt hours per year.

STEP 16: Calculate Lighting Cost Saved

This Step calculates the dollar value of the lighting energy saved.

[Find the average cost of electricity, including demand charges, from your local utility.] Multiply the cost by the lighting energy saved to arrive at lighting cost saved.

Lighting Energy Savings Graphs

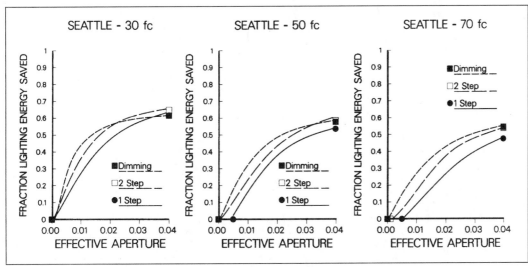

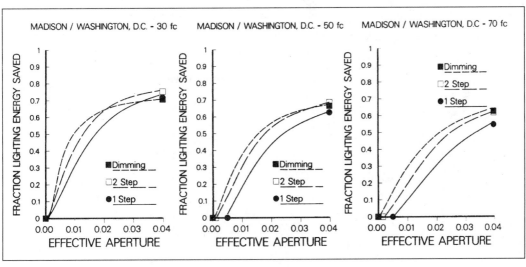

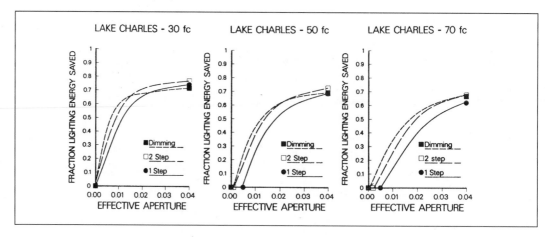

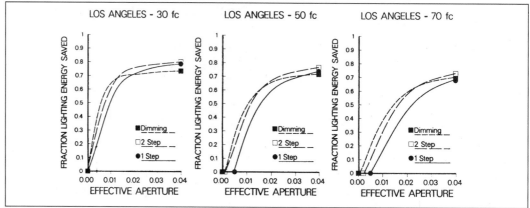

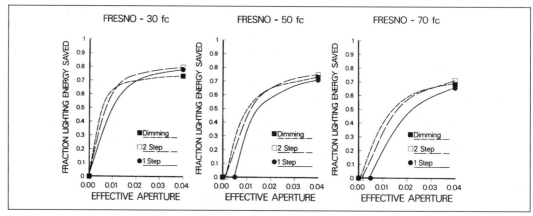

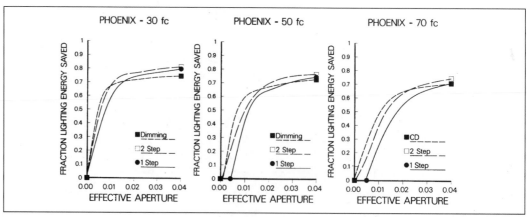

WORKSHEET 4

Note: See [Lighting Savings Worksheet, pages 52–54] for more information and an example of the use of this form. Some "Step" numbers refer to previous Form information.

STEP 13: Finding Full Load Lighting Hours

The default value corresponds to typical office working hours, as shown in the schedule in [the previous section]. If that schedule differs greatly from the schedule in your building, refer to [Appendix E] for the procedure for finding your full load operating hours. Otherwise, use the default value.

Full load lighting hours = $\boxed{2600}$ hrs.
$\qquad$ (default: 2600)

STEP 14: Find Fraction of Lighting Energy Saved

Use the graph from [the Lighting Energy Savings Graphs, pages 53–54] corresponding to your Representative Location (Step 1) and your Desired Average Illuminance (Step 2). Enter graph at the EA value (Step 12) corresponding to your skylight design. Draw a line up to the curve for your Daylighting Control System (Step 2), then across to the fraction of lighting energy saved. Enter the fraction below.

EA = 0.022 (Step 12)
Fraction of Lighting Energy Saved $\boxed{0.55}$

STEP 15: Calculate Lighting Energy Saved

$$\frac{\text{LPD (Step 2)}}{1000} \times \text{Gross Floor Area} \times \text{Full Load Hours} \times \text{Fraction Saved} = \text{Lighting Energy Saved (kWh)}$$
$$\qquad\qquad\quad \text{(Step 2)} \qquad\qquad \text{(Step 13)} \qquad\qquad \text{(Step 14)}$$

$$\frac{\boxed{1.5}}{1000} \times \boxed{10,000} \times \boxed{2,600} \times \boxed{0.55} = \boxed{21,450} \text{ kWh/yr}$$

STEP 16: Calculate Lighting Cost Saved

. . . If actual electricity costs are not known, [contact your local utility for a current rate schedule].

$$\text{Lighting Energy Saved} \times \text{Average Electricity Cost} = \boxed{21,450} \times \boxed{0.073} = \boxed{\$1,566.}$$
$$\quad \text{(Step 15)} \qquad\qquad\quad (\$/\text{kWh}) \qquad\quad \text{kWh/yr} \quad \$/\text{kWh} \quad \$/\text{yr}$$

WORKSHEET 5
Cooling Calculation Worksheet

This Worksheet helps you to estimate the cooling energy and cost effects from your skylight system. These effects result primarily from reduced internal gains when the electric lighting is automatically turned off by the daylight control system, and reflect the additional solar heat gains that enter through the skylight. These effects should be added to the lighting cost savings calculated in Step 16, to arrive at the combined savings.

In general, the cooling effects will be small compared to the lighting savings. It is even possible for the cooling effects to be negative, i.e., there is an increase in cooling costs. This would indicate that the skylight system may be oversized. If, however, the combined lighting and cooling savings are still substantial, it indicates that the lighting savings far outweigh the increased cooling costs due to skylighting.

Instructions
STEP 17: Note Representative City

As in the earlier calculations, a representative city is used here. Check off the representative city that you selected in Step 1. This is for reference when performing the following cooling calculations.

STEP 18: Find Coefficients for Representative City

The numbers in the table are used in the next step to calculate the cooling energy effects for the representative city. Circle the numbers for the cooling city you have chosen.

STEP 19: Calculate Cooling Energy and Cost Effects

Perform the calculation as shown, using the numbers circled in Step 18. The Cooling Energy Effect is found first. This is multiplied by the Average electricity cost to find the Cooling Cost Effect. You should use the same electricity cost as was used in Step 16. A negative value is an added cooling cost; a positive value represents a saving.

As discussed above, the Cooling Cost Effect should be added to the Lighting Cost Saved to obtain total savings.

WORKSHEET 5

Note: See [Cooling Calculation Worksheet, page 56] for more information and an example of the use of this form. Some "Step" numbers refer to previous Form information.

STEP 17: Note Representative City

This calculation makes use of the same representative cities selected in Step 1. Check off your selection again here, for reference:

- ☐ Seattle, WA
- ☐ Madison, WI
- ☑ Washington, DC
- ☐ Lake Charles, LA
- ☐ Los Angeles, CA
- ☐ Fresno, CA
- ☐ Phoenix, AZ

STEP 18: Find Coefficients for Representative Cooling City

	B1	B2
Seattle, WA	0.19	11.5
Madison, WI	0.31	16.6
Washington, DC	0.42	21.1
Lake Charles, LA	0.66	30.8
Los Angeles, CA	0.53	28.1
Fresno, CA	0.51	36.9
Phoenix, AZ	0.68	47.3

STEP 19: Calculate Cooling Energy and Cost Effects

B1 (Step 18)		Fraction Saved (Step 14)		LPD (Step 2)		Temporary Value #1
0.42	×	0.55	×	1.5	=	0.347

B2 (Step 18)		Effective Aperture (Step 12)		Skylight Effic. (Step 5)		Temporary Value #2
21.1	×	0.022	÷	1.02	=	0.455

Temporary Value #1		Temporary Value #2		Unit Cooling Energy Effect		Gross Floor Area		Cooling Energy Effect
0.347	−	0.455	=	−.108	×	10,000	=	−1,080
(from above)		(from above)		kWh/yrsf		(Step 2)		kWh/yr

		Cooling Energy Effect		Average Electricity Cost		Cooling Cost Effect
		−1,080	×	0.073	=	−79.
		kWh/yr (from above)		(Step 18) $/kWh		kWh/yrsf

Limits of Analysis

The estimation method contained in the Worksheets and presented in this [section] was derived from an extensive body of computer analysis. (The technical basis for the work is contained in a series of papers published by Lawrence Berkeley Laboratory. . . .) As with any such analysis effort, a set of common assumptions were used to establish a base case building. From this base, the most important variables were systematically changed, such as Effective Aperture and Lighting Power Density. The results of this body of computer simulations were distilled into the graphs and procedures presented in these Guidelines.

In choosing the base case and the variables for this study, care was taken to make assumptions that are broadly applicable to typical commercial buildings. As a result, the information presented is valid for many, if not most, commercial skylighting applications. For buildings that differ significantly from the typical buildings used in this study, however, the results may be less meaningful.

These results are generally valid when the following conditions are true:

- Climate conditions similar to those in the representative cities.
- Occupancy schedules and characteristics similar to office occupancies, i.e., daytime operation, ordinary internal heat gains, ordinary lighting requirements. See [Lighting Savings Worksheet, pages 52–54] for more information.
- Generally even lighting requirements, with no major differences in task illuminance.
- Flat and low-slope roof systems (<4:12 pitch).
- Roughly even skylight distribution across roof.
- No significant shading from adjacent buildings or vegetation.

- Skylight spacing less than or equal to 1.5 times ceiling height.
- Effective aperture less than 0.05.
- Skylight glazings that are at least partially diffusing.
- Daylighting controls for lighting.

Buildings that differ greatly from these conditions may require a detailed analysis to accurately estimate their skylighting performance.

The following [section] presents additional technical information on other energy considerations for skylighting, such as heating load and peak electricity demand. That information may cause you to adjust your skylight design to a different optimum than was selected with these Worksheets. If that is the case, you can return to the Worksheets and work through your new design comparing it to the original.

Daylight Economic Analysis

The preceding sections presented a set of worksheets that can be used to estimate the lighting and cooling energy and cost savings from skylighting. This savings information is important, because it shows that skylighting reduces operating costs, in addition to its other benefits to occupants. For many applications, this may be sufficient to justify using skylights. To make a complete economic evaluation, however, requires more information.

The savings estimates derived above assumed a simple, flat rate for electricity. . . . however, utility rate structures are more complicated than flat rates, and may require more detailed breakdowns of energy consumption to accurately estimate. This becomes even more so when all the energy effects of skylighting are included, such as heating energy and peak demand changes. . . . [A] complete analysis of energy and cost savings could require detailed computer simulations. . . .

In addition to cost savings, or "benefits," from skylighting, we need to know the "costs" of the skylighting system. These costs include two primary elements: the costs of the skylights and of the daylighting controls, along with the associated labor to install them. There are also other costs that may be included, such as maintenance costs or long-term replacement costs. There may also be associated savings, such as increased life of lighting equipment.

The primary costs can be accurately predicted by the building contractor or hardware supplier; the "softer" costs must be estimated as best they can.

Once the costs and benefits of skylighting have been quantified, they can be compared to each other, and also to the costs and benefits of alternative systems. The easiest comparison is the "simple payback," which is the first cost divided by the annual savings, and is a crude measure of the number of years it will take for the savings to pay back the initial investment. More sophisticated analyses take into account the time value of money, estimates of general inflation and energy cost inflation, and lifetime of the equipment until replacement. A complete analysis would compare the life cycle costs and benefits of a "no skylighting" design with one or more skylighting and daylight control systems. This would provide clear guidance in selecting the final skylighting system.

A complete economic analysis can quantify the dollar benefits and costs of skylighting; it cannot quantify the less tangible, but nevertheless valuable, benefits of skylights such as occupant satisfaction and delight. This is left to the judgment and sensibility of the owner, designer, contractor, and occupants. In a well designed system, these benefits can far outweigh the straight economic benefits.

[Note: A thorough discussion of this calculation methodology is presented in the American Architectural Manufacturers Association (AAMA) Skylight Handbook. For additional information, it can be obtained from: AAMA, 1540 East Dundee Rd., Palatine, IL 60067. Telephone: (708) 202–1350]

3.2 COMPUTER PROGRAMS

Computer programs have existed for practitioners to investigate various aspects of daylighting since programmable calculators first became available. Over the years, the cost of hardware has been steadily decreasing while the speed and storage have been increasing. Several simulation programs are discussed that many practitioners who regularly design and integrate daylighting strategies into buildings implement at strategic phases of the design process.

More general information on a wide range of tools is displayed later in the text in the design tools survey section compiled by Lawrence Berkeley Laboratory.

RADIANCE

The Windows and Lighting Program at the Lawrence Berkeley Laboratory in Berkeley,

California is charged by the U.S. Department of Energy with developing new technologies for the energy-efficient use of daylight and electric lighting in buildings. One of the group's major thrusts is the development of design tools to help architects and engineers produce better building designs using existing technology.

One such project is the collection of lighting simulation and analysis routines called RADIANCE. RADIANCE has been developed in a UNIX environment over a period of nine years and consists of more than 100 separate routines that provide numerous functions and capabilities for lighting and daylighting design and research.

RADIANCE is an advanced lighting simulation program that uses a ray-tracing methodology to accurately predict the behavior of light in spaces. Users describe the geometry of the space and the characteristics of surface materials and light sources. The program then uses the mathematics of the physical behavior of light to calculate luminances in the scene. The output is a photo-realistic color image that contains numeric predictions of light levels at any point in the scene.

The ability to view an illuminated space without having to physically construct it is of immeasurable value not only to designers but to researchers as well. The RADIANCE program has the potential to promote energy-efficient lighting design by demonstrating the visual effect of new lamp technologies, daylighting, and intelligent controls. Many innovative lighting designs have been rejected by clients who thought the modest energy consumption would result in dark, unrentable spaces. A proven tool for predicting visibility in a form everyone can understand, "a picture" could allay such doubts and clear the path to more efficient and reliable designs. As computers

become faster and cheaper, and as computer-aided design becomes more common, design studies will rely increasingly on simulation to explore innovative architectural and lighting solutions.

RADIANCE can be used at any point in a design process. It needs only a single light source and a single surface to calculate an image. Of course, the more detail the user provides, the more accurate and interesting the final image. The user describes the color and other optical properties of each surface. Typically, a library of standard materials (e.g., wood, copper, glass) is maintained. Surface textures and patterns can also be applied. An easy technique to improve the realism of the final image is to digitize photos of fabrics or other patterns and apply them in a scene. Textures are defined mathematically, and patterns can be created this way as well; for example, a very realistic wood grain pattern can be created simply with a function. Next, the user adds photometric data for electric light sources and, if daylight modeling is desired, also provides time of day, latitude, longitude, and calendar day. Once the calculation of the final scene is complete, the user specifies viewpoint, exposure, and other parameters for the image and lets the software work for several hours (very complex images can take 24 hours to produce). This process can be done in batch mode in the background, keeping the machine free for other tasks. To help establish view points and to spot mistakes in the model, RADIANCE has a lower-grade imaging utility that is interactive. As it progressively refines an image on the screen, it allows the user to manipulate view parameters or check lighting values.

The final output is an image that can be displayed on the screen or copied onto video, paper, or film. Sequences of stills can be captured on video for animated walk-through. In addition, any kind of lighting data can be obtained, and these can be plotted or otherwise manipulated in any manner.

The RADIANCE program has been used to produce synthetic images of many indoor and outdoor lighting situations, with an emphasis on calculations that were previously considered too difficult to resolve with other methods. These include daylit office spaces with penetrating beam sunlight and venetian blinds, building atria, and rooms with many glass and metal surfaces (see Figures 3.2.1 and 3.2.2).

Computational Methodology

Accurately modeling the behavior of light in real environments with thousands of reflective surfaces is a challenge to current computational techniques. RADIANCE uses a technique called ray tracing to follow light backward from an observer to the light source(s) of a hypothetical scene. Once a path has been found, the luminance associated with each ray is computed from the candle power distribution of the light source and the reflective properties of the intervening surfaces (see Figures 3.2.3 and 3.2.4). Accuracy is obtained with a computational model that handles many types of surfaces (e.g., matte, shiny, or glass) and objects of high geometric complexity. With the use of advanced sorting techniques, scenes containing thousands of objects can be rendered efficiently. Unlike other relighting programs that are limited to calculations of illuminance in purely diffuse environments, RADIANCE accurately handles reflections from shiny surfaces, permitting the realistic rendition of highlights. The lighting model has been further enhanced with the calculation of inter-reflections between surfaces and contributions from spatially distributed sources such as the sky.

Figure 3.2.1
Radiance output showing an interior without fenestration control and the corresponding direct beam penetration. (Courtesy of Greg Cunningham, AIA and Associates.)

Figure 3.2.2
Radiance output showing an interior view with exterior horizontal fenestration controls to limit direct beam penetration. (Courtesy of Greg Cunningham, AIA and Associates.)

A synthetic image consists of thousands of pixels (picture elements), and several rays are needed to compute the luminance value at each one. A high-resolution image

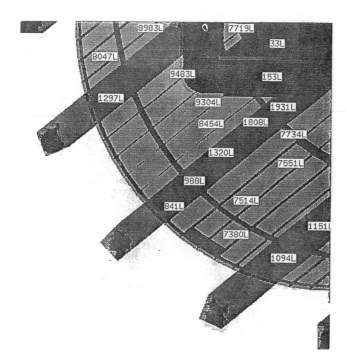

Figure 3.2.3
Floor plan showing lux without fenestration control. (Courtesy of Greg Cunningham, AIA and Associates.)

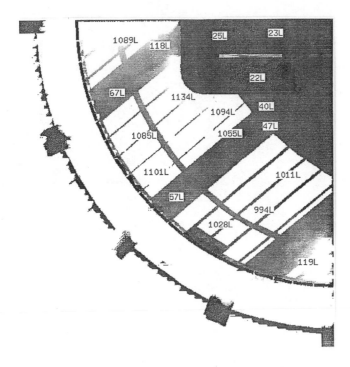

Figure 3.2.4
Floor plan showing lux with horizontal fenestration controls. (Courtesy of Greg Cunningham, AIA and Associates.)

therefore requires millions of computations. On a microcomputer workstation, an image may take several central processing unit (CPU) hours to generate, thus jobs are usually run overnight.

Although the real-time generation of high-resolution images is beyond the capability of today's workstations, low-resolution images can be completed interactively using a technique called "adaptive refinement." One of the RADIANCE programs uses this technique to trace rays continuously on a color workstation, progressively increasing the resolution of the displayed image while the user looks on. During the typical calculation, the display evolves at a rate of 50 pixels per second and represents far more information than could be obtained from a physical model or a hand calculator through conventional photometry. The user can interrupt the program at any time to move the viewpoint, adjust the exposure, or display individual luminance values. In a few minutes, an experienced designer can get a good idea of how the environment will look in a final rendering or in real life.

Limitations

RADIANCE is not a user-friendly program in its current form. The first step is creating the scene geometry. For example, walls, windows, and furniture are described. This is ideally done with a three-dimensional drawing program. However, RADIANCE works only with text files. In other words, a cube must be given to RADIANCE as a text field containing the numeric spatial coordinates of the cube's six surfaces. Technicians are currently developing software to translate commercial CAD files for RADIANCE input, and several of them are now available. Typically, a user will convert the CAD file to a text format and then translate this text to a RADIANCE text file; this does not free the user from interacting with

RADIANCE text, because some fine tuning of the geometry may be desired and additional data must be added to the CAD output. Information about materials, lights, and geographic location are not included in the base CAD file. Also, many CAD packages have a limited range of geometric forms that they can easily create; RADIANCE not only handles any kind of geometry but also contains many tools to easily create complex forms. Users may find it highly desirable to leave difficult shapes for RADIANCE and not attempt them with the CAD software.

Because most CAD packages handle strictly metric data, it is necessary to manually apply optical properties to every surface drawing in CAD. (Some drawing packages allow additional attributes to be added to surfaces; this means a material code number could be included in the CAD text file to be used by RADIANCE.) Once the CAD geometry has been translated for RADIANCE, materials must be created and applied to surfaces. This requires working with the text form of a scene that the user is accustomed to viewing in three dimensions, which makes exact identification of specific parts of the scene difficult. Some vendors are working on interfaces to ease this process. A functional prototype for an interface that helps the user "map" materials onto surfaces in the three-dimensional model is available. This interface also provides a more intuitive way to create materials; for example, colors are selected from a color wheel rather than described by their red-green-blue numeric values.

Lights must also be placed in the scene. This requires describing their photometric properties and locating them correctly. There are some tools to assist in entering the data, but complex lighting conditions can require considerable lighting expertise. In terms of placing simple sources when working with a CAD program, the user can place dummy "markers" in the three-dimensional file for replacement by RADIANCE with something more appropriate.

Prerequisites

Because of the compelling images RADIANCE produces and because of its potential to increase one's overall understanding of the behavior of light in spaces, RADIANCE is an invaluable tool for anyone involved in architectural or lighting design. However, it takes a tremendous commitment to become a RADIANCE user, at least until significant improvement has been made in the area of program's ease of use. At a minimum, you must (1) be familiar with the UNIX operating system; (2) be familiar with a UNIX text editor; (3) have a reasonable understanding of photometries; and (4) have a UNIX-running computer available for long time periods. Designers who answer no to any of these and who want RADIANCE only for its graphic output should carefully consider the difficulties involved. It takes a lot of work to create a RADIANCE image, but the results are rich with information. If you do not need all of that information, perhaps such a complex program is not the best choice for you. On the other hand, others will find the effort is worth it.

Software Links

RADIANCE comes with translators for the following file types: Architrion Text File; AutoCAD DXF; GDS Things File; IES Luminaire Data; Sun 8 and 24-bit Rasterfiles; and Targa 8, 16, and 32-bit images.

Graphics Support

RADIANCE supports the following graphics interfaces: X11 8-bit color or gray-scale and 24-bit color displays, X10 8-bit color or gray-scale displays, Sunview 8-bit color gray-scale displays, NeWS color or gray-scale displays, and AED 512 color and graphics terminals.

Hardware Support

RADIANCE should compile without modification on any UNIX system with X11 support. RADIANCE has been tested on the following hardware platforms: Sun 3, Sun 4 workstations, DEC station running ULTRIX, Silicon Graphics IRIS, and Mac II running AUX.

How to Obtain a Copy

To obtain a copy, write to:

> Windows and Lighting Program
> Attention: Greg Ward
> Building 90-3111, Lawrence Berkeley
> Laboratory
> University of California
> Berkeley, CA 94720
> Telephone: (510) 486–5605

SUPERLITE

The SUPERLITE program is a state-of-the-art computer program for predicting illuminance in buildings. The program addresses the need to accurately model geometrically complex fenestration systems in architecturally complex building spaces.

This program's free geometric system is capable of calculating illuminance levels for virtually any building configuration that can be defined by walls and windows of trapezoidal geometry. This allows the program to model complicated building shapes, such as A-frame structures, L-shaped rooms with internal obstructions (e.g., partitions), and external obstructions such as overhangs or adjacent buildings.

In addition to calculating daylighting levels from diffuse sources of outdoor illumina-

tion, the sky and ground, SUPERLITE accounts for the effect of direct sunlight in the room. The window glazing can be either clear or diffusing glass with a diffusing sheer curtain or shade.

The solar and weather data input for the program can be supplied in three ways. The first option allows the user to supply the appropriate sky condition. The sky models available in this program are (1) the uniform sky; (2) the CIE standard overcast sky; and (3) the CIE standard clear sky, with or without direct sun. The second option involves specifying geographic data, such as latitude and longitude, and the time and date of the simulation using the stipulated sky conditions. This option allows a series of simulations to be conducted for given times of the day and year. The third option requires specifying the solar location under predetermined sky conditions.

Illuminance data are calculated for nodal points on arbitrary work planes located and oriented as specified by the user. These data can be provided numerically in terms of illuminance level or daylight factor in tabular format. Analyses are conducted for different sky conditions, different hours, and various times of the year to study the annual performance of fenestration systems combined with daylighting.

Calculational Methodology

SUPERLITE adopts a very detailed point-by-point illumination calculation for the date, time, and sky conditions specified. The daylight illumination on any arbitrary work surface inside a room depends on three quantities: the direct illumination from the sky and sun, illumination from external reflections, and illuminance from internal reflections. To determine the contribution of each of these quantities, the luminance distribution of the sky and each internal and external reflector must be known.

The luminance distribution of the sky depends on weather conditions, the time of day, and the time of year. It is estimated from an empirical formula. The luminance distribution of any external or internal surface depends on both the quantity of light received from the sky and reflections from surrounding surfaces. For internal surfaces, this includes light from the sky and external reflections, which is attenuated on transmission through windows. By calculating light-exchange factors for each surface, one can calculate the light impinging from sky and surrounding reflectors on any surface.

Limitations

Like RADIANCE, SUPERLITE is not a user-friendly program in its current form. The entire geometry of the space to be analyzed is defined in terms of numerical coordinates. The input file is a string of numbers without any explanations. Hopefully, in the near future, several CAD interfaces will be available.

In the present stage of development, SUPERLITE has a number of limitations. The first limitation is the assumption that all reflected light is assumed to be perfectly diffuse, whereas some building surfaces may be semispecular. A second assumption is that the luminous flux entering a room has a uniform spectral composition and that its reflection by surfaces is uniform over the entire visible spectrum. Also, the modeling of the sky is limited to the three theoretical sky distributions described previously; therefore, partly cloudy skies cannot be simulated.

Typically these limitations are not of great concern for normal daylighting studies;

however, the capabilities of the program are being expanded to allow modeling of everchanging design strategies and system technologies for which these limitations would be significant.

Prerequisites

SUPERLITE is a valuable tool for anyone involved in architectural or lighting design. However, it takes a significant commitment to become a SUPERLITE user, at least in the present form. At a minimum, one must (1) be familiar with the operating system; (2) be familiar with the compilation procedure for compiling FORTRAN routines, and (3) have a reasonable understanding of the three-dimensional geometrical coordinate system. Designers who require reliable lighting predictions for a complex space, without spending a lot of money, can resort to SUPERLITE. Also, SUPERLITE does not directly produce any graphic output. The user is able to take the information from SUPERLITE to any other plotting software for development of contour plotting.

Software Links

An interface called ADELINE is under development. This is a graphic interface for SUPERLITE and DOE2. Only a prototype is available at this time.

Graphics Support

Superlite cannot communicate with any other graphics software directly.

Hardware Support

SUPERLITE was developed on a VAX/VMS platform. It is also tested under the following platforms: Sun 3 and Sun 4 workstations and IBM PCs.

How to Obtain a Copy

To obtain a copy, write to:

Windows and Lighting Program
Building 90-3111,
Lawrence Berkeley Laboratory
University of California
Berkeley, CA 94720-USA
Telephone: (510) 486–4096
Fax: (510) 486–4089

PowerDOE

PowerDOE (formerly DOE2.1E, DOE2.1D, etc.), was specifically developed for evaluating the energy performance of buildings on an hour-by-hour basis and is one of only a few detailed building energy simulation programs that incorporates detailed hourly daylighting analysis.

For many years, architects and engineers have used scaled models, and hand calculator programs, and sophisticated mainframe computer programs to determine levels of interior daylight for different building configurations. However, none of these tools determines the annual energy savings from daylighting, information that could have an important effect on design decisions.

Difficulties were overcome by adding daylighting simulation algorithms to the original DOE2.1B version in about 1982. Taken into account are such factors as window size, glass transmittance, inside surface reflectances, sun control devices such as blinds and overhangs, and the luminance distribution of the sky.

DOE2 daylighting calculations are essentially used to perform energy analysis of buildings with energy savings potentials by using daylight through various types of building apertures.

When thermal zones of the building under analysis are defined, daylighting elements such as window location, glass transmittance, interior and exterior shades, other external shades, reflectances of walls, roof, floor, and so on are identified. Based on the type of visual task of the space, required illumination level is prescribed for the space. The control scheme for the lighting zone (e.g., stepped or continuously dimmed) is specified. The thermal zone can be divided into one or two lighting zones controlled by individual lighting sensors (reference points). During an hourly simulation, depending on the available daylight in the specified reference point and daylighting controls, electric lighting is either dimmed or switched off. The direct energy savings achieved by reducing the hours of operation of lights and the cooling energy savings from the reduction of the internal heat gain (from lights) is corrected and accounted by DOE2. Hence, on an annual basis, the user can predict the energy savings associated with daylighting.

Computational Methodology

The DOE2 daylighting model, in conjunction with the thermal loads analysis, determines the energy impact of daylighting strategies based on hour-by-hour analysis of daylight availability, site conditions, window management in response to sun control and glare, and various lighting control strategies.

The daylighting calculation has three main stages. In the first stage a preprocessor calculates daylight factors for later use in the hourly loads calculation. The user specifies the coordinates of one or two reference points in a space. DOE2 then integrates over the area of each window to obtain the contribution of direct light from the window to illuminance at the reference points and the contribution of light that reflects from the surfaces before reaching the reference point. Taken into account are such factors as the luminance distribution of the sky, window size, orientation, glass transmittance, and internal and external shades. The calculation is carried out for standard CIE clear and overcast sky conditions for a series of 20 different solar altitude and azimuth values covering the range of annual sun positions in the sky vault. Similarly, daylight factors for glare are also calculated and stored.

In the second stage, an hourly daylighting calculation is performed every hour that the sun is up. The illuminance from each window is found by interpolating the stored daylight factors using the current hour exterior horizontal illuminance. If the glare control option has been specified, the program will automatically close window blinds or drapes to decrease glare below a predefined comfort level. A similar option uses window shading devices to automatically control solar heat gain.

In the last stage, the program simulates the lighting control system (which may be either stepped or continuously dimmed) to determine the electrical lighting energy needed to make up the difference between the daylighting level and the design illuminance. Finally, the zone lighting electrical requirements are passed to the thermal calculation portion of the simulation, which determines hourly heating and cooling loads.

Limitations

Because DOE2 interpolates daylight factor values from precalculated solar positions for each hour of the day, a small amount of error is associated with the interpolation. The interior reflected component of the daylight factor in DOE2 is calculated based on the split flux principle. In this method, the daylight transmitted by the windows is split into two parts: a downward flux, which falls on the floor and the portions of the walls below the imaginary horizontal plane passing through the center of the window; and an upward flux, which strikes the ceiling and portions of the walls above the window midplane. This split flux principle works well when the window geometry is simple and the reflectance variation between the surfaces are not extreme. However, this methodology cannot reliably predict the inter-reflected component if the window has special devices for reflecting light such as light shelves. Also, the luminous distribution of the sky is calculated based on the cloud cover, cloud type, and solar radiation using empirical relationship. This calculated daylight level may be different from the actual daylight available.

Prerequisites

The DOE2 daylighting program is suitable for professionals who want to analyze the impact of daylighting controls on the overall energy consumption of the building. Because it is coupled with the energy analysis program, the user has to learn to use the program as a whole rather than just for the daylighting analysis portion. DOE2 has its own input syntax, and learning it might be time consuming.

Software Links

A graphical interface called ADELINE is under development.

Graphics Support

PowerDOE cannot communicate with any other graphics software directly.

Hardware Support

DOE2 was developed on the VAX/VMS platform. It is also tested under the following platforms: Sun 3 and Sun 4 workstations and IBM PCs.

How to Obtain a Copy

To obtain a copy, write to:

Building Energy Simulation Group
Lawrence Berkeley Laboratory
University of California

Berkeley, CA 94720
Telephone (510) 486–5711

PC versions are available from several private vendors.

3.3 DAYLIGHTING DESIGN TOOL SURVEY*

A broad range of design tools and calculation methodology exists to evaluate daylight related issues. The following survey identifies many that are available to the designer along with a brief description of the attributes of each program.

Table 3.3.1
Nomographs

TOOL/LAST UPDATE/CONTACT	DESCRIPTION	COST
DAYLIGHTING NOMOGRAPHS (1984) Building Technologies Program Lawrence Berkeley Laboratory 1 Cyclotron Road, Bldg 90-3111 Berkeley, CA 94720 (510) 486–4761 Fax: (510) 486–4089	Assist designers in determining potential daylighting benefits and costs; checking strategy for energy conservation and load management.	$ Free. No support.
ENERGY MONOGRAPHS (1984) Burt Hill Kosar Rittelmann 400 Morgan Center Butler, PA 16001 (412) 285–4761 Contact: Al Sain	Useful in early design analysis on commercial buildings; capable of total building energy analysis, including savings from daylight and heating/cooling loads. Note: Free within TVA region.	$50.00 for notebook and enlarged, reusable nomograph set from TVA, Div. of Conservation & Energy Management, Commercial & Industrial Branch, 3S D Signal Place, Chattanooga, TN 37401

*The four tables in this section are reprinted with permission from Lawrence Berkeley Laboratory.

Table 3.3.2
Protractors/Tables

TOOL/LAST UPDATE/CONTACT	DESCRIPTION	COST
CLEAR SKY DAYLIGHT TABLES (1979) Harvey Bryan 48 Agassiz Avenue Belmont, MA 02178 (617) 484–0854	Determines sky component contribution to the illumination of an interior point for a given window geometry and glazing description. Most useful at an early design stage, when scale drawings are not available yet.	$25.00
CLEAR SKY WALDRAM DIAGRAMS (1979) Harvey Bryan 48 Agassiz Avenue Belmont, MA 02178 (617) 484–0854	Assist in determination of sky component contribution to the illumination of an interior point, accounting for angle of incidence losses for vertical glazing and obstructions. Graphic method is useful in early design stages.	$25.00
DAYLIGHT FACTOR DOT CHARTS (1985) *Concepts and Practice of Architectural Daylighting* by Fuller Moore, Van Nostrand Reinhold Co., New York City, N.Y. 1985, p. 234	Determines sky component of the daylight factor at a given interior reference point through overlay with an obstruction mask.	$30.00 approx.
LBL PROTRACTORS (1984) Harvey Bryan 48 Agassiz Avenue Belmont, MA 02178 (617) 484–0854	Allows for determination of the sky component contribution to the illumination of an interior point for an interior point of finite height under overcast sky conditions.	$25.00
LUME PROTRACTOR (1983) Lighting Research Laboratory P.O. Box 6193 Orange, CA 92613-6193 (714) 771–1312 Contact: Bill Jones	Useful in early design analysis.	$5.00
UW GRAPHIC DAYLIGHTING DESIGN METHOD (1980) Department of Agriculture Gould Hall JO-20 University of Washington Seattle, WA 98105 (206) 543–4180 Contact: Marietta Millet	Determines daylight patterns for a room based on the proportions of the window openings, providing illumination level, distribution, and gradient. For more info see: B. Stein and J. Reynolds, *Mechanical and Electrical Equipment for Buildings (MEEB),* 8th Edition, John Wiley & Sons, New York, N.Y., 1992, or G.Z. Brown et al., *Inside Out,* 2nd Edition, John Wiley & Sons, New York, N.Y., 1992.	$30.00 approx.

Table 3.3.3
Micros

TOOL/LAST UPDATE/ CONTACT	DESCRIPTION	HARDWARE	SOFTWARE/COST
AAMASKYI AND SKYLIGHT HANDBOOK (1988) Architectural Aluminum Manufacturers Association (AAMA) 1540 E. Dundee Road, Suite 310 Palatine, IL 60067 (708) 202–1350	Skylight design analysis with emphasis on optimizing for energy efficiency, incorporating both a worksheet and Lotus spreadsheet tool.	IBM PC or compatible	$50.00/software pkg. Lotus 1-2-3, $50.00/handbook, $100.00/handbook + software (Half price for AAMA members.)
ADM-DOE2 (1989) Adm Associates, Inc. 3299 Ramos Circle Sacramento, CA 95827 (916) 363–8383 Fax: (916) 363–1788 Support: Sekhar Krishnamurti Sales: Marla Sullivan	Micro version of DOE 2.1D mainframe program, with additional enhancements.	IBM 386 or compatible, 80837 math-coprocessor.	2MB RAM, $295.00 with one free weather data file and supplement manuals to DOE 2.1D.
AWNSHADE 1.0 (1991) Florida Solar Energy Center 300 State Road 401 Cape Canaveral, FL 32920 (407) 783–0300, Ext. 134 Fax: (407) 783–2571 Contact: Ross McCluney	Calculates the unshaded fraction of a rectangular window shaded by an awning for any given solar position.	IBM PC or compatible.	MS QuickBASIC 3.0 MS-DOS, $35.00.
BUILDING ENERGY ESTIMATION MODULE (BEEM™)–Electric Power Research Institute (EPRI) (1993) Requests for copies should be directed to your local electric utility company. Ask for the person in charge of commercial lighting programs.	Useful in early design stages; evaluates energy impact, including energy use, peak demand, costs, of window and lighting control configurations.	IBM PC or compatible, mouse desirable, but not required.	BASIC 512KB RAM, No charge or nominal cost (max. $50.00), EPRI/BEEM Support Line for registered users.
CONTROLITE 1.0 (1985) Building Technologies Program Lawrence Berkeley Laboratory 1 Cyclotron Road, Bldg 90-3111 Berkeley, CA 94720 (510) 486–4089 Fax: (510) 486–4089 Contact: Francis Rubinstein	Calculates energy savings and cost-benefit of using lighting controls in buildings. QUICKLITE incorporated.	IBM PC XT, IBM PC AT, or true compatible.	256KB RAM, MS-DOS 2.0, or later. $ Free. No support.
DAYLIT (1988) Murray Milne	Calculates daylight considering fins,	IBM PC or compatible.	FORTRAN, 256 KB RAM,

TOOL/LAST UPDATE/ CONTACT	DESCRIPTION	HARDWARE	SOFTWARE/COST
School of Architecture UCLA 1317 Perloff Hall 405 Hillgard Avenue Los Angeles, CA 90025-1467	overhangs, skylights and lightshelves. Calculates electric light for 3 zones with 5 control strategies. Plots hourly and annually data based on IES method.		MS-DOS 3.0. Manual on disk. $ Info on request.
DAYLITE 2.2 (1991) Solarsoft/Kinetic Software 12672 Skyline Boulevard Woodside, CA 94062 (415) 851–4484 Contact: Bill Ashton	Daylighting design takes into account overhangs, fins, and skylights; calculates electric lighting demand.	IBM PC or compatible, MacIntosh.	PASCAL. $489.00
DOE-PLUS (1992) ITEM Systems P.O. Box 5218 Berkeley, CA 94705-0218 (510) 428-0803 Fax: (510) 428–0324 Contact: Steve Byrne	Pre-/Post-processor for micro version of DOE-2.1 D mainframe program, interactive input, error checking, context-sensitive help and 3-D view of building. Plots DOE-2 results.	IBM 386 or compatible, 80387 math-coprocessor, hard disk, color VGA monitor and mouse highly recommended.	C, 4 MB RAM, $495.00 for DOE-PLUS only, $790.00 for DOE-PLUS and micro version of DOE-2.1D (FORTRAN).
ENSAR (Custom built) Ensar Group 2305 Broadway Avenue Boulder, CO 80304 Contact: Greg Franta, FAIA	Used with physical model; analysis capability flexible to room configurations.	Custom built.	Custom built. $ Info on request.
LUMEN-MICRO 6 (1993) Lighting Technologies 2540 Frontier Street, Suite 107 Boulder, CO 80301 (303) 449–5791 Fax: (303) 449–5864 Contact: David DiLaura	Analyzes complex interior lighting systems including daylight, direct/indirect lighting, mixed and even aimed luminaires. DXF file editor, user friendly input, animated walk-through. Limited to rectangular spaces.	IBM 386 or compatible w/high density floppy drive, 8 MB hard disk space, 80387 math-coprocessor, VGA or SVGA Graphics	FORTRAN, 2MB RAM, MS-DOS 3.3 or later, $595.00. $129 for upgrade from Lumen-Micro 5 until December 1993.
MICRO-DOE 2 (1989) Acrosoft International, Inc. 9745 E. Hampden Avenue, #230 Denver, CO 80231 (303) 368-9225 Fax: (303) 368-5929 Contact: Gene Tsai	Micro version of DOE-2.1D mainframe program, with additional enhancements.	*Regular DOS Version:* IBM 386 or compatible, Intel math-coprocessor. *Extended DOS Version:* IBM 486 or compatibles, Intel or Weitek math-coprocessor.	640KB RAM MS-DOS 2.1 or later. $495.00 with 2 free weather data files. 3MB RAM, MS-DOS 3.0 or later. $625.00 with 2 free weather data files.

Table 3.3.3 (*Continued*)
Micros

TOOL/LAST UPDATE/ CONTACT	DESCRIPTION	HARDWARE	SOFTWARE/COST
MICROLITE 1.0 (1983) Harvey Bryan 48 Agassiz Avenue Belmont, MA 02178 (617) 484–0854	Analyzes the daylight illumination for rectangular rooms with vertical glazing in exterior walls. Obstructions are not accounted for.	IBM PC or compatible, APPLE II.	BASIC. IBM: 128KB RAM. APPLE: 40 KB RAM. $25.00
PRC-DOE2 (1992) Partnership for Resource Conservation 140 South 34th Street Boulder, CO 80303 (303) 499–8611 Fax: (303) 499–8611 Contact: Paul Reeves	Micro version of DOE-2.1D mainframe program, with additional enhancements. Custom-built PRC-TOOLS available.	IBM 386 or compatible, 80387 math-coprocessor. Color VGA monitor highly recommended.	FORTRAN, 4MB RAM, $295.00 for program and 2 weather files. $195.00–$695.00 for additional custom tools. $25.00 for additional weather file.
QUICKLITE 1.0 (1985) Building Technologies Program Lawrence Berkeley Laboratory 1 Cyclotron Road, Bldg 90-3111 Berkeley, CA 94720 (510) 486–5605 Fax: (510) 486–4089	A relatively quick, crude estimator of daylight levels in simple rectangular rooms.	TRS 80, TI-59.	BASIC, FORTRAN, $ Free. No support.
SUNPATH 1.2 (1993) Florida Solar Energy Center 300 State Road 401 Cape Canaveral, FL 32920 (407) 783–0300, Ext. 134 Fax: (407) 783–2571 Contact: Ross McCluney	Calculates solar coordinates, sunrise and sunset, sunpath for a sequence of days, solar-to-standard-time conversions and vice versa. Includes graphic program PATHPLOT and editable library of 233 U.S. cities.	IBM PC or compatible. EGA or VGA monitor needed for PATHPLOT screen display but will output HPGL files for importing into presentation programs w/o graphics monitor.	SUNPATH: MS QuickBASIC. PATHPLOT: MS Visual BASIC. 350KB RAM, MS-DOS $35.00.
SUNSPEC 1.1 (1993) Florida Solar Energy Center 300 State Road 401 Cape Canaveral, FL 32920 (407) 783–0300, Ext. 134 Fax: (407) 783–2571 Contact: Ross McCluney	Calculates clear sky solar direct and diffuse spectral irradiances on horizontal or tilted planes, integrated broad-band irradiances, luminances and luminous efficacies. Files can be read by WINDOW 4.0. Includes graphic program SPECPLOT.	IBM PC or compatible. EGA or VGA monitor needed for SPECPLOT screen display but will output HPGL files for importing into presentation programs w/o graphics monitor.	SUNSPEC: MSQuickBASIC, SPECPLOT MSVisual BASIC 300KB RAM, MS-DOS, $35.00.

TOOL/LAST UPDATE/ CONTACT	DESCRIPTION	HARDWARE	SOFTWARE/COST
SUPERLITE 2.0 (1993) Building Technologies Program Lawrence Berkeley Laboratory 1 Cyclotron Road, MS 90-3111 Berkeley, CA 94720 (510) 486–4154 Fax: (510) 486–4089 Contact: Rob Hitchcock or Werner Osterhaus	Updated version of SUPERLITE PC 1.01. Now analyzes daylight and electric lighting for various room geometries. Max. 5 windows. Tabulated output, no graphics.	IBM PC or compatible with 8087 or better math-coprocessor chip.	FORTRAN, MS-FORTRAN 3.2 compiler, 640 KB RAM. $ Free. No support.
WINDOWS 4.0 (1992) Bostik Construction Products P.O. Box 8 Huntingdon Valley, PA 19006	A public-domain program developed by Lawrence Berkeley Laboratory for analyzing heat transfer through window systems. U-value and shading coefficient are calculated.	IBM PC or compatible.	256KB RAM, MS DOS 2.1 or higher, Math-coprocessor decreases calculation time. $ Free.

Table 3.3.4
Mainframes

TOOL/LAST UPDATE/ CONTACT	DESCRIPTION	HARDWARE	SOFTWARE/COST
DOE-2.1E (1993) Supersedes DOE-2B, C, D. Building Technologies Program Lawrence Berkeley Laboratory 1 Cyclotron Road, MS 90-3147 Berkeley, CA 94720 (510) 486–5711 Fax: (510) 486–4089 Contact: Kathy Ellington	Daylighting and glare calculation integrated with hourly energy simulation and window management.	DEC, Sun-4.	FORTRAN, $ info on request. Some support. Documentation ordered from NTIS at additional cost.
RADIANCE 2.1 (1992) Building Technologies Program Lawrence Berkeley Laboratory 1 Cyclotron Road, MS 90-3147 Berkeley, CA 94720 (510) 486–5711 Fax: (510) 486–4089 Contact: Greg Ward	A ray-tracing program that accurately predicts light levels and produces photo realistic images of architectural space in all sky conditions.	Sun Microsystems, DEC, MacIntosh w/(AUX), CRAY. Other UNIX machines.	C, $ Free to anyone who wishes to develop further.
UWLIGHT (1986) Department of Architecture Gould Hall JO-20 University of Washington Seattle, WA 98105 (206) 543–2132 Contact: Brian Johnson	Useful as an educational tool. Analyzes daylight and electric lighting for rectangular rooms. Output primarily text, minimal graphics.	VAX/VMS host computer.	FORTRAN 5, $150.00 for 9-track tape. tape. $100.00 for MS-DOS or MacIntosh formatted disks.

3.4 PHYSICAL MODELING

The physics of illumination is such that light behaves exactly the same way in a model as it does in a full-scale building. If a scaled model duplicates the full-scale building, and if it is tested under analogous sky conditions, the results in the model will be identical to those of the full-scale building. The technical issues surrounding daylighting design do not require the use of expensive equipment or excessive data analysis to answer a simple question.

Physical models can be built and studied at all stages of the design process and on all budgets. Fundamentally, daylighting models are design tools that answer questions not only of daylighting issues but of many other aspects of building design.

Design options can be explored through physical modeling by changing one variable at a time, such as aperture size, placement, or orientation. The most desirable conditions can be recognized, and decisions based on the information gathered from the quantitative and qualitative results can influence the building design.

Model simulations can be performed under an artificial sky, where conditions can be held constant or under the actual sky. Outdoor testing is the least expensive but is often more time consuming because of unpredictable sky conditions. Indoor testing, on the other hand, requires an artificial sky or a heliodon. The artificial sky simulator is able to produce a controlled lighting environment. The light will simulate natural sky conditions in a controlled environment. After the initial expense, testing is quite simple. Several artificial sky domes exist throughout the country. The University of California at Berkeley has one type of artificial sky dome (see Figure 3.4.2). Many designers have found it very beneficial to make use of the facility early in the design process.

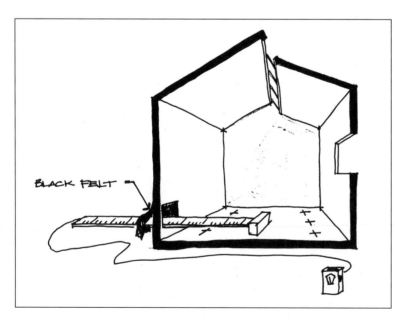

Figure 3.4.1
Model test with inexpensive handheld light meter.

Figure 3.4.2
Sky simulator facility measuring 24 ft in diameter allows architects, researchers, and students to accurately test building models. It is located on the U.C. Berkeley campus. The facility is operated by the Building Technologies Program at Lawrence Berkeley Laboratory. (Photograph courtesy of Lawrence Berkeley Laboratory, Berkeley, California.)

Model building is a routine activity in most architectural offices. Only slight modifications to this normal practice are necessary for using these models for daylight studies. The instrumentation required to get the quantitative measurements are simple and usually inexpensive. There is also an opportunity for qualitative evaluation through visual observation, photography, and video recording. The subsequent analysis of photographs typically satisfies the modeling objectives. Simple and inexpensive hand-held meters can provide adequate illuminance data for analysis. Several things can be accomplished through model studies:

- They can be constructed for visual observations and aesthetic analysis.
- Comparisons can be made between modifications of designs.
- Window areas can be changed to test impacts of usable daylight, as can different types of wall treatments.
- Illumination levels resulting from different design schemes can be compiled and used to project energy savings.

Sky Conditions

The type of sky conditions that will exist at a site should be understood. Appendix C graphically presents weather data, including cloud cover for five different climate zones throughout the United States.

The illumination produced by natural sky conditions tends to change constantly. Interior illumination values will not be very meaningful if the sky changes significantly between tests. It is recommended that coincident light levels be recorded during a model testing session, both in the model and outside the model at a horizontal surface. This will give you the opportunity to normalize illumination levels in the model relative to the instantaneous sky conditions.

Model testing under partly cloudy conditions is not recommended because of the rapid changes in sky conditions. A clear or uniformly cloudy condition is more suitable.

There are five types of sky conditions: uniform sky, overcast sky, clear sky, partly cloudy sky, and direct sunlight.

Uniform Sky

The uniform sky provides an equal amount of illuminance in all directions. Hand calculation or an artificial sky simulator is best suited to test under uniform sky conditions.

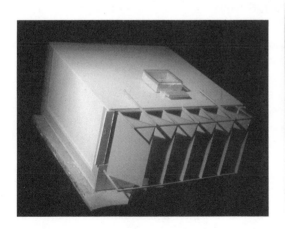

Figure 3.4.3
Direct beam model test.

Figure 3.4.4
Direct beam model test.

Overcast Sky

In overcast sky conditions, water particles diffusely refract and reflect all wavelengths of sunlight. As a result, the zenith is three times brighter than at the horizon.

Clear Sky

The light is diffuse because it is refracted and reflected as the sunlight passes through the atmosphere. Under these conditions, the sky is brighter along the horizon and less intense at the zenith.

Partly Cloudy Sky

The illuminance level varies depending on the position of the clouds relative to the sun. Higher horizontal illuminance may result under partly cloudy sky than under a clear sky.

Direct Sunlight

Direct sunlight is perpendicular to the surface. It is viewed largely that direct sunlight is too intense for task illumination.

To simulate the effect of daylighting for various times of the day and year with the sun in a different position with respect to the window wall, a solution is to put the model on a tilt table (see Figure 3.4.5). Adjustments are made to the tilt table with respect to the sun to simulate solar penetration at various times of the year using a sun dial to verify the simulated date and time. The position of the sun in the sky is measured by its "altitude" angle (angle from horizon) and its "azimuth" angle (horizontal angle east or west of south). The solar azimuth and altitude are dictated by the site latitude, day of the year, and time of the day.

Tilting a daylighting model to simulate different months and hours may cause distorted results if the window sees different

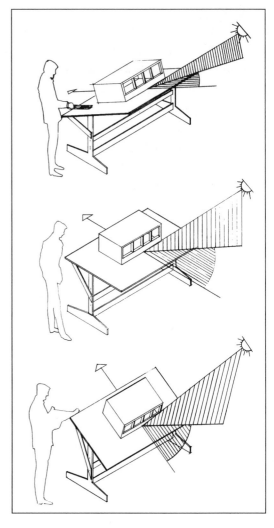

Figure 3.4.5
Tilt table simulating different seasons.

portions of the sky vault and ground as it is tilted. When the measurements are made in the winter and the model is tilted downward to simulate a higher summer sun, the amount of error increases the more the model is tilted. This can be minimized by doing the measurements on a roof top or in the summer when the sun is high. In this case, the model is tilted upward to simulate the low winter sun. This will be much more accurate when enough of a ground base is constructed to act as a horizon.

An advantage of simulating daylighting with models under summer sky conditions instead of during the winter is that the amount of error is not only smaller but is also constant for all of the studies. Unfortunately, models with skylights cannot be tilted to simulate the time of year, because they receive light from the entire hemispherical sky vault. In this case, tilting a skylight model decreases the available sky vault and produces incorrect results.

When windows or clerestories are facing different directions and tilting is desired, the daylighting levels can be measured separately for each orientation and the results added together. The windows or clerestories not facing the direction under study are covered with opaque black to account for light lost through the window to the outside. This is repeated for each of the building orientations with windows or clerestories. The individual results are added together. A grid system of light measurement points is necessary to do this with accuracy. After light meter readings are completed, a diagram can be plotted to illustrate the relation between the amount of light and the building cross section. Peaks and valleys of the light level can be located and altered by changes in the solar control design. By graphing the light levels of different options on the same graph, one can easily compare.

Scales

Models for studying daylight can be constructed at any convenient scale. Generally it is difficult to reproduce details accurately in very small models, and the relative size of the illumination meter-probe to be used may cause excessive absorption and reflection when inserted into a small model. However, a small scale model is useful at an early stage of design development. Typically $\frac{1}{16}$ or $\frac{1}{8}$ in. per 1 ft is a practical scale to provide a sense of massing, solar access, reflection, or obstruction of daylight. Mid-

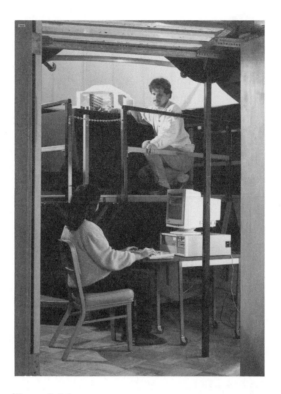

Figure 3.4.6
Researchers test a scale model of a hotel atrium using light sensors linked to a data collection program. (Photograph courtesy of Lawrence Berkeley Laboratory, Berkeley, California.)

Figure 3.4.7
Researchers select a series of roof shading designs in a hotel atrium to evaluate solar access properties. (Photograph courtesy of Lawrence Berkeley Laboratory, Berkeley, California.)

and full-scale models are used for detail refinements. At 1 in. per ft to full-scale mock-ups, effective photography analysis can be accomplished. At mid to full scale, critical daylighting details are evaluated in accordance with the building's desired performance. A scale of 1 in. per foot also produces a convenient size model for studying a room. This scale may be too large to handle conveniently if several rooms or adjacent parts of the building must be included in the study. A scale of ½ or ⅜ in. may be used if care is exercised in construction. Models at lesser scales are difficult to build to scale and to measure using available light-sensing cells.

Materials

Materials of the model are important only in terms of their transparency or opacity (light transmitted or blocked), their reflectance (light reflected or absorbed), and their texture (glossy or diffusing).

The illuminance levels may be affected by the reflectance of the interior surfaces and furnishings. The reflectance of the surfaces and furnishings must be recognized, but the accuracy of representation should be determined at each stage of the design process. A method of approximating reflectance with a light meter is described in Figure 3.4.8.

The texture of materials affects the quality and quantity of light distributed in a space.

Color is of no significance if it is measured with a properly corrected light meter. These instruments do not differentiate between colors but measure only the quantity of light reflected from these surfaces. Thus, gray paint or dark and light patterns can be used to simulate colored surfaces, provided a reflectometer is available for

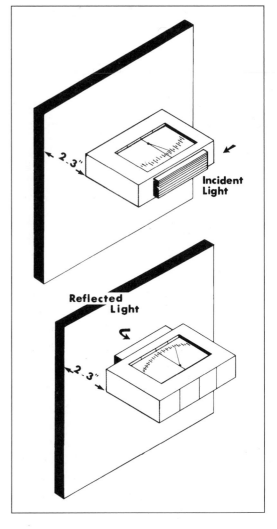

Figure 3.4.8
Method to estimate reflectance values.

measuring and watching the paint's reflectance properties.

Walls can be built of plywood, foamboard, or cardboard and painted appropriately. Foamboards are often not completely opaque and must be painted or covered with foil or some other opaque material to prevent the penetration of unwanted light. The construction joints and material opacity are two sources of light leaks. Window glass can be simulated in the model with real glass, or for relatively simple openings, glass may be altogether omitted from the model and a multiplication factor applied to the measured illumination levels to compensate for the light reflection and absorption of the glass. For the simulation of a glass with a transmission of 80%, for instance, the illumination levels in the model without glass may be reduced by a factor of 0.20. Although the glass does not, in fact, reduce illumination uniformly throughout the interior space, the distribution effect is relatively minor except when direct sun is on the fenestration, in which case actual glass or acetate should be used in the model to account for specular reflection off of the glass. The model builder is safe in using the actual materials where possible.

The integration of electric lighting into physical models is a difficult task. To incorporate the aspects of electric lighting one should calculate the additional light provided from electric sources after the daylighting values have been measured.

Measurement Equipment

Illuminance meters are used to find qualitative and quantitative results in daylighting models (see Figure 3.4.10). The illuminance meter is particularity useful in calculating Daylight Factors (the amount of light inside the model versus outside the model).

When illuminance is measured, the illuminance meter's unfiltered photocells respond to the total energy spectrum differently than the human eye, which responds to the "visible" portion of the spectrum. The photocell responds to other portions of the energy spectrum as well. For comparative studies of models, this discrepancy is not significant. The relative merits of two design schemes being compared are still valid. However, for absolute measurements (actual illumination levels) the photocell must be adapted with a color corrector

Figure 3.4.9
Model test with light sensors.

(often referred to as a "viscor filter"), which causes its response to match that of the average human eye. Because the addition of the color correction device seldom alters significantly the price to the purchaser, it is recommended that it be included in any new purchase.

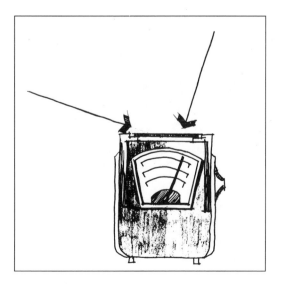
Figure 3.4.10
Typical hand-held light meter used in determining illuminance levels.

Photocells are also subject to the "cosine law of illumination," that is, they are not as sensitive to light striking the cell at a low incident angle as from a high or more direct angle. This produces incorrect measurements when the instrument is used for general lighting studies. Most manufacturers of photometers can provide a cosine correction device for their photocells. It is absolutely necessary that photometers for lighting studies be equipped with a cosine correction device.

There are three types of cosine correction geometry: domed diffuser, partial cosine correction, and full cosine correction.

Domed Diffuser

The meter is a hemispheric "photographic type" equally sensitive to light from all directions. However, a domed diffuser is intentionally not cosine corrected and thus is not ideal for light measurements.

Partial Cosine Correction

The meter is a simple flat diffuser that approximates cosine correction. However, it tends to reflect too much light at low angles. Also, the meter undermeasures light at high angles of incident.

Full Cosine Correction

Extra light is allowed to strike the edge or side of the diffuser to compensate for higher diffuser reflectance at lower angles.

Data Analysis

Following the quantitative results, the designer must evaluate the accumulated data. Typically the data are presented graphically to measure the quality and distribution of light. In the process, the performance of the various proposed design schemes are considered. Graphically, two formats are generally used: the Iso-Lux contour plan and the Daylight Factor graph/section.

An Iso-Lux contour is a graph that plots the contours of equal Daylight Factors over a building's floor plan. Under this method, the designer can measure the distribution of illuminance throughout a space. For instance, if the contours are spaced closely together, a strong illuminance gradient exists.

The Daylight Factor graph/section is presented in a building section cut through the fenestration. The average illuminance is found in the total area under the curve. This allows the designer to compare the total illumination on the work plane. Graphically, a flatter curve indicates a uniform distribution of daylight. However, a flatter curve may result in contrast glare in the user's field of vision. The slope of the curve indicates the amount and rate of illuminance change.

Model Performance

Model performance can be used for energy calculations in conjunction with hourly simulation computer programs such as DOE2, Trace, and Blast. Several methods can be implemented to accomplish this, including modifying the radiation component of the weather tape relative to daylight in the model or modifying the performance of the electric lighting system.

Most hourly simulation programs such as DOE2 have profile numbers that represent a percent of maximum load (see Table 3.4.1). You simply input a watts/square foot

Table 3.4.1
Electric Lighting Schedule from PowerDOE (DOE2)

LIGHTING SCHEDULE FOR INTERIOR ZONE

Lights: DS1 = Day-schedule

Hours = (1, 7)	Values = (0.05)
Hours = (8, 11)	Values = (.1, .9, .9, .95)
Hours = (12, 15)	Values = (.95, .8, .8, .9)
Hours = (16, 19)	Values = (.9, .95, .8, .7)
Hours = (20, 24)	Values = (.6, .4, .3, .2, .2)

LIGHTING SCHEDULE FOR NORTH PERIMETER DAYLIGHT ZONE

Lights: DS1-N = Day-schedule

Hours = (1, 7)	Values = (0.05)
Hours = (8, 12)	Values = (.1, .39, .39, .42, .33)
Hours = (13, 17)	Values = (.28, .28, .39, .39, .42)
Hours = (18, 24)	Values = (.8, .7, .6, .4, .3, .2, .2)

LIGHTING SCHEDULE FOR SOUTH PERIMETER DAYLIGHT ZONE

Lights: DS1-S = Day-schedule

Hours = (1, 7)	Values = (0.05)
Hours = (8, 12)	Values = (.1, .34, .34, .37, .29)
Hours = (13, 17)	Values = (.24, .24, .34, .34, .37)
Hours = (18, 24)	Values = (.8, .7, .6, .4, .3, .2, .2)

LIGHTING SCHEDULE FOR EAST PERIMETER DAYLIGHT ZONE

Light: DS1 = Day-schedule

Hours = (1, 7)	Values = (0.05)
Hours = (8, 12)	Values = (.1, .27, .27, .29, .32)
Hours = (13, 17)	Values = (.27, .27, .39, .39, .42)
Hours = (18, 24)	Values = (.8, .7, .6, .4, .3, .2, .2)

LIGHTING SCHEDULE FOR WEST PERIMETER DAYLIGHT ZONE

Lights: DS1 = Day-schedule

Hours = (1, 7)	Values = (0.05)
Hours = (8, 12)	Values = (.1, .39, .39, .42, .42)
Hours = (13, 17)	Values = (.27, .27, .27, .27, .29)
Hours = (18, 24)	Values = (.8, .7, .6, .4, .3, .2, .2)

(power density) value for the building or thermal zone, and on an hourly basis, the program will take a fraction of that power density for the thermal calculations.

If you can reduce these profile numbers relative to the daylight levels in the physical model, the program will factor this electric lighting reduction into the hourly calculations.

Typically one would take footcandle readings in the physical model at least three times during the day or simulated day when a tilt table is used. For example, 9 A.M., noon, and 3 P.M. can be used to simulate the day. Ideally one would also like to test four seasons, which would represent the entire year. Readings during a equinox period (March 21 or September 21) will give an average condition for an annual calculation.

Table 3.4.2
Methodology to Modify Electric Lighting Schedules in Hourly Simulation Programs*

For Dimming Control

$$MDL_{hr,or} = (PC_{yr} \times FC_{clr,hr,or}) + (PO_{yr} \times FC_{or,hr,or})$$

$$DRF_{hr,or} = \text{Minimum} \begin{cases} \dfrac{MDL_{hr,or}}{DL} \\ 1.00 \end{cases}$$

$$PRF_{hr,or} = \text{Maximum} \begin{cases} \dfrac{MDL_{hr,or}}{CF} \end{cases}$$

$$NPN_{hr,or} = OPN_{hr,or} \times PRF_{hr,or}$$

For an On/Off Control

$$MDL_{hr,or} = (PC_{yr} \times FC_{clr,hr,or}) + (PO_{yr} \times FC_{or,hr,or})$$

$$DRF_{hr,or} = \frac{MDL_{hr,or}}{DL}$$

$$PRF_{hr,or} = \begin{cases} CF & DRF \geq 1.00 \\ 1.00 & DRF < 1.00CF \end{cases}$$

$$NPN_{hr,or} = OPN_{hr,or} \times PRF_{hr,or}$$

WHERE:

PC =   PERCENTAGE OF CLEAR SKY CONDITIONS (SEE APPENDIX C).

FC$_{CLR/OC,HR,OR}$ =   AVERAGE CLEAR OR OVERCAST DAY FOOTCANDLES LEVEL AT HOUR AND ORIENTATION (FROM MODEL TEST).

PO =   PERCENTAGE OF OVERCAST SKY CONDITIONS (SEE APPENDIX C).

MDL$_{HR,OR}$ =   MEAN DAYLIGHT LEVEL AT HOUR AND ORIENTATION.

DL =   DESIGN LEVEL. (THIS IS THE ILLUMINATION LEVEL REQUIRED IN FOOT-CANDLES.)

DRF$_{HR,OR}$ =   DAYLIGHT REDUCTION FACTOR AT HOUR AND ORIENTATION (MUST NOT EXCEED 1.00).

CF =   CONTROL FACTOR. (THIS IS THE MINIMUM SETPOINT THAT A DIMMING SYSTEM WILL REDUCE TO, TYPICALLY AROUND 0.50. THIS CORRESPONDS TO A DIMMER GOING DOWN TO 50% FULL LOAD.)

PRF$_{HR,OR}$ =   POWER REDUCTION FACTOR AT HOUR AND ORIENTATION (MUST BE AT LEAST EQUAL TO CF).

OPN$_{HR,OR}$ =   OLD PROFILE NUMBER AT HOUR AND ORIENTATION.

NPN$_{HR,OR}$ =   NEW PROFILE NUMBER AT HOUR AND ORIENTATION.

---

*clr = clear; hr = hour; or = orientation.

Actual summer performance will be better than spring or fall performance, whereas winter performance will actually be worse because of shorter days and lower sun positions. Hence, winter and summer measurements offset each other. For most cases, data for September 21 at 9 A.M., noon, and 3 P.M. can be used to modify electric lighting schedules. The methodology for modifying the profile numbers or the percent of maximum load for dimming control and an on/off control is shown in Table 3.4.2.

CHAPTER 4

CASE STUDIES

The sensitivity with which light is allowed to enter into a space remains a design issue. The methods of light control, its entry into spaces, and its impact on surfaces all are dependent on the designer's understanding of light.

The case study section summarizes a variety of buildings implementing daylighting strategies. Performance specifications are included to help evaluate each project for its energy efficiency. Each example includes a short written description, building graphics and photographs, a building energy performance summary, and a pollution avoidance summary (refer to Chapter 1).

RETAIL BUILDINGS

Montebello Town Center (see Figures 4.1–4.11)

Building Type:	Retail Mall
Location:	Montebello, California
Building Area:	950,000 ft^2 (120,000 ft^2 circulation/atrium)
Daylighting Strategies:	Gable beam/vaulted skylights with diffusing panels
Lighting Power Density	1.0 watts/ft^2
Electric Lighting Controls:	On/off
Architect	Gruen Associates, Robert Lesmett (partner), Greg Moe (project architect)
Engineer:	Store Matakovich and Wolfbert, Tom Davis (project manager), Bob Kuisel (project engineer)
Summary:	The Montebello Town Center in Montebello, California, is a 950,000 ft^2 shopping center designed by Gruen Associates. The shopping center includes 165 specialty shops, three department stores, and a food court with 17 restaurants.

The retail stores are organized around a linear plan that utilizes three anchor stores at either end of the center and one opposite the entrance. A barreled acrylic dome and diffusing panels are used to allow daylight to penetrate the linear circulation spine. The daylight not only illuminates the circulation spine but also provides enough light for the live trees and plants in the space. The barreled acrylic dome permits reflected daylight to reach the open spaces, whereas the diffusing panels control direct beam penetration. During certain seasons, a thin linear slice of light enters the building and hits the floor, which helps direct shoppers through the circulation spine while adding visual contrast and interest.

The combination of reflected, diffuse, and direct daylight improves the visual quality of the interior environment and, in addition, reduces lighting, HVAC, and peak demand loads. The Montebello Town Center was able to reduce its peak demand charge from a typical 503 kW (without daylighting) to 264 kW while enhancing the retail environment.

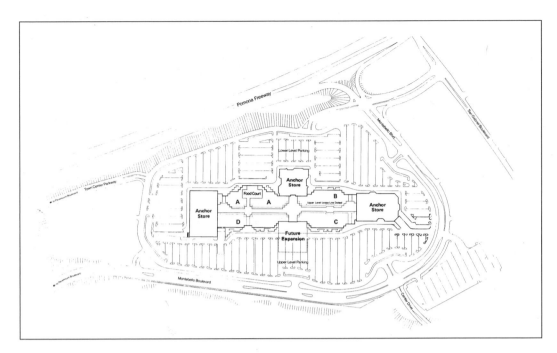

Figure 4.1
Site plan.

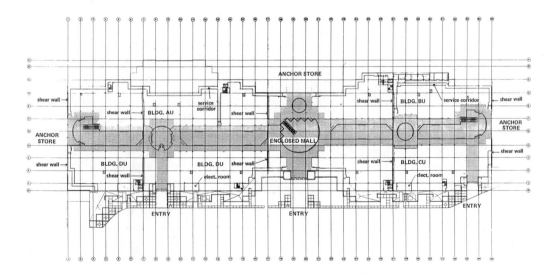

Figure 4.2
Upper level plan.

MONTEBELLO TOWN PLAZA

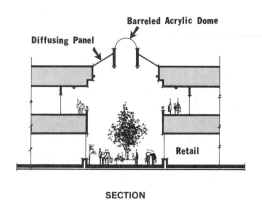

Figure 4.3
Section through circulation area.

Figure 4.4
Facade showing entrance.

Figure 4.5
Toplighting strategy over food court area.

Figure 4.6
Interior view showing diffusing and transparent apertures.

Figure 4.7
Interior showing a slice of light.

Figure 4.8
Diffusing barrel vault.

Figure 4.9
Exterior roof detail.

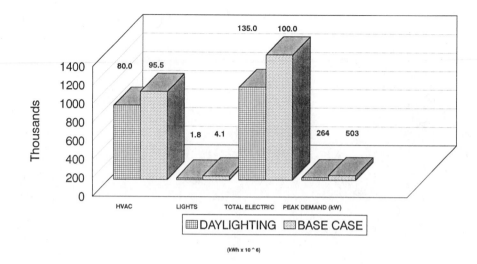

Figure 4.10
Building energy performance summary (annual kilowatt hours) (Montebello Town Center).

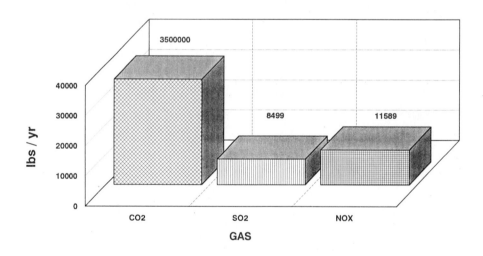

Figure 4.11
Pollution avoidance values (Montebello Town Center).

Salzer's Video (see Figures 4.12–4.21)

Building Type:	Small retail
Location:	Ventura, California
Building Area:	8000 ft^2
Daylighting Strategies:	Toplighting, skylights, sidelighting, windows with overhangs, and clerestories
Light Design Level:	50 footcandles
Lighting Power Density:	1.5 watts/ft^2
Electric Lighting Controls:	On/off
Mechanical System:	Roof-mounted heat pumps
Architect:	Scott Ellinwood and Associates, Scott Ellinwood, FAIA
Landscape Architect:	William Morgan
Engineers:	Malcolm Lewis and Associates (mechanical/electrical), John Oeltman, Engineers (structural)
Summary:	The Salzer's Video store in Ventura, California, incorporated every element of lighting that influences retail design. The architect, Scott Ellinwood, considered fenestration, daylighting systems, electric lighting, and mechanical systems. To verify their energy-saving solutions, they used the DOE computer analysis tool extensively.

Fenestration was incorporated in a manner that was sympathetic to both the fundamentals of daylighting and the requirements of retail design. The south and east elevations are glazed from ground level to 16 ft with an 8-ft overhang. The overhang allows some direct sun during the early morning but is shaded during the remainder of the day. The west elevation is designed without fenestration because of glare and heat gain considerations. The north facade has clerestories for each of the interior levels. Skylights are incorporated to provide most of the daylight for the deep interior spaces.

Practical daylighting solutions were incorporated into a retail space to provide energy savings, effective street exposure, and a pleasant retail environment (see Figures 4.12–4.21).

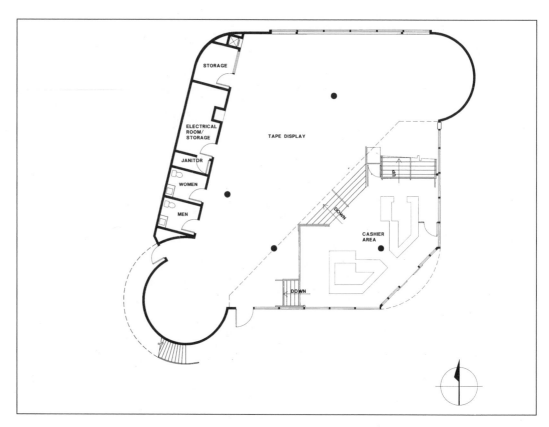

Figure 4.12
First floor plan.

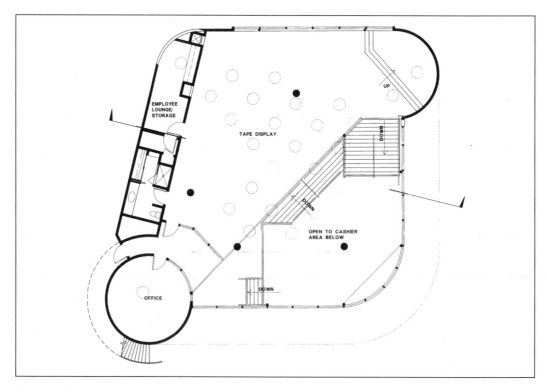

Figure 4.13
Second floor plan.

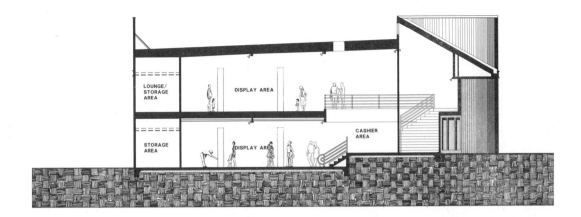

Figure 4.14
Building section through display area.

Figure 4.15
Elevation. (Photo by Scott Ellinwood, FAIA.)

Figure 4.16
Elevation. (Photo by Scott Ellinwood, FAIA.)

Figure 4.17
Entrance. (Photo by Mike Urbanek.)

Figure 4.18
Interior showing round skylights and clerestory. (Photo by Scott Ellinwood, FAIA.)

Figure 4.19
Interior. (Photo by Mike Urbanek.)

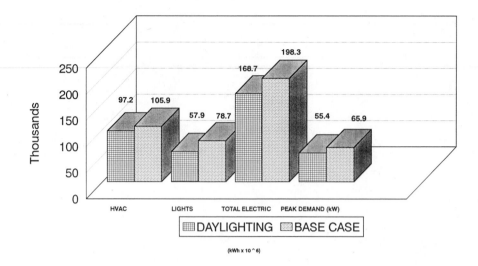

Figure 4.20
Building energy performance summary (annual kilowatt hours) (Salzer's Video).

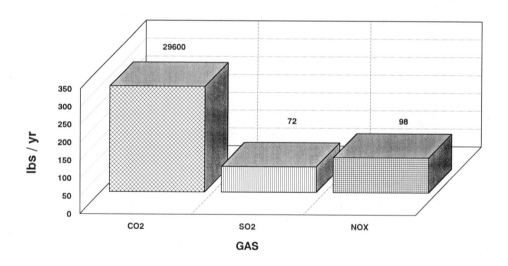

Figure 4.21
Pollution avoidance values (Salzer's Video).

Wal-Mart (see Figures 4.22–4.26)

Building Type:	Retail
Location:	Lawrence, Kansas
Building Area:	120,000 ft^2
Daylighting Strategies:	Toplighting with skylights and light scoops
Lighting Power Density:	1.4 watts/ft^2
Electric Lighting Controls:	Dimming
Architects:	BSW International
Engineers:	CEI Consultants, Inc. (mechanical/electrical)
Consultants:	Rocky Mountain Institute, William McDonough Architects
Summary:	The Wal-Mart store in Lawrence, Kansas, was designed to address many issues toward a sustainable society. The daylighting system includes new prototype units designed by Andersen Windows. The system incorporates solar optic films, which spread daylight more evenly into the space. The manufacturer claims that fewer skylights are needed compared with traditional skylights and that there is an increased amount of sales in the daylighting zones under the roof apertures.

In addition to the daylighting strategy, the building incorporates an engineered wood beam system, a refrigeration system with a non–ozone depletion refrigerant, recycling of both gray and storm water, and a package recovery area for recycling material used for packaging items sold in the store. Many other sustainable strategies were included in the design and construction of this facility.

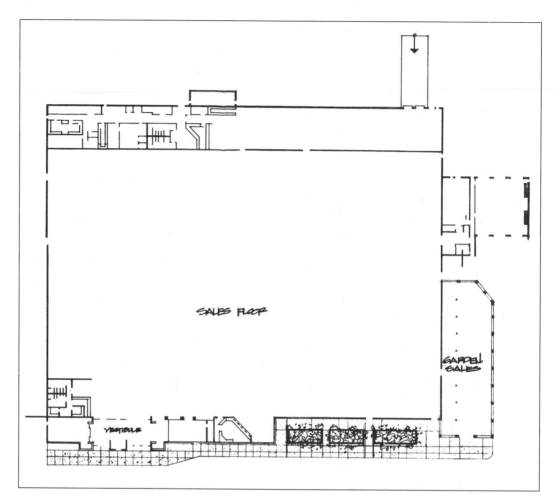

Figure 4.22
Floor plan.

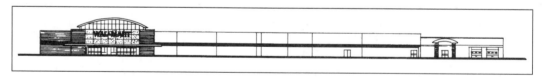

Figure 4.23
Front elevation.

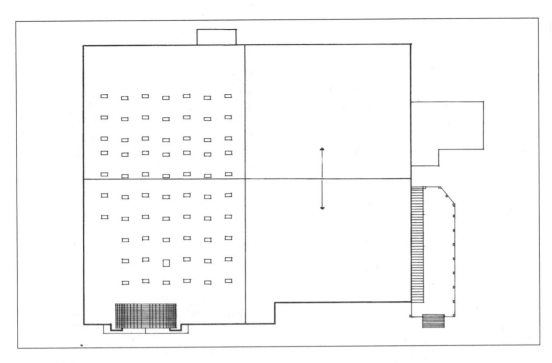

Figure 4.24
Roof plan.

Figure 4.25
Roof aperture. (Photo by Jon B. Peterson.)

Figure 4.26
Roof aperture. (Photo by Jon B. Peterson.)

OFFICE BUILDINGS

Southcoast Air Quality Management District (see Figures 4.27–4.39)

Building Type:	Regulatory offices, laboratory, and conference center
Location:	Diamond Bar, California
Building Area:	370,000 ft^2
Daylighting Strategies:	Sidelighting with horizontal shading devices, clerestories
Architect:	Meyer & Allen Associates
Engineers:	Hayakowa Engineers (mechanical/electrical), Fluor Daniel (construction manager)
Summary:	The South Coast Air Quality Management District Headquarters in Diamond Bar, California, designed by architects Meyer & Allen Associates includes a 60,000-ft^2 Conference Center, a two-story, 60,000-ft^2 laboratory building, and a five-story, 250,000-ft^2 office building. The new headquarters accommodates all of the personnel and activities that were once located in various locales.

Detailed simulations and physical model tests were performed to optimize the fenestration. South elevation shading devices were implemented to reduce glare in the office spaces, and high-performance glazing was specified. The laboratory integrated a north-facing clerestory, resulting in a relatively uniform distribution within this space.

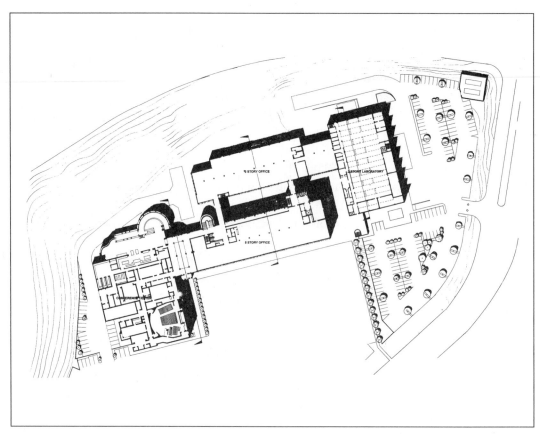

Figure 4.27
First level/partial site plan.

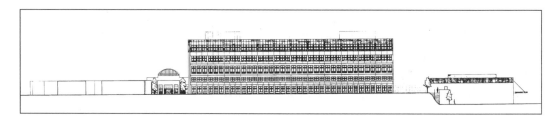

Figure 4.28
South elevation.

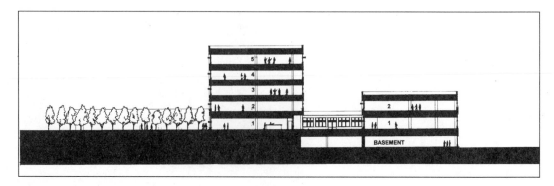

Figure 4.29
Section through office towers.

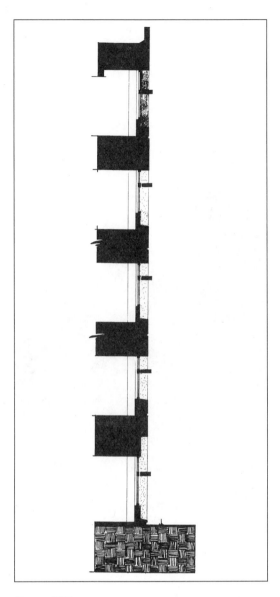

Figure 4.30
Section through south-facing facade.

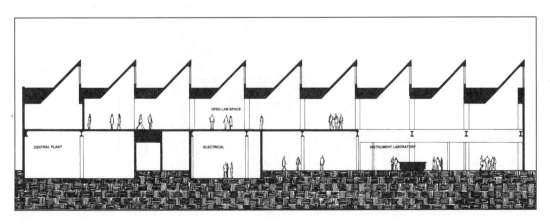

Figure 4.31
Section through laboratory space.

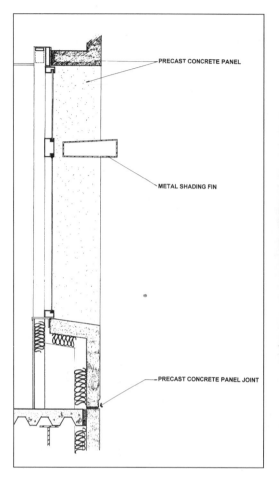

Figure 4.32
Detail of south-facing window wall.

Figure 4.33
Courtyard facade. (Photo by Paul Bielenberg.)

Figure 4.34
Interior showing toplighting and sidelighting.

Figure 4.35
Clerestories over laboratory space.

Figure 4.36
Roof apertures.

Figure 4.37
Window details.

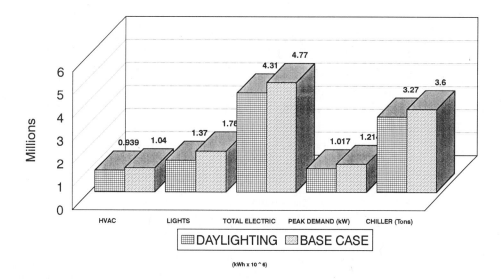

Figure 4.38
Building energy performance summary (annual kilowatt hours) (SCAQMD Building).

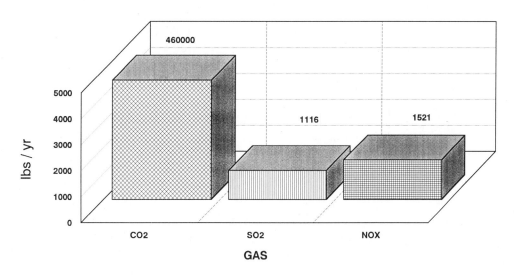

Figure 4.39
Pollution avoidance values (SCAQMD Building).

Emerald People's Utility District Headquarters Building (see Figures 4.40–4.47)

Building Type:	Office
Location:	Eugene, Oregon
Building Area:	24,000 ft^2
Daylighting Strategies:	Clerestories, light shelves, shading controls
Architect:	Equinox Design, Inc., John S. Reynolds, AIA; W. E. Group Architects and Planners, Dick Williams, AIA
Engineers:	Warner Engineering (electrical), Rogers and Associates (mechanical)
Consultant:	Virginia Cartwright (daylighting)
Interior Designer:	McCarter, Boczkaj
Landscape Architect:	Lloyd Bond and Associates
Summary:	The Emerald People's Utility District Headquarters in Eugene, Oregon, is a public utility company that promotes conservation and advocates renewable energy resources. In accord with the EPUD's philosophy, their 24,000-ft^2 headquarters was designed with similar principles in mind.

In plan, the building is C shaped with attenuated east and west wings. On the wing-sloped roofs, the south facing clerestories allow daylight to penetrate deep into the interior spaces. The windows are shaded by vine-covered trellises during the summer months. Light shelves divide the top and bottom parts of the T-shaped windows on the south elevation. Below the light shelves, horizontal louvers are used for additional shading. The north elevation does not use fenestration controls for shading but incorporates the light shelves to reflect daylight into the spaces. To reduce solar heat gain, the east and west facing glazing is kept to a minimum.

The fenestration controls, daylighting features, and other energy-saving devices allow the EPUD building to save more than half the energy used by conventional buildings of equal size.

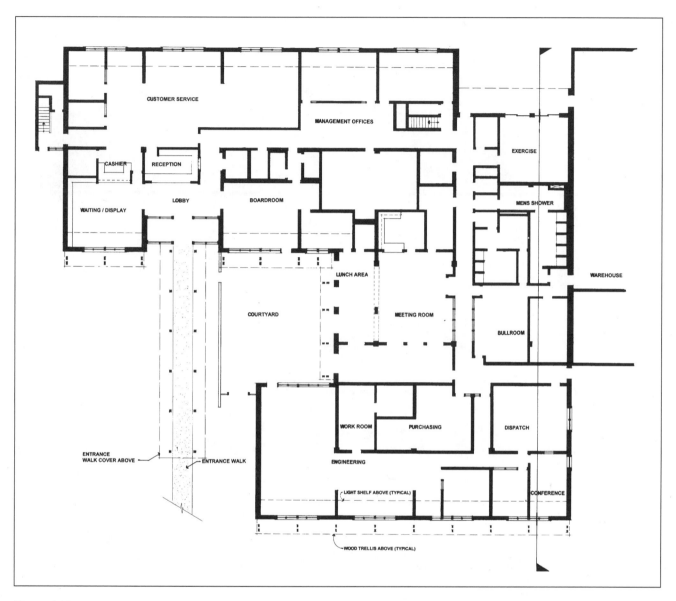

Figure 4.40
First floor plan.

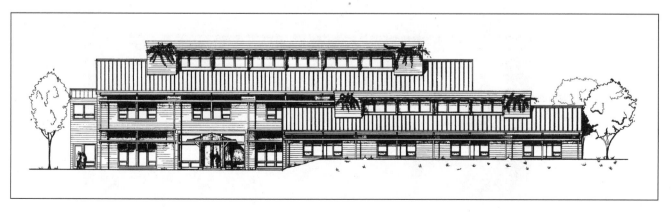

Figure 4.41
South elevation.

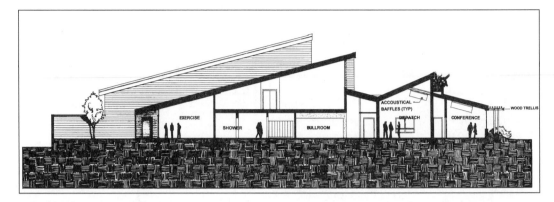

Figure 4.42
Building section looking east.

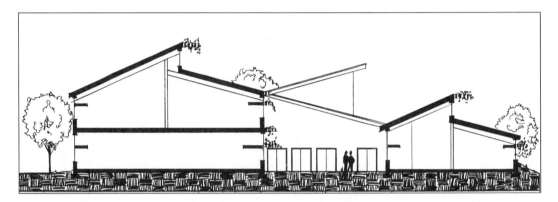

Figure 4.43
Building section.

Figure 4.44
Interior office space. (Photo by Richard A. Cooke.)

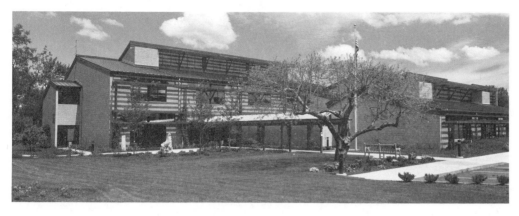

Figure 4.45
Exterior elevation. (Photo by Richard A. Cooke.)

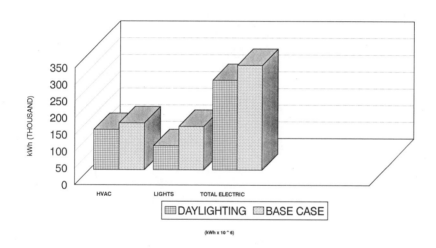

Figure 4.46
Building energy performance summary (Emerald People's Utility District).

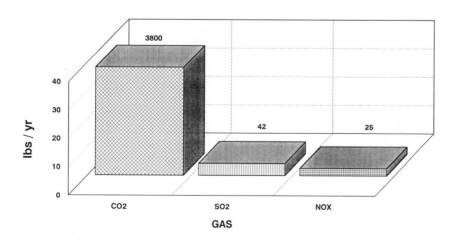

Figure 4.47
Pollution avoidance values (Emerald People's Utility District).

Way Station (see Figures 4.48–4.55)

Building Type:	Mental Health Care Facility
Location:	Frederick, Maryland
Building Area:	30,000 ft^2
Daylighting Strategies:	Sidelighting, light shelves, clerestories, skylights
Architect:	Ensar Group, Inc., Gregory Franta, FAIA (partner in charge)
Landscape Architect:	Treeland Nursery
Engineers:	Engineering Economics (mechanical/electrical), Clanton Engineering (lighting)
Interior Designer:	Kate Duininck
Contractor:	Callas Contractors
Cost:	$3.3 million
Photographer:	Harriet Wise
Summary:	Way Station, Inc., is a nonprofit organization in Frederick, Maryland, that provides a program to rehabilitate patients with mental illnesses. The ENSAR Group was commissioned to design a new 30,000-ft^2 mental health center for Way Station.

The facility was designed to be extensively daylit and energy efficient while enhancing the occupants' psychological and physical well-being. On two levels, office and program spaces line the edges of internal light courts. Light shelves are integrated on the south elevation to provide shading that reduces brightness and solar heat gains but also allows daylight to enter deep into the space. In addition, daylighting enters from roof light monitors, which illuminate the building's interior, especially the atrium. Interior colors were specified to complement the daylighting concepts.

The building's design allows for significant energy savings. The new facility consumes only one third of the energy used by a conventional building because the design responded to the local environment and used daylighting, high-performance windows, and energy-efficient mechanical/electrical systems. The payback period is expected to be 5 to 10 years.

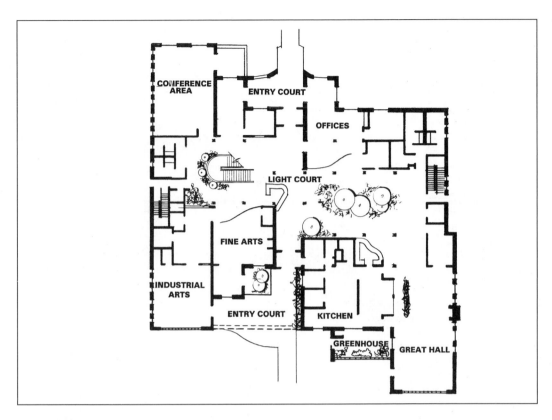

Figure 4.48
First floor plan.

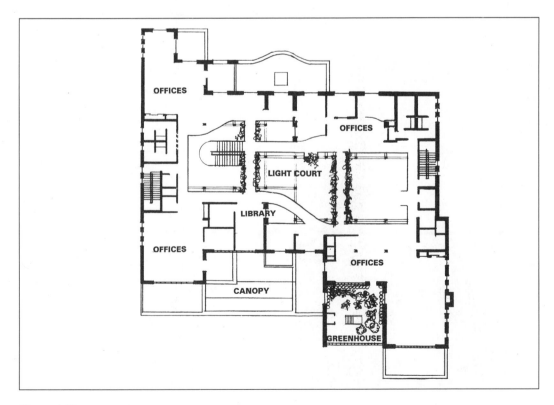

Figure 4.49
Second floor plan.

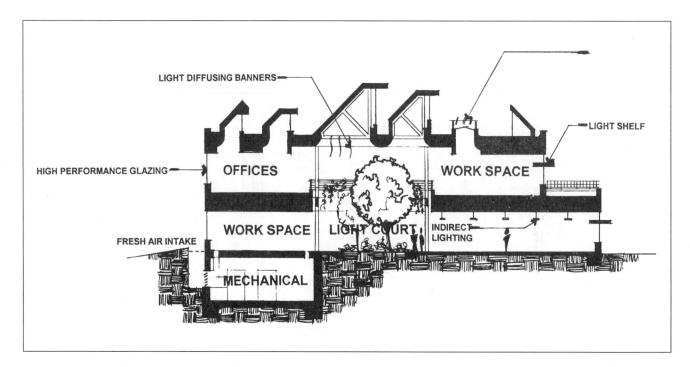

Figure 4.50
Building section.

Figure 4.51
Open interior. (Photo by Harriet Wise.)

Figure 4.52
Window wall. (Photo by Harriet Wise.)

Figure 4.53
Building interior. (Photo by Harriet Wise.)

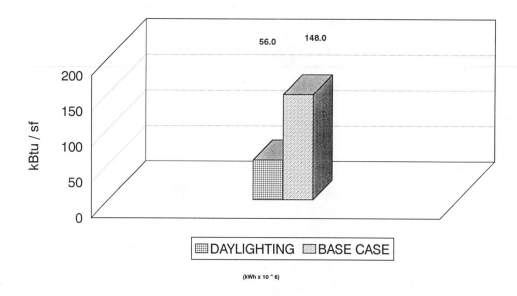

Figure 4.54
Building energy performance summary (Way Station).

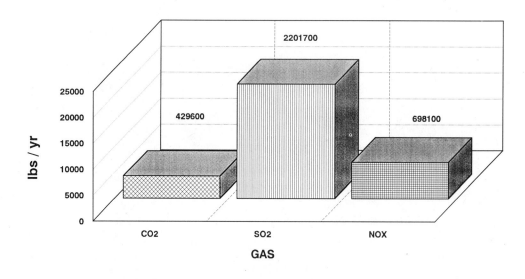

Figure 4.55
Pollution avoidance values (Way Station).

INSTITUTIONAL BUILDINGS

Peter Boxenbaum Arts Education Center
Crossroads School (see Figures 4.56–4.65)

Building Type:	Secondary School
Location:	Santa Monica, California
Building Area:	15,000 ft^2
Daylighting Strategies:	Ridged cupola, skylights with louvers, side windows
Architect:	Moore, Ruble, Yudell Architects and Planners,
	Leon Goult (project manager)
Summary:	The Boxenbaum Art Education Center in Santa Monica, California, was designed by Moore, Ruble, Yudell Architects. The 15,000-ft^2 building overlooks the Santa Monica Freeway and is placed within a row of former warehouses.

At first glance, windows appear to be lacking, but daylighting finds its way through a ridged cupola extending the entire length of the main gallery space. The cupola integrates arched windows that reflect diffuse daylight into the double-height space. Only reflected and diffuse light is allowed to enter most spaces, whereas direct beam daylighting is used to articulate and direct pedestrian circulation. The perimeter studio spaces use skylights with horizontal louvers to reflect daylight and avoid direct beam penetration.

The architects' strategy incorporated daylighting as a design feature to both enhance the space and reduce energy consumption. They were sensitive to direct beam and solar heat gain while using many of the benefits of daylighting design. The architects have produced a design that finds its delight from daylighting and sensible planning.

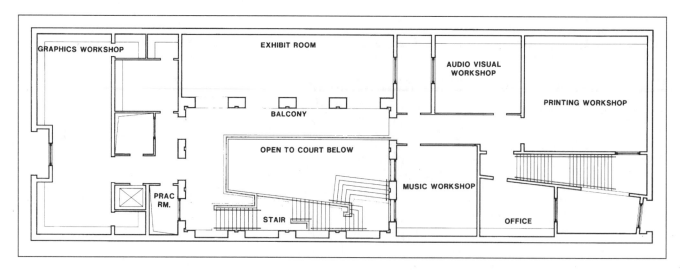

Figure 4.56
Floor plan.

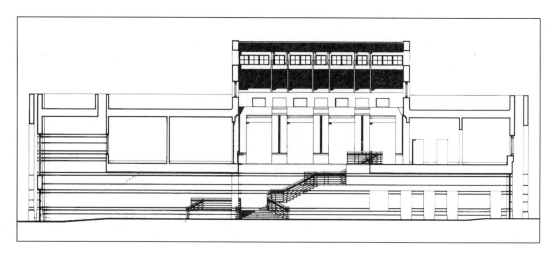

Figure 4.57
Building section.

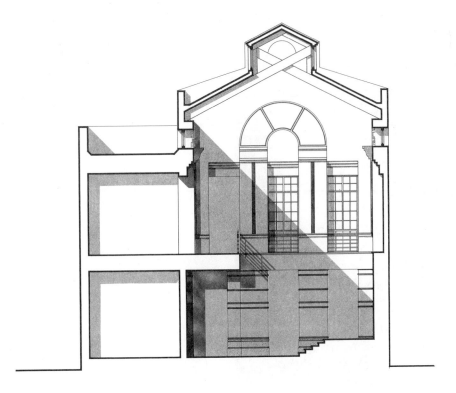

Figure 4.58
Section.

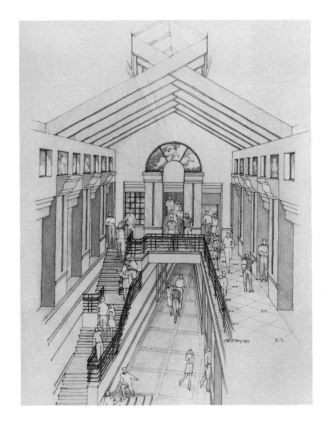

Figure 4.59
Interior perspective.

Figure 4.60
Main circulation space. (Photo by Timothy Hursley.)

Figure 4.61
Stairwell with roof monitor above for high light intensity to
draw circulation to the second level. (Photo by Timothy
Hursley.)

Figure 4.62
Skylights with sheet metal louvers.

Figure 4.63
Roof monitor behind parapet for wall wash.

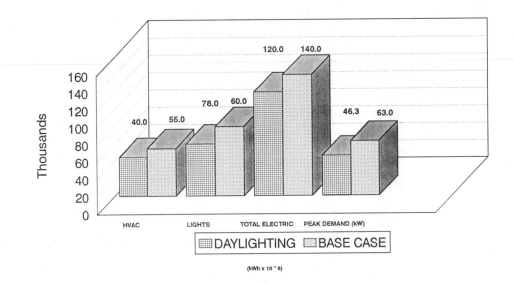

Figure 4.64
Building energy performance summary (annual kilowatt hours) (Crossroads Fine Arts School).

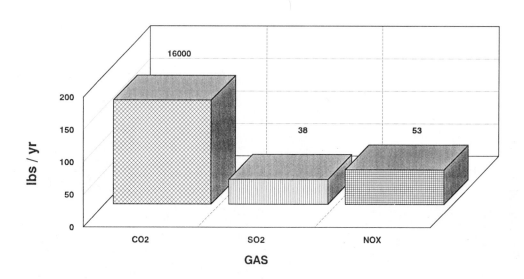

Figure 4.65
Pollution avoidance values (Crossroads Fine Arts School).

Evergreen State College
College Activities Building (see Figures 4.66–4.80)

Building Type:	College Activity Building
Location:	Olympia, Washington
Building Area:	9000 ft^2 (addition)
Daylighting Strategies:	Clerestory and windows with a horizontal perforated metal eyebrow
Architects:	Olson/Sundberg Architects, Rick Sundberg/Walter Schacht (principals); Mark Snyder, Kristen Murray, Grace Schlitt (project architects)
Engineers:	Tres West Engineering (electrical), Ratti, Swenson, Perbix (structural)
Consultants:	Loveland/Millet (lighting design)
Summary:	The rooftop addition to the College Activities Building at Evergreen State College in Olympia, Washington, was designed by Olson/Sundberg Architects. The 9000-ft^2 addition is used by the student activities offices.

The architects included interior and exterior light shelves on the perimeter of the building. The light shelves enabled daylight to reflect deep into the interior spaces while reducing summer solar heat gains and controlling brightness. The common interior space is a vaulted interior with a curved ceiling that is illuminated with daylighting through south-facing clerestories that extends 120 ft from east to west. The daylighting in the south-, west-, and east-facing offices is controlled by horizontal overhangs that diffuse and control the lighting. As a result, the workstations and other spaces are free of glare and direct beam penetration.

The design was evaluated based on energy savings contributed by daylighting and other lighting control systems. The results concluded a net annual energy reduction of 18.7%, or approximately 23,700 Kwh/yr. Although the architects' design concept concentrated on low maintenance and energy costs, sustainable energy sources, and a comfortable environment, they were able to generate elegant design features that revealed an aesthetically pleasing, efficient, and functional building.

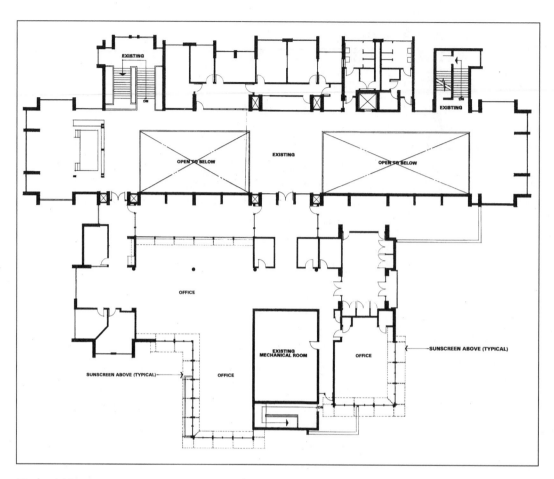

Figure 4.66
Third floor plan (Activities Building, Phase II).

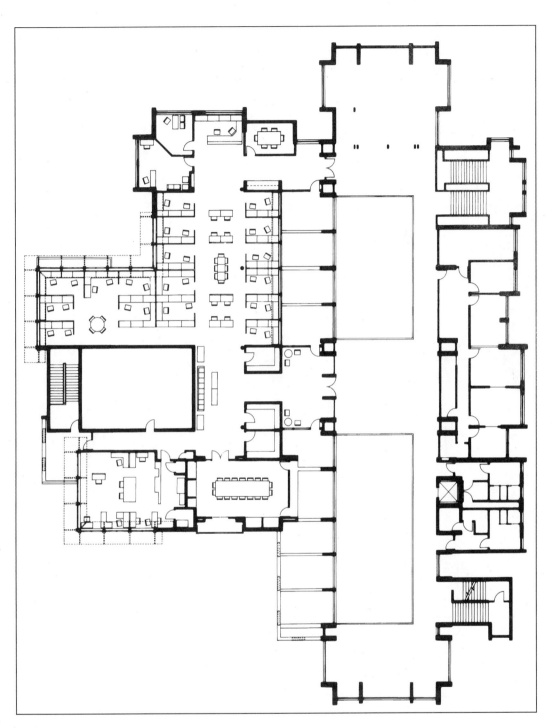

Figure 4.67
Floor plan.

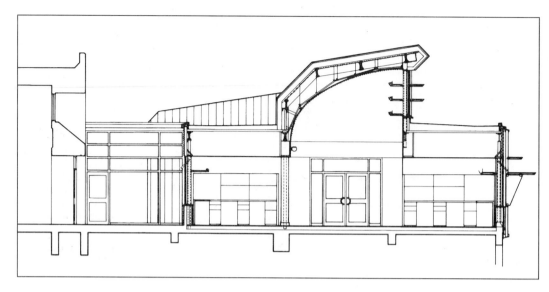

Figure 4.68
Building section.

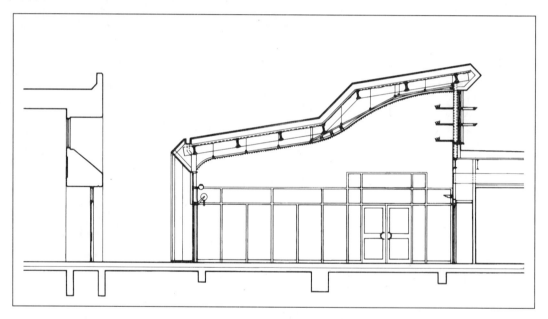

Figure 4.69
Building section.

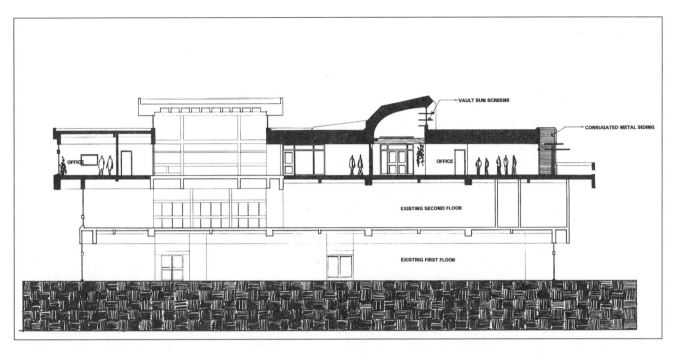

Figure 4.70
Section through vaulted clerestory.

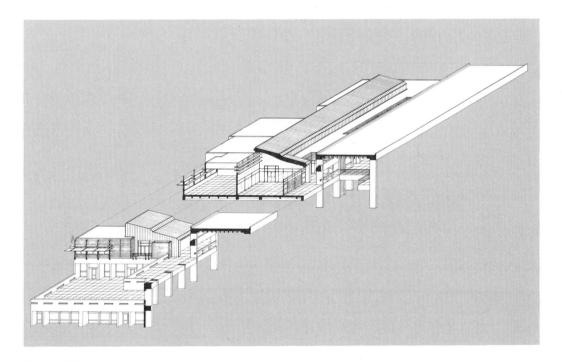

Figure 4.71
Building section.

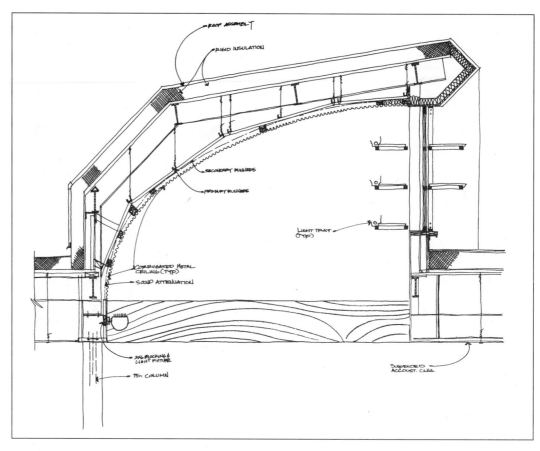

Figure 4.72
Detail section.

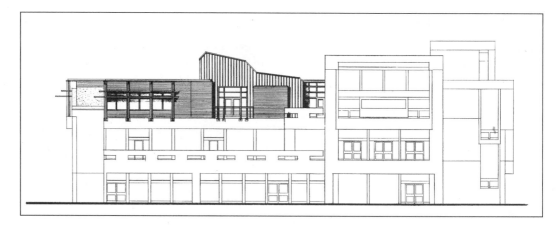

Figure 4.73
East elevation.

Figure 4.74
Elevation. (Photo by Olson/Sundberg Architects.)

Figure 4.75
Interior of clerestory. (Photo by Olson/Sundberg Architects.)

Figure 4.76
Interior space. (Photo by Olson/Sundberg Architects.)

Figure 4.77
Detail of fenestration controls. (Photo by Olson/Sundberg Architects.)

Figure 4.78
Detail of window treatment. (Photo by Olson/Sundberg Architects.)

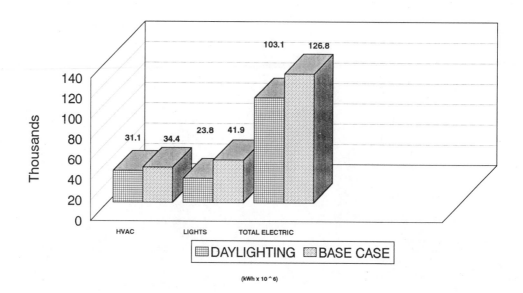

Figure 4.79
Building energy performance summary (annual kilowatt hours) (Evergreen College Addition).

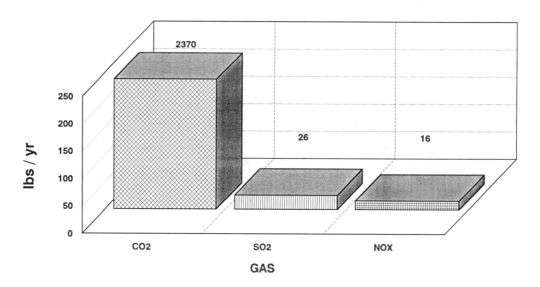

Figure 4.80
Pollution avoidance values (Evergreen College Addition).

Boulder Public Library (see Figures 4.81–4.90)

Building Type:	Library
Location:	Boulder, Colorado
Building Area:	53,000 ft^2
Daylighting Strategies:	Clerestories, window walls, light shelves, deep overhangs
Architect:	Midyette/Seieroe/Hartronft, Boulder, Colorado (design team: J. Nold Midyette, Vernon M. Seieroe, J. Erik Hartronft)
Associate Architect:	Eugene Aubry
Landscape Architect:	Gage Davis International/Terrasan
Engineers:	JVA, Inc. (structural), Engineering Economics (mechanical/electrical), AEC, Inc. (energy)
Contractor:	Pinkard Construction Company
Cost:	$9.5 million ($116/ft^2)
Photographer:	Andrew Kramer, AIA
Summary:	The 53,000-ft^2 addition to the Boulder Public Library in Boulder, Colorado, was conceived as an environmentally sensitive expression of the community's values. The firm, Midyette/Seieroe/Hartronft, incorporated daylighting techniques and other energy-conserving measures in the design.

The L-shaped volume complements the site and the surrounding vernacular with carefully selected materials and architectural expressive forms that respond to Boulder's Flatirons (rock outcroppings). The entrance is defined by a halved-conical form clad in glass. Included in the design are stepped clerestory roof monitors, deep overhangs on the south and west elevations, and light shelves that reflect daylighting into the interior spaces. Instead of skylights, vertical glazing on the northeast elevation provided adequate illumination levels while not increasing cooling loads. For their purposes, skylights provided too much illumination during the summer months, increasing the cooling load, and too little illumination during the winter months, increasing the electric lighting loads.

The two-story addition increases the square footage by 140% but increases energy consumption by only 40%. Previously the electric lighting loads accounted for 54.6% of the total annual energy loads, whereas the cooling loads consumed 15.5%. Consequently, if the electric lighting loads are reduced, the cooling loads will follow similar reductions. As a result, the energy-conserving measures are expected to reduce the total energy loads by more than 30%.

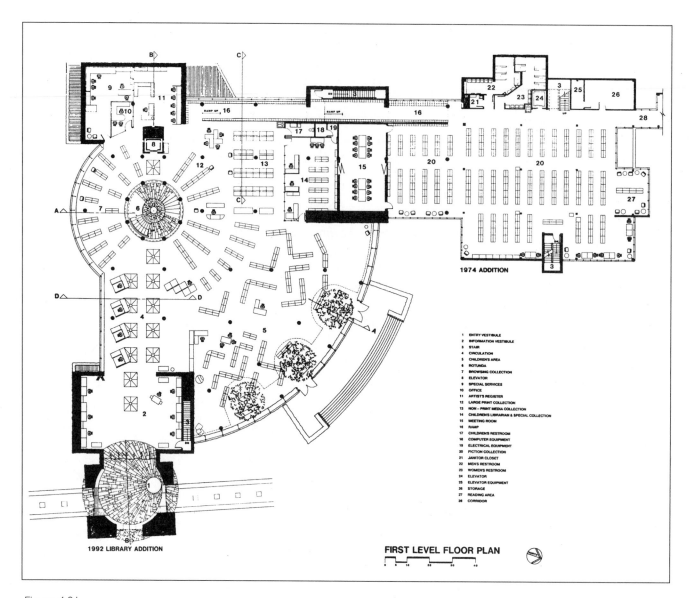

1   ENTRY VESTIBULE
2   INFORMATION VESTIBULE
3   STAIR
4   CIRCULATION
5   CHILDREN'S AREA
6   ROTUNDA
7   BROWSING COLLECTION
8   ELEVATOR
9   SPECIAL SERVICES
10   OFFICE
11   ARTIST'S REGISTER
12   LARGE PRINT COLLECTION
13   NON – PRINT MEDIA COLLECTION
14   CHILDREN'S LIBRARIAN & SPECIAL COLLECTION
15   MEETING ROOM
16   RAMP
17   CHILDREN'S RESTROOM
18   COMPUTER EQUIPMENT
19   ELECTRICAL EQUIPMENT
20   FICTION COLLECTION
21   JANITOR CLOSET
22   MEN'S RESTROOM
23   WOMEN'S RESTROOM
24   ELEVATOR
25   ELEVATOR EQUIPMENT
26   STORAGE
27   READING AREA
28   CORRIDOR

FIRST LEVEL FLOOR PLAN

Figure 4.81
First level floor plan.

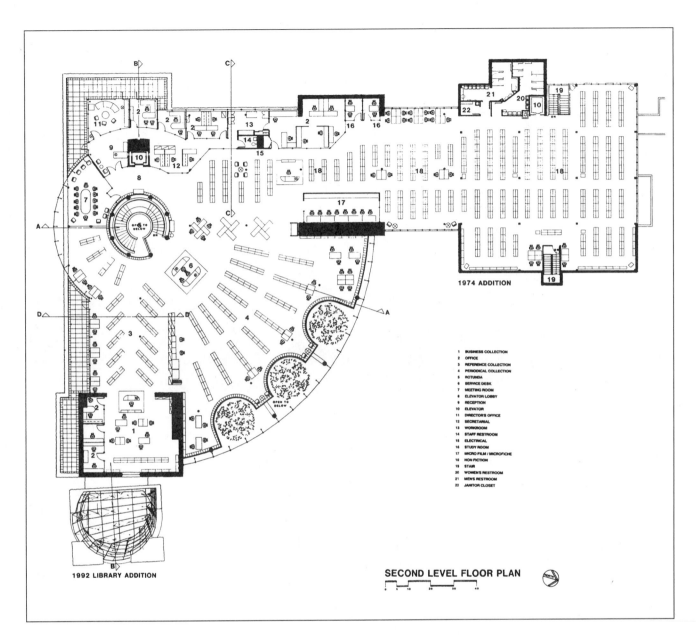

1   BUSINESS COLLECTION
2   OFFICE
3   REFERENCE COLLECTION
4   PERIODICAL COLLECTION
5   ROTUNDA
6   SERVICE DESK
7   MEETING ROOM
8   ELEVATOR LOBBY
9   RECEPTION
10 ELEVATOR
11 DIRECTOR'S OFFICE
12 SECRETARIAL
13 WORKROOM
14 STAFF RESTROOM
15 ELECTRICAL
16 STUDY ROOM
17 MICRO FILM / MICROFICHE
18 NON FICTION
19 STAIR
20 WOMEN'S RESTROOM
21 MEN'S RESTROOM
22 JANITOR CLOSET

1974 ADDITION

1992 LIBRARY ADDITION

SECOND LEVEL FLOOR PLAN

Figure 4.82
Second level floor plan.

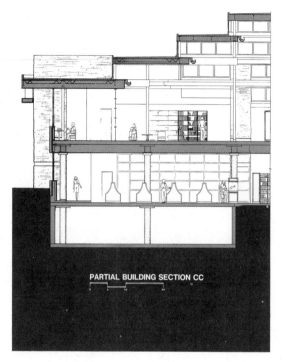

PARTIAL BUILDING SECTION CC

PARTIAL BUILDING SECTION DD

Figure 4.83
Building sections.

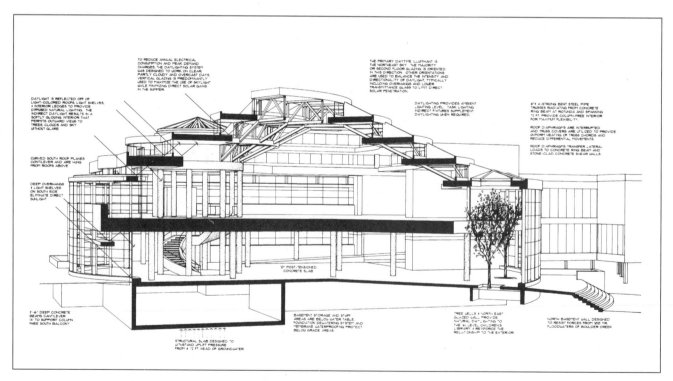

Figure 4.84
Break-away section.

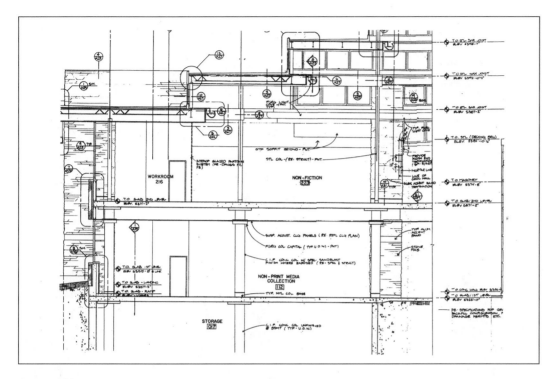

Figure 4.85
Detail of apertures.

Figure 4.86
Building exterior. (Photo by Andrew Kramer, AIA.)

Figure 4.87
Building exterior. (Photo by Andrew Kramer, AIA.)

Figure 4.88
Interior view of clerestories. (Photo by Andrew Kramer, AIA.)

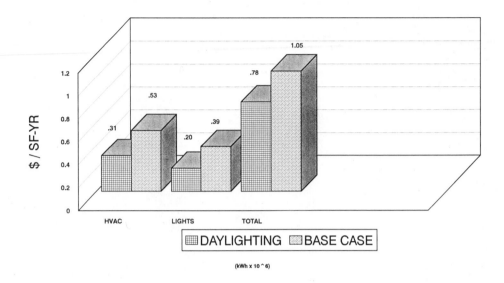

Figure 4.89
Building energy performance summary (Boulder Library Addition).

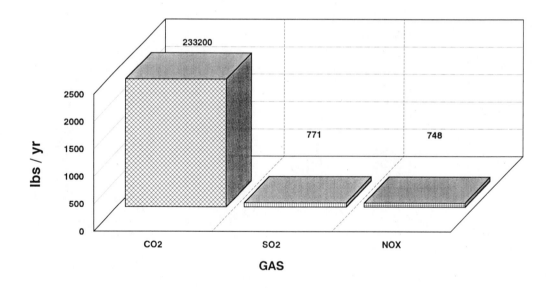

Figure 4.90
Pollution avoidance values (Boulder Library Addition).

CLA Building (see Figures 4.91–4.110)

Building Type:	Classroom, Laboratory, and Administrative Offices
Location:	Pomona, California
Building Area:	183,000 ft^2
Daylighting Strategies:	Sidelighting with high-performance glass
Electric Lighting Control Type:	Dimming
Architect:	Antoine Predock (principal in charge); Cameron Erdmann, W. Anthony Evanko (project architects)
Engineer:	Timmerman Evans Schrieber (mechanical/electrical), ESS, Inc. (energy)
Summary:	The CLA Building consists of an administrative tower with a sloping triangular roof, a connected student services wing, and a classroom and laboratory wing. The academic computer center to be used by all university students and faculty includes an instruction support computer technology center. A second component provides offices for university administrative and student service departments, which need to be accessible and convenient to the existing student population, prospective students, and off-campus visitors. The third component provides instructional spaces for lectures, self-instructional laboratories in computing and information processing, instructional television facilities, and faculty offices. Careful analysis with several simulation tools was performed to compare different glass types in the computer rooms. As a result, a glazing system with a visible transmittance of 0.50 was specified. It was believed that a higher value would have allowed more light but would have produced glare on the computer monitors; less light was let in to prevent occupants from closing the drapes and interdicting the system.

The central courtyard allows controlled daylight to enter in these adjacent spaces.

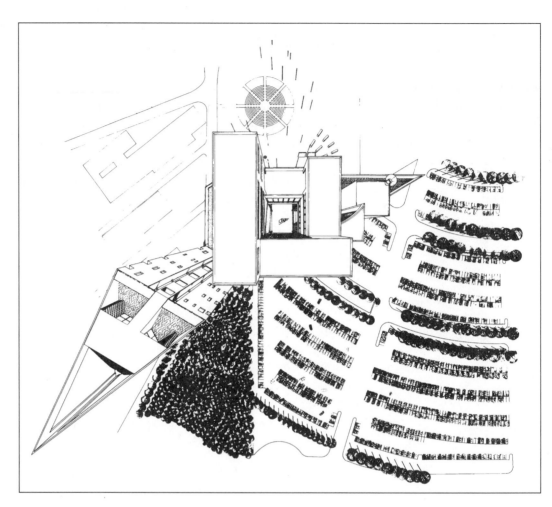

Figure 4.91
Perspective from above.

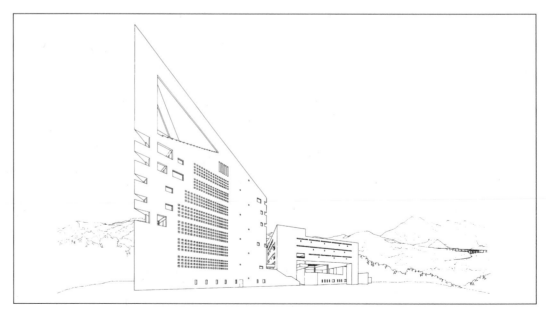

Figure 4.92
Perspective from southwest.

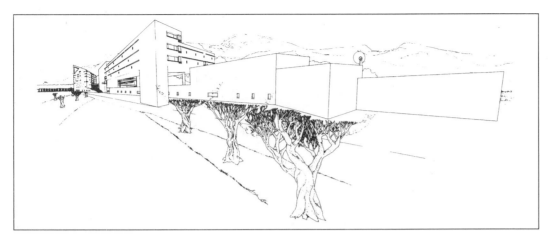

Figure 4.93
Perspective from southeast.

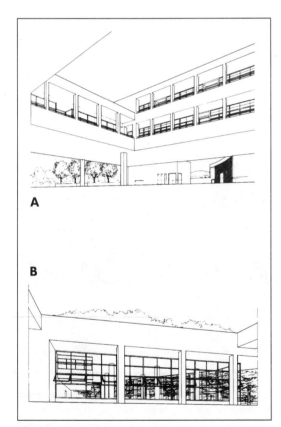

Figure 4.94
Perspective from central courtyard (A) and registration area (B).

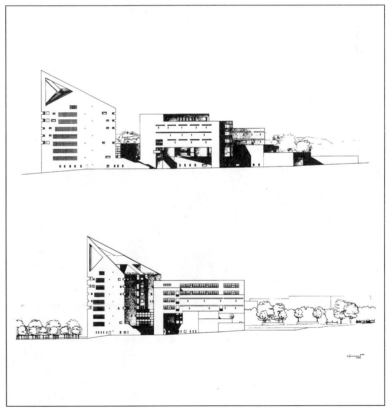

Figure 4.95
Elevations.

Figure 4.100
Exterior.

Figure 4.101
Window wall.

Figure 4.102
Courtyard.

Figure 4.103
Exterior facade.

Figure 4.104
Window detail.

Figure 4.105
Courtyard.

Figure 4.106
Courtyard space.

Figure 4.107
Window detail.

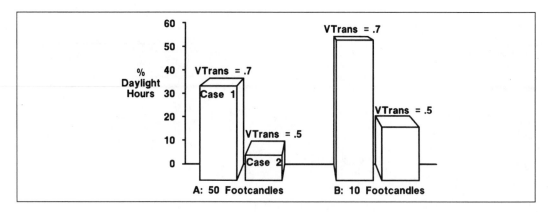

Figure 4.108
Percent of daylight hours greater than maximum recommended glare as a function of visible transmittance.

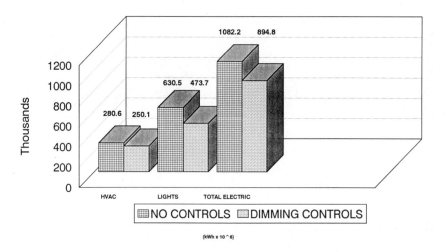

Figure 4.109
Building energy performance summary (annual kilowatt hours) (CLA Building).

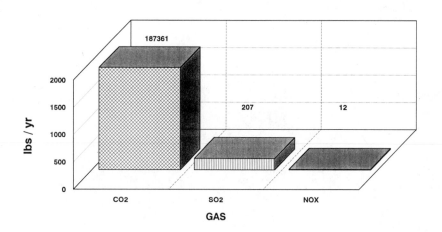

Figure 4.110
Pollution avoidance values (CLA Building).

INDUSTRIAL BUILDINGS

Precision Tool Company (see Figures 4.111–4.115)

Building Type:	Industrial Building
Location:	Santa Fe Springs, California
Building Area:	69,710 ft^2
Daylighting Strategies:	Skylights (toplighting)
Electric Lighting Control Type:	On/off
Electric Lighting Power Density:	1.30 watts/ft^2
Space Conditioning System:	Roof-mounted package units
Summary:	Precision Tool Company is a 70,000-ft^2 tilt-up concrete industrial building. This type of building is popular for industrial occupancies because it can be built for an inexpensive \$35 to \$75/ft^2 and is commonly built in 50 to 90 days. This company fabricates components for the aerospace industry and houses large machinery and some storage space. The daylighting strategy is a simple 4 × 8 ft skylight equal to approximately 5% of the roof area. The skylight is an acrylic domed skylight with a transmittance of approximately 50%. This diffusing aperture will completely scatter the direct beam sunlight that falls incident on it, resulting in a daylight space without any hot spots. These simple installations are often very cost effective.

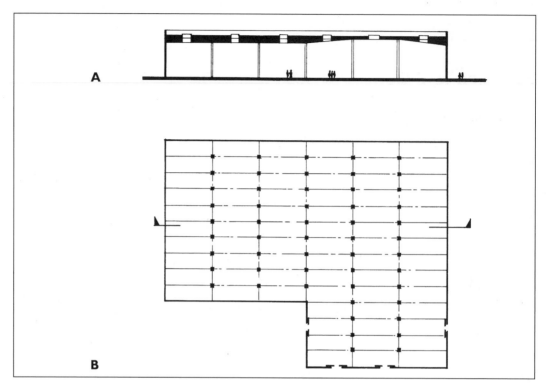

Figure 4.111
Floor plan (A) and section (B).

Figure 4.112
Building interior.

Figure 4.113
Roof landscape.

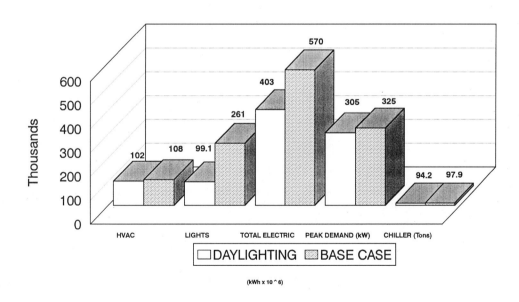

Figure 4.114
Building energy performance summary (annual kilowatt hours) (Precision Tool Company).

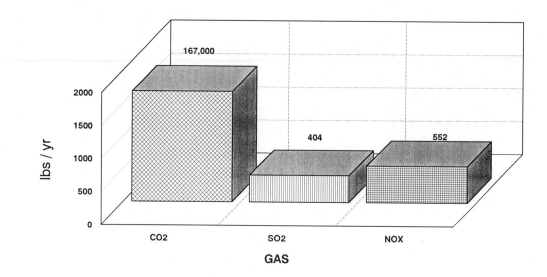

Figure 4.115
Pollution avoidance values (Precision Tool Company).

Appendix A

Daylighting Feasibility Worksheets and Data*

WORKSHEET I

(Note: See [Trial Design Worksheet, pages 39–41] for more information and an example of the use of the form.)

STEP I: Choose Representative Location

The map shows zones of roughly equal daylight availability. Each has a representative city. Choose the zone that contains your own location. Note: For Zone 2, data is provided for both Madison, WI and Washington, DC. Choose the location whose climate, especially for cooling, is most similar to that of your location.

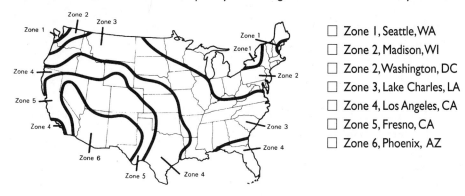

☐ Zone I, Seattle, WA

☐ Zone 2, Madison, WI

☐ Zone 2, Washington, DC

☐ Zone 3, Lake Charles, LA

☐ Zone 4, Los Angeles, CA

☐ Zone 5, Fresno, CA

☐ Zone 6, Phoenix, AZ

STEP 2: Find Basic Building Information

Occupancy [_____]
(office, retail, etc.)

Desired Average Illuminance (default: 50 fc) [_____] fc

Gross Floor Area [_____] sf
(with daylighting)

Lighting Power Density (default: 1.5) [_____] W/sf

Daylighting Control System: (Continuous Dimming) ☐ I-Step ☐ 2-Step ☐

(Note: Ceiling height does not enter into this calculation. It is assumed that skylight spacing is less than or equal to 1.5 times ceiling height. . . .)

STEP 3: Select Trial Skylight

If possible, list the following details for a trial skylight. If not, enter the default values and skip to end of Step 4.

---

*Excerpted with permission from the *American Architectural Manufacturers Association Skylight Handbook—Design Guidelines* (SHDB–1) with P.C. disk. Available: $100.00 (book only $50.00). Write to AAMA, 1540 East Dundee Road, Palatine, IL 60067. Call (708) 202–1350.

Area of typical skylight opening (individual unit) [   ] sf
(default: 16)

Visible transmittance, VT = [   ]
(default: 50)

Shading coefficient, SC = [   ]
(default: 44)

STEP 4: Determine Trial Well Factor (WF)

If possible, perform this analysis with a trial light well design. If not, use [the following] default well factor. . . . Sketch trial design below: List the well dimensions:

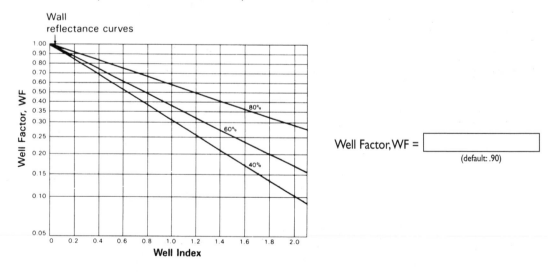

Well Height (in.), H = [   ]
(default: 18)

Maximum Well Width (ft.), W = [   ]
(default: 5)

Maximum Well Length (ft.), L = [   ]
(default: 5)

Well Wall Reflectance [   ]
(default: .80)

Calculate Well Index, using well dimensions listed above:

$$\text{Well Index} = \frac{H \times (L + W)}{24 \times W \times L} = \frac{\Box \times \Box + \Box}{\Box \times \Box \times \Box} = \boxed{0.30}$$
(default: .3)

Use the graph to find Well Factor, using values listed above. Start at Well Index. Draw up to appropriate wall reflectance curve, and across to find Well Factor; enter result below.

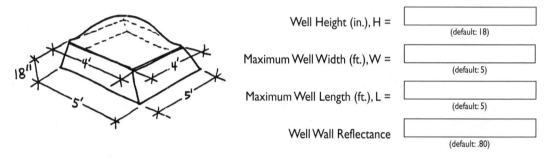

Well Factor, WF = [   ]
(default: .90)

STEP 5: Determine Skylight Efficacy (SE)

Use values listed above in Steps 3 and 4 to calculate SE. . . .

$$\text{Skylight Efficacy} = \frac{WF \times VT}{SC} = \frac{\Box \times \Box}{\Box} = \boxed{1.02}$$
(default: 1.02)

WORKSHEET 2

Note: Use [page 159] of this form (Steps 6–9) for first cut estimates of skylight area; use [page 160] (Steps 10–12) for subsequent analysis, when actual skylight sizes are known. See [Skylight Area Worksheet, pages 44–47] for more information and an example of the use of this form. Some "Step" numbers refer to Form 1 information.

STEP 6: Find Trial Effective Aperture (EA)

Choose the graph from [pages 45–47 that] corresponds to your Representative Location (Step 1) and to your Desired Average Illuminance (Step 2). Enter the graph at the LPD for your design (Step 2). Draw up to the dashed line curve that is closest to your SE (Step 5); mark the intersection points (you may interpolate between dashed curves). Repeat this step for the solid line curves. Draw horizontal lines from these points to find minimum and maximum Effective Apertures (EA). Enter these numbers in Step 7 below.

STEP 7: Determine Trial Skylight-to-Floor Ratio (SFR)

Minimum EA = [   ]   Maximum EA = [   ]

$$SFR = \frac{Max\ EA}{VT \times WF} = \frac{[\quad]}{[\quad] \times [\quad]}$$
            (Step 3) (Step 4)

$$SFR = \frac{Max\ EA}{VT \times WF} = \frac{[\quad]}{[\quad] \times [\quad]}$$
            (Step 3) (Step 4)

Minimum SFR = [   ]   Maximum SFR = [   ]

STEP 8: Determine Trial Skylight Area

Minimum Total Skylight Area:
Min. Area = Min. SFR × Gross Area = [   ] × [   ]
                (Step 7)   (Step 2)   sf
Minimum Area = [   ] sf

Maximum Total Skylight Area:
Max. Area = Max. SFR × Gross Area = [   ] × [   ]
                (Step 7)   (Step 2)   sf
Maximum Area = [   ] sf

STEP 9: Determine Trial Number of Skylights

Minimum Number of Skylights:
Min. Nmbr = Min. Area ÷ Unit Area = [   ] ÷ [   ]
                (Step 8)   (Step 3)   sf
Minimum Number = [   ]
                (round up)

Maximum Number of Skylights:
Max. Nmbr = Max. Area ÷ Unit Area = [   ] ÷ [   ]
                (Step 8)   (Step 3)   sf
Maximum Number = [   ]
                (round up)

Note: The following three steps are used to calculate Effective Aperture (EA) when the number of skylights, the well factor, and the visible transmittance of the skylight are known. . . .

STEP 10: Determine Total Skylight Area

Number of Skylights $\times$ Unit Area = $\boxed{}$ $\times$ $\boxed{}$ $\times$ $\boxed{}$ Total Skylight Area
     (#)   (sf each)   #   sf each   sf
                   (Step 3)

STEP 11: Determine Skylight-to-Floor Ratio (SFR)

Total Skylight Area $\div$ Gross Floor Area = $\boxed{}$ $\div$ $\boxed{}$ = $\boxed{}$ Skylight-to-Floor Ratio (SFR)
   (Step 10)   (Step 2)   sf   sf

STEP 12: Determine Effective Aperture (EA)

$\boxed{}$ $\times$ $\boxed{}$ $\times$ $\boxed{}$ = $\boxed{}$ Effective Aperture
SFR   VT   WF   EA
(Step 11) (Step 3) (Step 4)

WORKSHEET 4

Note: See [Lighting Savings Worksheet, pages 52–54] for more information and an example of the use of this form. Some "Step" numbers refer to previous Form information.

STEP 13: Finding Full Load Lighting Hours

The default value corresponds to typical office working hours, as shown in the schedule in [the previous section]. If that schedule differs greatly from the schedule in your building, refer to [Appendix E] for the procedure for finding your full load operating hours. Otherwise, use the default value.

Full load lighting hours = ☐ hrs.
                        (default: 2600)

STEP 14: Find Fraction of Lighting Energy Saved

Use the graph from [the Lighting Energy Savings Graphs, pages 53–54] corresponding to your Representative Location (Step 1) and your Desired Average Illuminance (Step 2). Enter graph at the EA value (Step 12) corresponding to your skylight design. Draw a line up to the curve for your Daylighting Control System (Step 2), then across to the fraction of lighting energy saved. Enter the fraction below.

EA = 0.022 (Step 12)
Fraction of Lighting Energy Saved ☐

STEP 15: Calculate Lighting Energy Saved

$$\frac{LPD\ (Step\ 2)}{1000} \times Gross\ Floor\ Area \times Full\ Load\ Hours \times Fraction\ Saved = Lighting\ Energy\ Saved\ (kWh)$$
                        (Step 2)   (Step 13)   (Step 14)

$$\frac{\boxed{\ }}{1000} \times \boxed{\ } \times \boxed{\ } \times \boxed{\ } = \boxed{\ }\ kWh/yr$$

STEP 16: Calculate Lighting Cost Saved

. . . If actual electricity costs are not known, [contact your local utility for a current rate schedule].

Lighting Energy Saved × Average Electricity Cost = ☐ × ☐ = ☐
    (Step 15)   ($/kWh)   kWh/yr $/kWh $/yr

WORKSHEET 5

Note: See [Cooling Calculation Worksheet, page 56] for more information and an example of the use of this form. Some "Step" numbers refer to previous Form information.

STEP 17: Note Representative City

This calculation makes use of the same representative cities selected in Step 1. Check off your selection again here, for reference:

☐ Seattle, WA
☐ Madison, WI
☐ Washington, DC
☐ Lake Charles, LA
☐ Los Angeles, CA
☐ Fresno, CA
☐ Phoenix, AZ

STEP 18: Find Coefficients for Representative Cooling City

	B1	B2
Seattle, WA	0.19	11.5
Madison, WI	0.31	16.6
Washington, DC	0.42	21.1
Lake Charles, LA	0.66	30.8
Los Angeles, CA	0.53	28.1
Fresno, CA	0.51	36.9
Phoenix, AZ	0.68	47.3

STEP 19: Calculate Cooling Energy and Cost Effects

$$
\begin{array}{cccccc}
\underset{\text{(Step 18)}}{B1} & \times & \underset{\text{(Step 14)}}{\text{Fraction Saved}} & \times & \underset{\text{(Step 2)}}{\text{LPD}} & = & \underset{\text{Value \#1}}{\text{Temporary}} \\
\boxed{} & & \boxed{} & & \boxed{} & & \boxed{}
\end{array}
$$

$$
\begin{array}{cccccc}
\underset{\text{(Step 18)}}{B2} & \times & \underset{\text{(Step 12)}}{\text{Effective Aperture}} & \div & \underset{\text{(Step 5)}}{\text{Skylight Effic.}} & = & \underset{\text{Value \#2}}{\text{Temporary}} \\
\boxed{} & & \boxed{} & & \boxed{} & & \boxed{}
\end{array}
$$

Temporary Value #1		Temporary Value #2		Unit Cooling Energy Effect		Gross Floor Area		Cooling Energy Effect
☐	−	☐	=	☐	×	☐	=	☐
(from above)		(from above)		kWh/yrsf		(Step 2)		kWh/yr

Cooling Energy Effect		Average Electricity Cost		Cooling Cost Effect
☐	×	☐	=	☐
kWh/yr (from above)		(Step 18) $/kWh		kWh/yrsf

Appendix B

Illuminance Selection*
Currently Recommended Illuminance Categories and Illuminance Values for Lighting Design—Targeted Maintained Levels

The following table is a consolidated listing of the IESNA's current illuminance recommendations. This listing is intended to guide the designer in selecting an appropriate illuminance.

Guidance is provided in Tables B.1 and B.2 as an *illuminance category,* representing a range of illuminances, and as an *illuminance value.* Illuminance categories are represented by letter designations A through I. Illuminance Values are given in *lux* with equivalents in *footcandles* and as such are intended as *target values* with deviations expected. These target values also represent *maintained* values. . . .

Table B.1 lists both illuminance categories and illuminance values for generic types of interior activities and normally is used when illuminance categories for a specific area/activity cannot be found in Table B.2.

In all cases the recommendations in the tables are based on the assumption that the lighting will be properly designed to take into account the visual characteristics of the task.

Table B.1
Illuminance Categories and Illuminance Values for Generic Types of Activities in Interiors

| Type of Activity | Illuminance Category | Range of Illuminances | | |
		Lux	Reference Work-Plane Footcandles	
Public spaces with dark surroundings	A	20-30-50	2-3-5	
Simple orientation for short temporary visits	B	50-75-100	5-7.5-10	General lighting
Working spaces where visual tasks are only occasionally performed	C	100-150-200	10-15-20	throughout spaces
Performance of visual tasks of high contrast or large size	D	200-300-500	20-30-50	
Performance of visual tasks of medium contrast or small size	E	500-750-1000	50-75-100	Illuminance on task
Performance of visual tasks of low contrast or very small size	F	1000-1500-2000	100-150-200	
Performance of visual tasks of low contrast and very small size over a prolonged period	G	2000-3000-5000	200-300-500	
Performance of very prolonged and exacting visual task	H	5000-7500-10,000	500-750-1000	Illuminance on a task, obtained by a combination of general and
Performance of very special visual tasks of extremely low contrast and small size	I	10,000-15,000-20,000	1000-1500-2000	local (supplementary) lighting)

*Published with permission. Source: IESNA Lighting Handbook. Published by the Illuminating Engineering Society of North America, 120 Wall Street, New York, NY 10005.

Table B.2
Illuminance Category for Particular Areas and Activities

Area/Activity	Illuminance Category	Area/Activity	Illuminance Category
Accounting (see **Reading**)		**Food service facilities**	
Air terminals (see **Transportation terminals**)		Dining areas	
Armories	C	Cashier	D
Art Galleries (see **Museums**)		Cleaning	C
Auditoriums		Dining	B
Assembly	C	Food displays (see **Merchandizing spaces**)	
Social activity	B	Kitchen	E
Banks (also see Reading)		**Garages—parking***	
Lobby		**Gasoline stations** (see **Service stations**)	
General	C	**Graphic design and material**	
Writing area	D	Coloring selection	F
Tellers' stations	E	Charting and mapping	F
Barber shops and beauty parlors	E	Graphs	F
Churches and synagogues*		Keylining	F
Club and lodge rooms		Layout and artwork	F
Lounge and reading	D	Photographs, moderate detail	E
Conference rooms		**Health care facilities**	
Conferring	D	Ambulance (local)	E
Critical seeing (refer to individual task)		Anesthetizing	E
Court rooms		Autopsy and morgue	
Seating area	C	Autopsy, general	E
Court activity area	E	Autopsy table	G
Dance halls and discotheques	B	Morgue, general	D
Depots, terminals, and stations		Museum	E
(see **Transportation terminals**)		Cardiac function lab	E
Drafting		Central sterile supply	
Mylar		Inspection, general	E
High contrast media; India ink, plastic		Inspection	F
leads, soft graphite leads	E	At sinks	E
Low contrast media; hard graphite leads	F	Work areas, general	D
Vellum		Processed storage	D
High contrast	E	Corridors	
Low contrast	F	Nursing areas—day	C
Tracing paper		Nursing areas—night	B
High contrast	E	Operating areas, delivery, recovery, and	
Low contrast	F	laboratory suites and service	E
Overlays		Critical care areas	
Light table	C	General	C
Prints		Examination	E
Blue line	E	Surgical task lighting	H
Blueprints	E	Handwashing	F
Sepia prints	F	Cystoscopy room	E
Educational facilities		Dental suite	
Classrooms		General	D
General (see **Reading**)		Instrument tray	E
Drafting (see **Drafting**)		Oral cavity	H
Home economics (see **Residences**)		Prosthetic laboratory, general	D
Science laboratories	E	Prosthetic laboratory, work bench	E
Lecture rooms		Prosthetic laboratory, local	F
Audience (see **Reading**)		Recovery room, general	C
Demonstration	F	Recovery room, emergency examination	E
Music rooms (see **Reading**)		Dialysis unit, medical	F
Shops*		Elevators	C
Sight-saving rooms	F	ECG and specimen room	
Study halls (see **Reading**)		Emergency outpatient	
Typing (see **Reading**)		General	E
Sports facilities*		Local	F
Cafeterias (see **Food service facilities**)		Endoscopy rooms	
Dormitories (see **Residences**)		General	E
Elevators, freight and passenger	C	Peritoneoscopy	D
Exhibition halls	C	Culdoscopy	D
Filing (refer to individual task)		Examination and treatment rooms	
Financial facilities (see **Banks**)		General	D

Area/Activity	Illuminance Category
Local	E
Eye Surgery	F
Fracture room	
General	E
Local	F
Inhalation therapy	D
Laboratories	
Specimen collecting	E
Tissue laboratories	F
Microscopic reading room	D
Gross specimen review	F
Chemistry rooms	E
Bacteriology rooms	
General	E
Reading culture plates	F
Hematology	E
Linens	
Sorting soiled linen	D
Central (clean) linen room	D
Sewing room, general	D
Sewing room, work area	E
Linen closet	B
Lobby	C
Locker rooms	C
Medical illustration studio	F
Medical records	E
Nurseries	
General	C
Observation and treatment	E
Nursing stations	
General	D
Desk	E
Corridors, day	C
Corridors, night	A
Medication station	E
Obstetric delivery suite	
Labor rooms	
General	C
Local	F
Birthing room	F
Delivery area	
Scrub, general	F
General	G
Resuscitation	G
Postdelivery recovery area	E
Substerilizing room	B
Occupational therapy	
Work area, general	D
Work tables or benches	E
Patients' rooms	
General	B
Observation	A
Critical examination	E
Reading	D
Toilets	D
Pharmacy	
General	B
Alcohol vault	D
Laminar flow bench	F
Night light	A
Parenteral solution room	D
Physical therapy departments	
Gymnasiums	D
Tank rooms	D
Treatment cubicles	D
Postanesthetic recovery room	
General	E

Area/Activity	Illuminance Category
Local	H
Pulmonary function laboratories	E
Radiological suite	
Diagnostic section	
General	A
Waiting area	A
Radiographic/fluoroscopic room	A
Film sorting	F
Barium kitchen	E
Radiation therapy section	
General	B
Waiting area	B
Isotope kitchen, general	E
Isotope kitchen, benches	E
Computerized radiotomography section	
Scanning room	B
Equipment maintenance room	E
Solarium	
General	C
Local for reading	D
Stairways	C
Surgical suite	
Operating room, general	F
Operating table*	
Scrub room	F
Instruments and sterile supply room	D
Clean up room, instruments	E
Anesthesia storage	C
Substerilizing room	C
Surgical induction room	E
Surgical holding area	E
Toilets	C
Utility room	D
Waiting areas	
General	C
Local for reading	D
Homes (see **Residences**)	
Hospitality facilities (see **Hotels**; **Food service facilities**)	
Hospitals (see **Health care facilities**)	
Hotels	
Bathrooms, for grooming	D
Bedrooms, for reading	D
Corridors, elevators, and stairs	C
Front desk	E
Linen room	
Sewing	F
General	C
Lobby	
General lighting	C
Reading and working areas	D
Canopy*	
Houses of worship*	
Kitchens (see **Food service facilities** or **Residences**)	
Libraries	
Reading areas (see **Reading**)	
Book stacks (vertical 760 mm [30 in.] above floor)	
Active stacks	D
Inactive stacks	B
Book repair and binding	D
Cataloging	D
Card Files	E
Carrels, individual study areas (see **Reading**)	
Circulation desks	D
Map, picture, and print rooms (see **Graphic design and material**)	

Table B.2 (*continued*)
Illuminance Category for Particular Areas and Activities

Area/Activity	Illuminance Category	Area/Activity	Illuminance Category
Libraries (*continued*)		Thermal print	E
Audiovisual areas	D	**Handwritten tasks**	
Audio listening areas	D	No. 2 pencil and softer leads	D
Microform areas (see **Reading**)		No. 3 pencil	E
Locker rooms	C	No. 4 pencil and harder leads	F
Merchandising spaces		Ballpoint pen	D
Alteration room	F	Felt-tip pen	D
Fitting room		Handwritten carbon copies	E
Dressing areas	D	Nonphotographically reproducible colors	F
Fitting areas	F	Chalkboards	E
Locker rooms	C	**Printed tasks**	
Stock rooms, wrapping, and packaging	D	6-point type	E
Sales transaction area (see **Reading**)		8- and 10-point type	D
Circulation*		Glossy magazines	D
Merchandise*		Maps	E
Feature display*		Newsprint	D
Show windows*		Typed originals	D
Motels (see **Hotels**)		Typed 2nd carbon and later	E
Municipal buildings—fire and police		Telephone books	E
Police		**Residences**	
Identification records	F	General lighting	
Jail cells and interrogation rooms	D	Conversation, relaxation, and entertainment	B
Fire hall	D	Passage areas	B
Museums		Specific visual tasks	
Displays of nonsensitive materials	D	Dining	C
Displays of sensitive materials*		Grooming	
Lobbies, general gallery areas, corridors	C	Makeup and shaving	D
Restoration of conservation shops and		Full-length mirror	D
laboratories	E	Handcrafts and hobbies	
Nursing homes (see **Health care facilities**)		Workbench hobbies	
Offices		Ordinary tasks	D
Accounting (see **Reading**)		Difficult tasks	E
Audiovisual areas	D	Critical tasks	F
Conference areas (see **Conference rooms**)		Easel hobbies	E
Drafting (see **Drafting**)		Ironing	D
General and private offices (see **Reading**)		Kitchen duties	
Libraries (see **Libraries**)		Kitchen Counter	
Lobbies, lounges and reception areas	C	Critical seeing	E
Mail sorting	E	Noncritical	D
Off-set printing and duplicating area	D	Kitchen range	
Spaces with VDTs*		Difficult seeing	E
Parking facilities*		Noncritical	D
Post offices (see **Offices**)		Kitchen sink	
Reading		Difficult seeing	E
Copied tasks		Noncritical	D
Ditto copy	E	Laundry	
Microfiche reader	B	Preparation and tubs	D
Mimeograph	D	Washer and dryer	D
Photograph, moderate detail	E	Music study (piano or organ)	
Thermal copy, poor copy	F	Simple scores	D
Xerograph	D	Advanced scores	E
Xerography, 3rd generation and greater	E	Substandard-sized scores	F
Electronic data processing tasks		Reading	
CRT screens	B	In a chair	
Impact printer		Books, magazines, and newspapers	D
good ribbon	D	Handwriting, reproductions and poor copies	E
poor ribbon	E	In bed	
2nd carbon and greater	E	Normal	D
Inkjet printer	D	Prolonged serious or critical	E
Keyboard reading	D	Desk	
Machine room		Primary task plane, casual	D
Active operations	D	Primary task plane, study	E
Tape storage	D	Sewing	
Machine area	C	Hand sewing	
Equipment service	E	Dark fabrics, low contrast	F

Area/Activity	Illuminance Category	Area/Activity	Illuminance Category
Light to medium fabrics	E	Sales room (see Merchandising space)	
Occasional, high contrast	D	Show windows*	
Machine sewing		Stairways (see Service spaces)	
Dark fabrics, low contrast	E	Storage rooms*	
Light to medium fabrics	E	Stores (see Merchandising spaces and Show windows)	
Occasional, high contrast	D	Television*	
Table games	D	Theater and motion picture houses*	
Restaurants (see Food service facilities)		Toilets and washrooms	C
Safety*		Transportation terminals	
Schools (see Educational facilities)		Waiting room and lounge	C
Service spaces (see also Storage rooms)		Ticket counters	E
Stairways corridors	C	Baggage checking	D
Elevators, freight and passenger	C	Rest rooms	C
Toilets and washrooms	C	Concourse	B
Service stations		Boarding area	C
Service bays*			

*Refer to the Illuminating Engineering Society of North America, IESNA Lighting Handbook, New York, 1993.

Appendix C

Weather Data

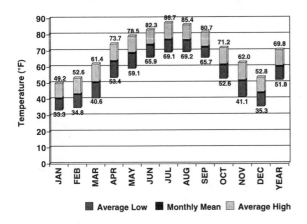

TEMPERATURE RANGE - ATLANTA

Average Low ■ Monthly Mean ■ Average High

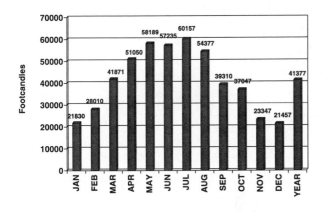

AVERAGE DAILY EXTERIOR ILLUMINANCE ATLANTA

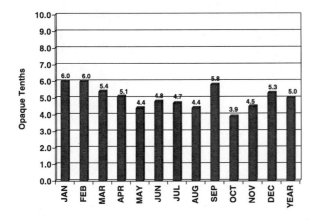

AVERAGE SKY COVER - ATLANTA

TEMPERATURE RANGE - CHICAGO

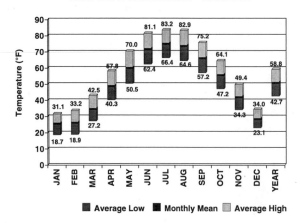

**AVERAGE DAILY EXTERIOR ILLUMINANCE
CHICAGO**

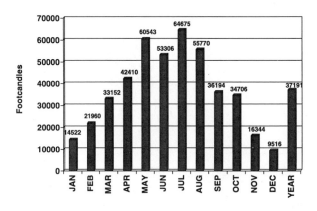

AVERAGE SKY COVER - CHICAGO

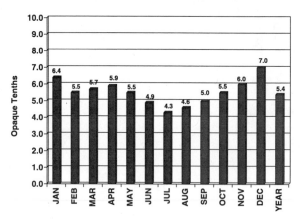

TEMPERATURE RANGE - DENVER

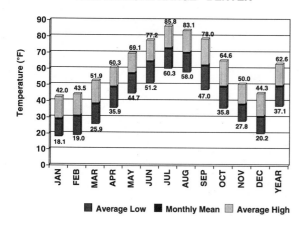

AVERAGE DAILY EXTERIOR ILLUMINANCE DENVER

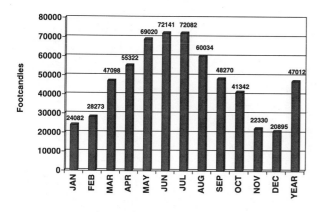

AVERAGE SKY COVER - DENVER

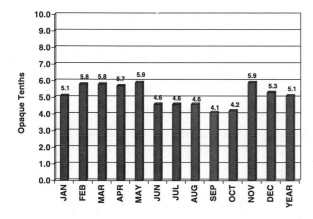

TEMPERATURE RANGE - LOS ANGELES

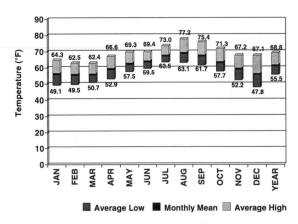

**AVERAGE DAILY EXTERIOR ILLUMINANCE
LOS ANGELES**

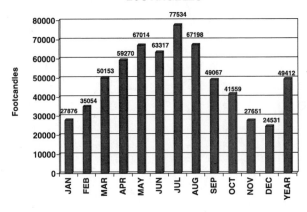

AVERAGE SKY COVER - LOS ANGELES

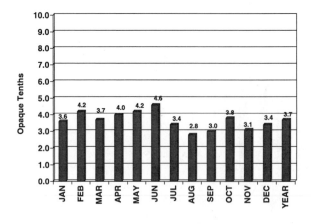

TEMPERATURE RANGE - NEW YORK

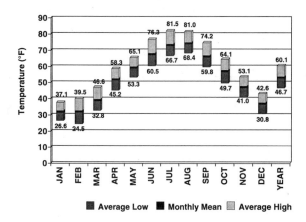

Temperature (°F)

| Average Low | Monthly Mean | Average High |

AVERAGE DAILY EXTERIOR ILLUMINANCE
NEW YORK

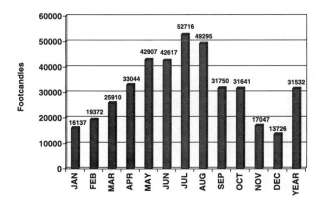

Footcandles

AVERAGE SKY COVER - NEW YORK

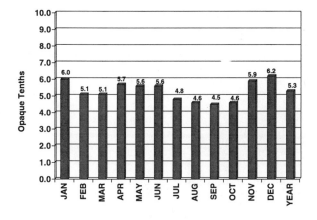

Opaque Tenths

TEMPERATURE RANGE - SEATTLE

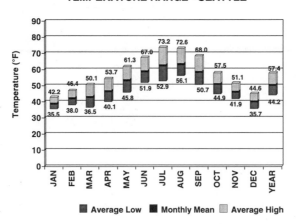

AVERAGE DAILY EXTERIOR ILLUMINANCE SEATTLE

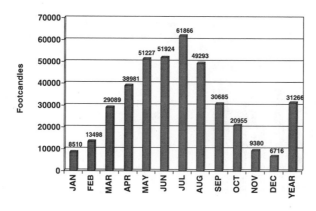

AVERAGE SKY COVER - SEATTLE

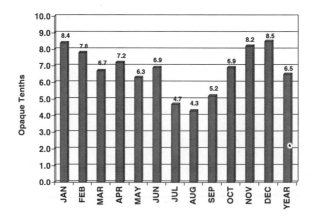

APPENDIX D

Glazing Material Properties

TYPICAL VISIBLE TRANSMITTANCE VALUES

MONOLITHIC GLASS CLEAR AND TINTED				
Glass	**Thickness**		**Transmittance**	
			Average Daylight (%)	Total Solar (%)
	in.	mm		
Sheet	SS	2.5	90	85
	DS 3	3	89	80
	3/16	5	89	78
Clear	1/8	3	89	80
	3/16	5	88	78
	1/4	6	87	75
	5/16	8	86	70
Clear heavy duty	3/8	10	84	67
	1/2	12	82	61
	5/8	15	80	56
	3/4	19	78	51
	7/8	22	75	48
Blue-green	1/8	3	83	63
	3/16	5	79	55
	1/4	6	75	47
Gray	1/8	3	61	63
	3/16	5	51	53
	1/4	6	44	46
	5/16	8	35	38
	3/8	10	28	21
	1/2	12	19	22
INSULATING GLASS				
(inboard light clear)				
Clear	1/8	3	80	69
	3/16	5	79	62
	1/4	6	77	59
Blue-green	1/8	3	75	52
	3/16	5	70	43
	1/4	6	66	36
Gray	1/8	3	55	52
	3/16	5	45	42
	1/4	6	39	35
Bronze	1/8	3	61	54
	3/16	5	53	43
	1/4	6	46	38

Note: check manufacturers' literature for specific values.

Appendix E

Alternative to Lighting Savings Graphs*

The procedure outlined in this appendix provides an alternative to the procedure for determining Lighting Energy Saved found on pages 52–53. It allows one to more accurately determine lighting energy savings for situations that differ significantly from those assumed in the analysis which underlies the worksheets. This procedure should be used where:

1) The Desired Average Illuminance (Step 2) is much greater than 70 footcandles, or much less than 30 footcandles, or
2) The operating schedule for the building is not similar to the default schedule shown on pages 52–53 (Step 13), which is a typical, 8–5 office schedule. Examples of dissimilar schedules would be elementary schools and retail stores.

It may also be used when:

3) You wish to develop a detailed profile of average daylighting illuminances.

This procedure is based on simulation data that gives the monthly average illuminance for each hour of the day in the skylighted space for a given Effective Skylight Area (EA). This data is shown for six representative daylighting climates, using an EA of 0.01. The representative climates are:

Seattle
Madison/Washington
Lake Charles
Los Angeles
Fresno
Phoenix

There is a separate data table for each of the locations (Figures E.6 to E.11), plus blank calculation tables which are filled in during the procedure (Figure E.12).

The illuminance in a space is very nearly proportional to the EA. For example, for an EA = .02, the illuminance in Figure E.1 would be double the values shown for each hour.

---

*Excerpted with permission from the *American Architectural Manufacturers Association Skylight Handbook— Design Guidelines* (SHDB-1) with P.C. disk. Available: $100.00 (book only $50.00). Write to: AAMA, 1540 East Dundee Road, Palatine, IL 60067. Call: (708) 202-1350.

This fact is the basis for this procedure; in essence, it has you adjust the illuminances for each hour, and project these values through to the hourly and total lighting energy savings. These adjustments are:

- Adjust illuminance levels for your actual EA
- Estimate lighting savings by your control system
- Determine full load lighting power
- Determine lighting energy savings

The details of the calculation follow:

1) Complete Forms 1, 2 & 3 to determine your trial skylight design. Note that the graphs in the analysis method to determine initial EA's for design (Step 6) were based on the typical, 8–5 schedule. If your operating schedule contains less daylighting hours, you should pick a smaller EA for initial design, such as the minimum EA found.

2) Select the data table for your Representative Location (Step 1) from Figures E.6 to E.11. For each value on the data table, multiply by the factor:

$$(\text{Value from table}) \times \frac{\text{EA}}{.01} = \text{new value}$$

and enter the result in the same location on a blank data table (Figure E.12). For example, the Washington, DC, value for hour 12 in January is 24 fc (see Figure E.7). If your EA is .02, multiply:

$$24 \text{ fc} \times \frac{.02}{.01} = 48\text{fc}$$

This number would be placed in the hour 12 location for January on a blank data table. The calculation would be repeated for each location on the worksheet. This should be labeled "Data Table 2, Average Daylight Illuminances" (see Figure E.2); it shows the monthly average daylight illuminance for each hour of an average day.

3) Based on the indicated illuminances, determine, for each hour of each month, the fraction of lighting energy that would be saved by your lighting control system. The following graphs illustrate how you could determine this for a dimming system and a two-step system. A similar analysis could be readily developed for different kinds of control systems. For example, use the graph below for a dimming system. If the daylighting illuminance were shown in Data Table 2 to be 40 footcandles for hour 10 in June, you would enter the graph at 40 fc, draw a vertical up to the sloped line, and thence horizontally to find the Lighting Fraction Saved to be 0.75. This value would be entered in a new blank data table for hour 10 in June. The procedure would be repeated for all hours. Note that in this example, many hours are at the minimum or maximum lighting savings values, and will not require calculation. The results of these calculations should be labeled "Data Table 3, Fraction of Lighting Energy Saved" (see Figure E.3).

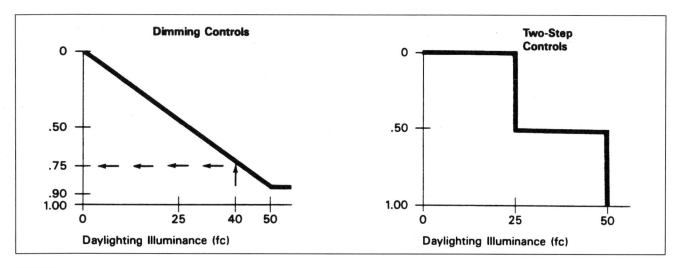

FIGURE E.1
Sample daylighting control operation.

4) Start with a new blank data table, labeled "Data Table 4, Full Load Lighting Power" (see Figure E.4). Determine the full load lighting power for the daylighted space by multiplying the Gross Floor Area times Lighting Power Density (both from Step 2). Determine your building's lighting schedule, as a decimal fraction of full load lighting for each hour of each month. For example, a typical building might require 85% of the lights on at noon, and only 50% of the lights on at 7 P.M. For each hour, multiply the lighting schedule decimal fraction times the full load lighting power times the number of operating days per month; divide by 1000. This will yield the number of kilowatt hours (kWh) used when there is no daylighting.

5) Start with another blank data table, labeled "Data Table 5, Lighting Energy Savings" (see Figure E.5). Determine the lighting energy saved by daylighting, multiplying the numbers in Data Table 3 by their corresponding values in Data Table 4. For example, if the value for hour 3 in December in Table 3 were .40, and the value for the same hour in Table 4 were 15,600, then you would enter the following value for hour 3 in December in Table 5:

$$.40 \times 15,600 \text{ kWh} = 6240 \text{ kWh}$$

6) Sum all the numbers in all columns and rows in Data Table 5. Carry this number back to Step 15 on Form 4; enter it as the answer, Lighting Energy Saved (kWh). Proceed on to Step 16 and the following forms.

The following pages include a worked example of this calculation (Figures E.2 to E.5). Following that are the source data tables (Figures E.6 to E.11), and a blank data table (Figure E.12).

Data Table No. 2
Title   Average Daylight Illuminances, EA = 0.02

Washington, DC
70 fc set point
1.8 W/sf Skylight SE = 1.0
Dimming system chosen for 1000 sf retail

	1	2	3	4	5	6	7	8	9	10	11	12	13	14	15	16	17	18	19	20	21	22	23	24
Jan.								2	12	24	38	46	48	42	30	16	4							
Feb.								6	20	40	60	72	72	64	48	30	12							
March							2	16	36	62	78	90	92	84	68	44	22	6						
April						2	16	36	60	80	94	102	102	94	76	56	34	14						
May						10	28	56	80	102	116	116	114	108	94	76	46	22	6					
June						12	30	58	88	108	122	130	124	122	112	92	62	32	12					
July							8	26	56	88	110	124	140	144	140	114	86	58	30	10				
Aug.							4	20	46	78	108	126	140	138	124	104	80	48	20	4				
Sept.							10	32	60	80	96	110	106	96	80	56	26	6						
Oct.								2	18	38	60	74	80	78	68	50	28	10						
Nov.								6	20	32	44	52	48	38	24	12								
Dec.								2	12	24	34	40	38	32	22	10								

FIGURE E.2
Example: Data Table 2.

Data Table No. 3
Title   Fraction Lighting Energy Saved

	1	2	3	4	5	6	7	8	9	10	11	12	13	14	15	16	17	18	19	20	21	22	23	24
Jan.								.03	.15	.31	.49	.59	.62	.54	.39	.21	.05							
Feb.								.08	.26	.51	.77	.90	.90	.82	.62	.39	.15							
March							.03	.21	.46	.80	.90	.90	.90	.90	.87	.57	.28	.08						
April						.03	.21	.46	.77	.90	.90	.90	.90	.90	.90	.72	.44	.18						
May						.13	.36	.72	.90	.90	.90	.90	.90	.90	.90	.90	.59	.28	.08					
June						.15	.39	.75	.90	.90	.90	.90	.90	.90	.90	.90	.80	.41	.15					
July						.10	.33	.72	.90	.90	.90	.90	.90	.90	.90	.90	.75	.39	.13					
Aug.						.05	.26	.59	.90	.90	.90	.90	.90	.90	.90	.90	.62	.26	.05					
Sept.							.13	.41	.77	.90	.90	.90	.90	.90	.90	.72	.33	.08						
Oct.							.03	.23	.49	.77	.90	.90	.90	.87	.64	.36	.13							
Nov.								.08	.26	.41	.57	.67	.62	.49	.31	.15								
Dec.								.03	.15	.31	.44	.51	.49	.41	.28	.13								

FIGURE E.3
Example: Data Table 3.

Data Table No. 4
Title   Full Load Lighting Power (KWH)

Open 7 days/week

1.8 W/sf, 1000 sf

Lighting schedule:
70%   10 A.M.–11 A.M.
100%   11 A.M.–7 P.M.
70%   7 P.M.–8 P.M.
50%   8 P.M.–9 P.M.

											Hours of Day												
	1	2	3	4	5	6	7	8	9	10	11	12	13	14	15	16	17	18	19	20	21	22	23	24
Jan.											39	56	56	56	56	56	56	56	56	39	28			
Feb.											35	50	50	50	50	50	50	50	50	35	25			
March											39	56	56	56	56	56	56	56	56	39	28			
April											38	54	54	54	54	54	54	54	54	38	27			
May											39	56	56	56	56	56	56	56	56	39	28			
June											38	54	54	54	54	54	54	54	54	38	27			
July											39	56	56	56	56	56	56	56	56	39	28			
Aug.											39	56	56	56	56	56	56	56	56	39	28			
Sept.											38	54	54	54	54	54	54	54	54	38	27			
Oct.											39	56	56	56	56	56	56	56	56	39	28			
Nov.											38	54	54	54	54	54	54	54	54	38	27			
Dec.											39	56	56	56	56	56	56	56	56	39	28			

FIGURE E.4
Example: Data Table 4.

Data Table No. 5
Title   Lighting Energy Savings (KWH)

											Hours of Day												
	1	2	3	4	5	6	7	8	9	10	11	12	13	14	15	16	17	18	19	20	21	22	23	24
Jan.											19	33	35	30	22	12	3	0	0	0	0			
Feb.											27	45	45	41	31	18	8	0	0	0	0			
March											35	50	50	50	49	32	16	4	0	0	0			
April											34	49	49	49	49	39	24	10	0	0	0			
May											35	50	50	50	50	50	33	16	4	0	0			
June											34	49	49	49	49	49	43	22	8	0	0			
July											35	50	50	50	50	50	42	22	7	0	0			
Aug.											35	50	50	50	50	50	35	15	3	0	0			
Sept.											34	49	49	49	49	39	18	4	0	0	0			
Oct.											35	50	50	49	36	20	7	0	0	0	0			
Nov.											22	36	33	26	17	8	0	0	0	0	0			
Dec.											17	29	27	23	16	7	0	0	0	0	0			

Total lighting savings = 3128 KWH/yr

FIGURE E.5
Example: Data Table 5.

	Hours of Day																							
	1	2	3	4	5	6	7	8	9	10	11	12	13	14	15	16	17	18	19	20	21	22	23	24
Jan.										1	10	12	13	12	9	5	1							
Feb.										10	18	21	22	21	17	11	5							
March									9	20	28	34	36	35	29	20	11	5						
April								9	24	31	41	48	51	49	41	32	23	12	3					
May								23	33	44	54	60	62	59	51	41	32	23	12	3				
June							8	22	31	46	58	64	64	63	55	45	34	22	9	3				
July							6	27	38	55	68	76	79	77	68	57	45	29	12	2				
Aug.								14	30	40	52	60	61	58	51	39	27	15	5					
Sept.								2	19	28	38	47	49	45	38	27	15	5						
Oct.									7	19	25	28	29	25	20	13	4							
Nov.										8	13	16	18	14	10	4	1							
Dec.										1	10	11	11	9	7	3								

FIGURE E.6
Representative daylighting illuminances (fc): Seattle. EA = 0.01.

	Hours of Day																							
	1	2	3	4	5	6	7	8	9	10	11	12	13	14	15	16	17	18	19	20	21	22	23	24
Jan.								1	6	12	19	23	24	21	15	8	2							
Feb								3	10	20	30	36	36	32	24	15	6							
March							1	8	18	31	39	45	46	42	34	22	11	3						
April						1	8	18	30	40	47	51	51	47	38	28	17	7						
May						5	14	28	40	51	58	58	57	54	47	37	23	11	3					
June						6	15	29	44	54	61	65	62	61	56	46	31	16	6					
July						4	13	28	44	55	62	70	74	70	57	43	29	15	5					
Aug						2	10	23	39	54	63	70	69	62	52	40	24	10	2					
Sept							5	16	30	40	48	55	53	48	40	28	13	3						
Oct							1	9	19	30	37	40	39	34	25	14	5							
Nov								3	10	16	22	26	24	19	12	6								
Dec								1	6	12	17	20	19	16	11	5								

FIGURE E.7
Representative daylighting illuminances (fc): Madison/Washington. EA = 0.01.

Hours of Day

Month	1	2	3	4	5	6	7	8	9	10	11	12	13	14	15	16	17	18	19	20	21	22	23	24
Jan.								1	8	18	27	33	34	33	28	18	7							
Feb.								4	14	26	36	42	45	42	35	24	12	3						
March								7	18	34	47	55	57	53	45	32	17	5						
April							4	15	33	48	59	63	64	60	50	36	19	7						
May								9	23	39	53	63	69	70	66	58	43	27	13	2				
June						1	10	25	43	57	69	74	74	66	60	49	32	15	3					
July								7	22	40	56	65	66	69	65	58	44	28	13	2				
Aug.								5	17	34	53	62	64	65	61	53	40	24	10	1				
Sept.								3	15	31	47	59	61	63	57	47	35	19	5					
Oct.								1	11	26	42	51	60	58	52	40	23	10	1					
Nov.								5	16	28	37	42	41	36	25	14	4							
Dec.								2	9	19	27	32	34	30	22	12	3							

FIGURE E.8

Representative daylighting illuminances (fc): Lake Charles. EA = 0.01.

Hours of Day

Month	1	2	3	4	5	6	7	8	9	10	11	12	13	14	15	16	17	18	19	20	21	22	23	24
Jan.								4	13	24	35	42	42	36	24	13	4							
Feb								7	18	33	46	52	52	46	36	21	9	1						
March							3	13	28	44	57	65	67	62	51	34	16	4						
April						1	9	22	39	56	67	72	71	68	56	42	22	8						
May							2	13	26	43	59	72	78	79	75	64	48	28	12	1				
June						4	14	27	43	57	67	74	76	74	64	49	30	14	4					
July							2	13	28	47	64	74	82	82	79	69	53	32	15	3				
Aug						1	9	22	43	60	73	80	81	76	64	47	26	10						
Sept							5	16	33	50	64	72	74	68	54	35	15	4						
Oct							3	12	25	39	49	56	57	50	37	19	7							
Nov							1	8	18	31	42	46	44	37	24	11	2							
Dec								4	13	23	33	39	39	32	20	9	2							

FIGURE E.9

Representative daylighting illuminances (fc): Los Angeles. EA = 0.01.

												Hours of Day												
	1	2	3	4	5	6	7	8	9	10	11	12	13	14	15	16	17	18	19	20	21	22	23	24
Jan.									6	15	23	29	30	26	19	11	3							
Feb.								3	11	22	33	39	39	36	28	18	8	1						
March								1	10	24	41	52	59	60	55	46	32	17	5					
April								9	23	43	59	70	75	75	71	61	47	27	12	1				
May							4	15	33	53	69	79	85	85	81	70	56	36	17	6				
June							6	18	39	59	75	85	91	91	88	79	64	45	23	9				
July							4	15	35	57	75	87	92	95	92	83	67	47	22	8				
Aug.								10	27	50	68	81	88	89	85	75	58	36	16	3				
Sept.								6	19	40	58	71	77	77	71	59	41	20	8					
Oct.								1	11	24	41	51	57	56	49	37	20	8						
Nov.								4	14	25	35	40	38	31	21	11	2							
Dec.									7	14	21	26	27	22	15	8								

FIGURE E.10
Representative daylighting illuminances (fc): Fresno. EA = 0.01.

												Hours of Day												
	1	2	3	4	5	6	7	8	9	10	11	12	13	14	15	16	17	18	19	20	21	22	23	24
Jan.									8	19	33	44	48	46	36	23	10	1						
Feb.								2	13	29	47	57	62	60	52	36	18	6						
March								8	26	49	65	74	76	73	62	47	27	10	1					
April							5	19	43	64	79	88	90	86	75	60	39	17	4					
May						1	10	29	55	75	90	97	97	95	86	70	50	24	8					
June						1	11	29	55	75	89	94	96	96	86	71	52	28	10	1				
July							5	22	49	69	84	91	94	95	89	74	53	25	7					
Aug.							4	19	43	65	82	91	94	93	84	68	46	20	5					
Sept.							2	14	36	61	77	86	87	82	70	52	29	10	1					
Oct.								8	24	45	60	68	69	65	54	34	15	2						
Nov.								3	13	29	45	56	57	53	38	21	7							
Dec.								1	8	19	31	41	45	40	29	16	6							

FIGURE E.11
Representative daylighting illuminances (fc): Phoenix. EA = 0.01.

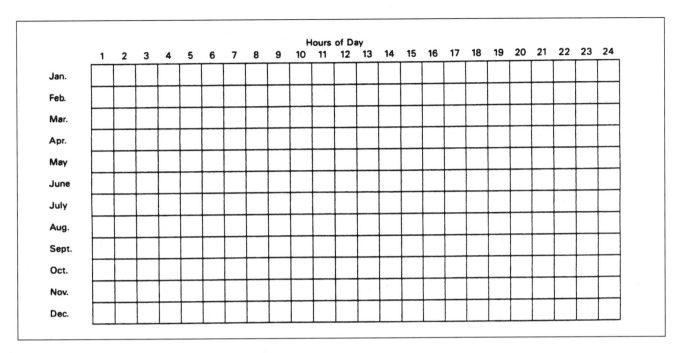

FIGURE E.12
Blank data table.

Appendix F

Daylight Parametrics

Appendix F describes a daylighting evaluation of a "typical" two-story office building. The purpose of the DOE2-based analysis was to evaluate and demonstrate the savings achievable through the use of automatic on/off daylighting controls in an otherwise standard two-story office building. Both perimeter daylighting and skylights were considered. The performance impacts of the daylight-controlled building were compared with an identical building without daylight controls in six weather locations: Chicago, New York, Atlanta, Denver, Los Angeles, and Seattle.

The base case building was assumed to be a "typical" two-story, 70,000-ft^2 office building with a 61% gross window-to-wall ratio on all orientations. The glass type was assumed to be double pane, light solar bronze (SC = 0.57, VT = 0.47) with shading provided by interior venetian blinds. Interior lighting consisted of fluorescent, two-lamp fixtures with energy-saving magnetic ballasts and energy-saving lamps (76 W/fixture). The installed lighting power density was modeled at 1.5 W/ft^2. Air conditioning is provided by rooftop unitary equipment (gas packs, SEER 10). A more complete building description is provided in Appendix F.1. The prototype building model is compliant with both Title-24 and ASHRAE 90.1 building energy standards.

Perimeter daylighting (Alternative 1) was modeled assuming a 15-ft perimeter zone and simple on/off daylight controls. Approximately 33% of the total building lighting is controlled by perimeter daylight controls. The benefit of adding skylights (Alternative 2) to provide daylighting to the core zone of the second floor was also investigated. The skylights (SC = 0.78, VT = 0.75) were modeled with a 4% skylight-to-roof area. Approximately 34% of the total building lighting is controlled by horizontal daylight controls. An illuminance setpoint of 50 footcandles was assumed for both the perimeter daylighting and skylight alternatives.

The incremental first cost of installing perimeter daylight controls was estimated to be $7,530. The incremental first cost for providing skylights and the associated controls on the second floor was estimated to be $20,145. This cost includes lighting control costs of $1,245 and skylight costs of $18,900. A more detailed breakdown of the capital costs is provided in Appendix F.2.

Utility costs were calculated assuming an average national cost of 7.2¢/kWh for electricity and 60.1¢/therm for natural gas. Note that the electric rate schedule used assumes a uniform annual energy charge and has no demand charges. A tax rate of 6% has been added to both the electric and gas charges.

The annual energy use in Appendix F.3 provides an energy summary for both the day-lighting and skylight alternatives. Each of the six sections (one per weather location) in Tables F.3.1 to F.3.6 are subdivided horizontally into three sections. The upper portion represents the *absolute* results. The middle and lower portions present *incremental* and *cumulative* savings for the current alternative compared with the previously implemented alternative. Therefore, the numbers given for skylights (Alternative 2) represent the incremental savings due to skylights after the perimeter daylighting (Alternative 1) has been implemented. Under the cumulative savings, each row represents savings relative to the base case (non-daylit) building. In both the incremental and cumulative savings sections, savings reported for perimeter daylighting are relative to the base case. Negative savings represent increased energy use.

The annual cost summary, also in tables in Appendix F.3, presents a utility cost summary and a simple payback analysis for both perimeter daylighting and skylights. Each of the six sections is subdivided with an *absolute* results section and an *incremental* and *cumulative* savings section. Under the incremental savings section, the simple payback for skylights (Alternative 2) assumes the perimeter daylight controls have already been implemented and therefore represents the payback for the skylights alone. Under the cumulative savings section, the simple payback for skylights (Alternative 2) represents the combined payback for both perimeter daylighting and skylights. Negative savings represent increased utility (natural gas) costs.

The light power reduction summary in Appendix 7.4 presents representative lighting power reduction results, and Appendix F.5 presents average illuminance in footcandles by month and time of day for each orientation and the second floor core zone (top lit) (courtesy of ESS, Inc.).

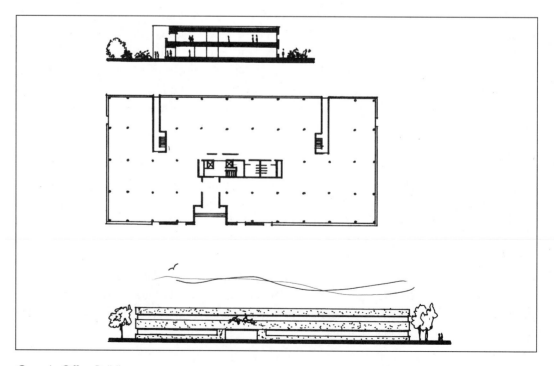

Generic Office Building.

Appendix F.1   Base Case Building Description

BASE CASE BUILDING DESCRIPTION GENERIC
OFFICE BUILDING DAYLIGHTING EVALUATION

Architectural

Building type	Two-story, office
Conditioned area	66,250 ft^2
Aspect ratio	2.12
Window-to-wall ratio	61%
Wall construction	Metal stud wall with brick facing
Wall R-value	7.0
Root construction	Built-up roofing on a metal deck
Root R-value	20
Window type	Double pane, solar bronze
Shading coefficient	0.57
Visible Transmittance	0.47

HVAC System

Type	Rooftop package units with gas furnace
Cooling efficiency	10 SEER
Furnace efficiency	80%
Cooling set point	74°F
Heating set point	70°F
Economizing	Yes
Outside air supply	20 ft^3/min/person

Building Operation and Internal Loading

Occupancy schedule	Monday–Friday:	7 A.M.–7 P.M.
	Saturday:	8 A.M.–12 P.M.
	Sunday and holidays:	Closed
Lighting density	1.5 W/ft^2	
Equipment density	1.5 W/ft^2	
Occupant density	250 ft^2/person	

Appendix F.2   Capital Cost Summary

CAPITAL COST SUMMARY GENERIC OFFICE BUILDING DAYLIGHTING EVALUATION

Perimeter Daylighting

Controller	8 × $560	$4,480
Transformer	12 × $45	540
Subtotal		5,020
Labor	(50%)	2,510
Total		$7,530

Skylights

Controller	1 × $560	$560
Transformer	6 × $45	270
		830
Labor	(50%)	415
Subtotal		$1,245
Skylights	21 × 250	5,250
Light well	21 × 400	8,400
Labor	21 × 250	5,250
Subtotal		$18,900
Total		$20,145

Appendix F.3   Annual Cost and Energy Use Summary

ATLANTA

			Site Energy				Utility Costs					
		Elect. (MWh)	N. Gas (Therms)	Total (MBtu)	Intensity (kBtu/ft²)	Electric ($)	Gas ($)	Total ($)	Intensity ($/ft²)	Capital Cost ($)	Simple Payback (Years)
Case	**Measures**										
Absolute Results											
	Base		865	2540	3210	48	65,990	160	66,150	1.00	na	na
Alt 1	Base	+ Daylighting	767	3070	2920	44	58,530	190	58,720	0.89	7530	na
Alt 2	Alt 1	+ Sky lights	710	3420	2770	42	54,210	210	54,420	0.82	27,675	na
Incremental Savings (relative to previously adopted measures; negative entries represent increases)											
Alt 1	Base	+ Daylighting	98	−530	290	4	7460	−30	7430	0.11	7530	1.0
Alt 2	Alt 1	+ Sky lights	57	−350	150	2	4320	−20	4300	0.06	20,145	4.7
Cumulative Savings (relative to DFE base; negative entries represent increases)											
Alt 1	Base	+ Daylighting	98	−530	290	4	7460	−30	7430	0.11	7530	1.0
Alt 2	Alt 1	+ Sky lights	154	−880	440	7	11,780	−50	11,730	0.18	27,675	2.4

			Site Energy				Source Energy				HVAC Energy			
		Elect. (MWh)	N. Gas (Therms)	Total (MBtu)	Intensity (kBtu/ft²)	Total (MBtu)	Intensity (kBtu/ft²)	Peak Demand (kW)	Light Elect. (MWh)	Elect. (MWh)	N. Gas (Therms)	Total (MBtu)	Peak Cooling (tons)
Case	**Measures**												
Absolute Results													
	Base		865	2540	3210	48	9116	138	350	306	376	2540	1540	133
Alt 1	Base	+ Daylighting	767	3070	2920	44	8168	123	305	237	347	3070	1490	117
Alt 2	Alt 1	+ Sky lights	710	3420	2770	42	7621	115	297	174	354	3420	1550	117
Incremental Savings (relative to previously adopted measures; negative entries represent increases)													
Alt 1	Base	+ Daylighting	98	−530	290	4	948	14	45	69	29	−530	50	16
Alt 2	Alt 1	+ Sky lights	57	−350	150	2	547	8	8	64	−7	−350	−60	1
Cumulative Savings (relative to DFE base; negative entries represent increases)													
Alt 1	Base	+ Daylighting	98	−530	290	4	948	14	45	69	29	−530	50	16
Alt 2	Alt 1	+ Sky lights	154	−880	440	7	1495	23	53	132	22	−880	−10	17

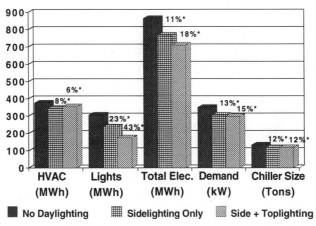

2 - STORY OFFICE BUILDING - ATLANTA

Legend: ■ No Daylighting   ▦ Sidelighting Only   ▨ Side + Toplighting

* Percentage savings (compared to base case)

CHICAGO

			Site Energy				Utility Costs				Capital Cost ($)	Simple Payback (Years)
		Elect. (MWh)	N. Gas (Therms)	Total (MBtu)	Intensity (kBtu/ft²)	Electric ($)	Gas ($)	Total ($)	Intensity ($/ft²)		
Case	*Measures*										
Absolute Results											
	Base	846	9640	3850	58	64,540	600	65,140	0.98	na	na
Alt 1	Base + Daylighting	758	10,660	3650	55	57,820	690	58,510	0.88	7530	na
Alt 2	Alt 1 + Sky lights	719	11,960	3650	55	54,900	740	55,640	0.84	27,675	na

Incremental Savings (relative to previously adopted measures; negative entries represent increases)

Alt 1	Base + Daylighting	88	−1020	200	3	6720	−90	6630	0.10	7530	1.1
Alt 2	Alt 1 + Sky lights	38	−1300	0	0	2920	−50	2870	0.04	20,145	7.0

Cumulative Savings (relative to DFE base; negative entries represent increases)

Alt 1	Base + Daylighting	88	−1020	200	3	6720	−90	6630	0.10	7530	1.1
Alt 2	Alt 1 + Sky lights	126	−2320	200	3	9640	−140	9500	0.14	27,675	2.9

			Site Energy			Source Energy				HVAC Energy			Peak Cooling (tons)
		Elect. (MWh)	N. Gas (Therms)	Total (MBtu)	Intensity (kBtu/ft²)	Total (MBtu)	Intensity (kBtu/ft²)	Peak Demand (kW)	Light Elect. (MWh)	Elect. (MWh)	N. Gas (Therms)	Total (MBtu)	
Case	*Measures*												
Absolute Results													
	Base	846	9640	3850	58	9631	145	336	306	357	9640	2180	116
Alt 1	Base + Daylighting	758	10,660	3650	55	8831	133	298	244	331	10,660	2200	101
Alt 2	Alt 1 + Sky lights	719	11,960	3650	55	8569	129	297	187	350	11,960	2390	103

Incremental Savings (relative to previously adopted measures; negative entries represent increases)

Alt 1	Base + Daylighting	88	−1020	200	3	800	12	38	62	26	−1020	−20	16
Alt 2	Alt 1 + Sky lights	38	−1300	0	0	262	4	1	57	−19	−1300	−190	−2

Cumulative Savings (relative to DFE base; negative entries represent increases)

Alt 1	Base + Daylighting	88	−1020	200	3	800	12	38	62	26	−1020	−20	16
Alt 2	Alt 1 + Sky lights	126	−2320	200	3	1062	16	39	119	7	−2320	−210	14

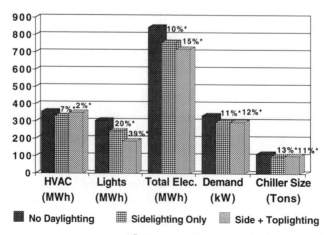

2 - STORY OFFICE BUILDING - CHICAGO

Legend: No Daylighting, Sidelighting Only, Side + Toplighting

* Percentage savings (compared to base case)

DENVER

			Site Energy				Utility Costs					
		Elect. (MWh)	N. Gas (Therms)	Total (MBtu)	Intensity (kBtu/ft²)	Electric ($)	Gas ($)	Total ($)	Intensity ($/ft²)	Capital Cost ($)	Simple Payback (Years)
Case	*Measures*										
Absolute Results											
	Base	832	6530	3490	53	63,500	400	63,900	0.96	na	na
Alt 1	Base	+ Daylighting	748	7410	3290	50	57,080	460	57,540	0.87	7530	na
Alt 2	Alt 1	+ Sky lights	696	8240	3200	48	53,130	510	53,640	0.81	27,675	na

INCREMENTAL SAVINGS (relative to previously adopted measures; negative entries represent increases)

Case		Measures	Elect. (MWh)	N. Gas (Therms)	Total (MBtu)	Intensity (kBtu/ft²)	Electric ($)	Gas ($)	Total ($)	Intensity ($/ft²)	Capital Cost ($)	Simple Payback (Years)
Alt 1	Base	+ Daylighting	84	−880	200	3	6420	−60	6360	0.10	7530	1.2
Alt 2	Alt 1	+ Sky lights	52	−830	90	1	3950	−50	3900	0.06	20,145	5.2

Cumulative Savings (relative to DFE base; negative entries represent increases)

Case		Measures	Elect. (MWh)	N. Gas (Therms)	Total (MBtu)	Intensity (kBtu/ft²)	Electric ($)	Gas ($)	Total ($)	Intensity ($/ft²)	Capital Cost ($)	Simple Payback (Years)
Alt 1	Base	+ Daylighting	84	−880	200	3	6420	−60	6360	0.10	7530	1.2
Alt 2	Alt 1	+ Sky lights	136	−1710	290	4	10,370	−110	10,260	0.15	27,675	2.7

			Site Energy				Source Energy				HVAC Energy			
			Elect. (MWh)	N. Gas (Therms)	Total (MBtu)	Intensity (kBtu/ft²)	Total (MBtu)	Intensity (kBtu/ft²)	Peak Demand (kW)	Light Elect. (MWh)	Elect. (MWh)	N. Gas (Therms)	Total (MBtu)	Peak Cooling (tons)
Case	*Measures*													
Absolute Results														
	Base		832	6530	3490	53	9181	139	336	306	344	6530	1830	142
Alt 1	Base	+ Daylighting	748	7410	3290	50	8407	127	295	246	319	7410	1830	123
Alt 2	Alt 1	+ Sky lights	696	8240	3200	48	7959	120	283	177	337	8240	1970	123

Incremental Savings (relative to previously adopted measures; negative entries represent increases)

Case		Measures	Elect. (MWh)	N. Gas (Therms)	Total (MBtu)	Intensity (kBtu/ft²)	Total (MBtu)	Intensity (kBtu/ft²)	Peak Demand (kW)	Light Elect. (MWh)	Elect. (MWh)	N. Gas (Therms)	Total (MBtu)	Peak Cooling (tons)
Alt 1	Base	+ Daylighting	84	−880	200	3	774	12	41	60	24	−880	0	19
Alt 2	Alt 1	+ Sky lights	52	−830	90	1	448	7	12	69	−17	−830	−140	−1

Cumulative Savings (relative to DFE base; negative entries represent increases)

Case		Measures	Elect. (MWh)	N. Gas (Therms)	Total (MBtu)	Intensity (kBtu/ft²)	Total (MBtu)	Intensity (kBtu/ft²)	Peak Demand (kW)	Light Elect. (MWh)	Elect. (MWh)	N. Gas (Therms)	Total (MBtu)	Peak Cooling (tons)
Alt 1	Base	+ Daylighting	84	−880	200	3	774	12	41	60	24	−880	0	19
Alt 2	Alt 1	+ Sky lights	136	−1710	290	4	1221	19	53	129	7	−1710	−140	18

2 - STORY OFFICE BUILDING - DENVER

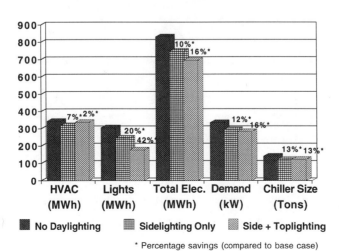

Legend: ■ No Daylighting   ▦ Sidelighting Only   ▨ Side + Toplighting

* Percentage savings (compared to base case)

LOS ANGELES

		Site Energy				Utility Costs				Capital Cost ($)	Simple Payback (Years)
		Elect. (MWh)	N. Gas (Therms)	Total (MBtu)	Intensity (kBtu/ft²)	Electric ($)	Gas ($)	Total ($)	Intensity ($/ft²)		
Case	**Measures**										
Absolute Results											
	Base	788	110	2700	41	60,160	10	60,170	0.91	na	na
Alt 1	Base + Daylighting	689	170	2370	36	52,570	10	52,580	0.79	7530	na
Alt 2	Alt 1 + Sky lights	616	190	2120	32	47,000	10	47,010	0.71	27,675	na
Incremental Savings (relative to previously adopted measures; negative entries represent increases)											
Alt 1	Base + Daylighting	100	−60	330	5	7590	0	7590	0.11	7530	1.0
Alt 2	Alt 1 + Sky lights	73	−20	250	4	5570	0	5570	0.08	20,145	3.6
Cumulative Savings (relative to DFE base; negative entries represent increases)											
Alt 1	Base + Daylighting	100	−60	330	5	7590	0	7590	0.11	7530	1.0
Alt 2	Alt 1 + Sky lights	173	−80	580	9	13,160	0	13,160	0.20	27,675	2.1

		Site Energy				Source Energy				HVAC Energy			
		Elect. (MWh)	N. Gas (Therms)	Total (MBtu)	Intensity (kBtu/ft²)	Total (MBtu)	Intensity (kBtu/ft²)	Peak Demand (kW)	Light Elect. (MWh)	Elect. (MWh)	N. Gas (Therms)	Total (MBtu)	Peak Cooling (tons)
Case	**Measures**												
Absolute Results													
	Base	788	110	2700	41	8090	122	311	306	300	110	1030	116
Alt 1	Base + Daylighting	689	170	2370	36	7076	107	264	232	274	170	950	90
Alt 2	Alt 1 + Sky lights	616	190	2120	32	6331	96	254	159	274	200	960	96
Incremental Savings (relative to previously adopted measures; negative entries represent increases)													
Alt 1	Base + Daylighting	100	−60	330	5	1014	15	47	74	25	−60	80	27
Alt 2	Alt 1 + Sky lights	73	−20	250	4	745	11	10	73	0	−30	−10	−6
Cumulative Savings (relative to DFE base; negative entries represent increases)													
Alt 1	Base + Daylighting	100	−60	330	5	1014	15	47	74	25	−60	80	27
Alt 2	Alt 1 + Sky lights	173	−80	580	9	1759	27	57	147	26	−90	70	20

2 - STORY OFFICE BUILDING - LOS ANGELES

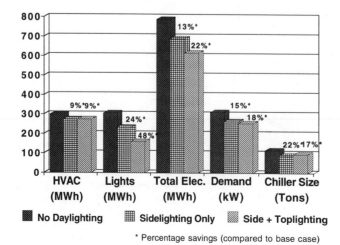

■ No Daylighting   ▥ Sidelighting Only   ▦ Side + Toplighting

* Percentage savings (compared to base case)

NEW YORK

			Site Energy				Utility Costs					
			Elect. (MWh)	N. Gas (Therms)	Total (MBtu)	Intensity (kBtu/ft^2)	Electric ($)	Gas ($)	Total ($)	Intensity ($/ft^2)	Capital Cost ($)	Simple Payback (Years)
Case	Measures											
Absolute Results												
	Base		819	6130	3410	51	62,470	380	62,850	0.95	na	na
Alt 1	Base	+ Daylighting	737	6850	3200	48	56,280	420	56,700	0.86	7530	na
Alt 2	Alt 1	+ Sky lights	699	7480	3140	47	53,380	430	53,810	0.81	27,675	na
Incremental Savings (relative to previously adopted measures; negative entries represent increases)												
Alt 1	Base	+ Daylighting	81	−720	210	3	6190	−40	6150	0.09	7530	1.2
Alt 2	Alt 1	+ Sky lights	38	−630	60	1	2900	−10	2890	0.04	20,145	7.0
Cumulative Savings (relative to DFE base; negative entries represent increases)												
Alt 1	Base	+ Daylighting	81	−720	210	3	6190	−40	6150	0.09	7530	1.2
Alt 2	Alt 1	+ Sky lights	119	−1350	270	4	9090	−50	9040	0.14	27,675	3.1

			Site Energy				Source Energy				HVAC Energy			
			Elect. (MWh)	N. Gas (Therms)	Total (MBtu)	Intensity (kBtu/ft^2)	Total (MBtu)	Intensity (kBtu/ft^2)	Peak Demand (kW)	Light Elect. (MWh)	Elect. (MWh)	N. Gas (Therms)	Total (MBtu)	Peak Cooling (tons)
Case	Measures													
Absolute Results														
	Base		819	6130	3410	51	9003	136	324	306	330	6140	1740	111
Alt 1	Base	+ Daylighting	737	6850	3200	48	8243	124	297	248	307	6850	1730	101
Alt 2	Alt 1	+ Sky lights	699	7480	3140	47	7916	120	298	196	321	7480	1840	103
Incremental Savings (relative to previously adopted measures; negative entries represent increases)														
Alt 1	Base	+ Daylighting	81	−720	210	3	761	12	27	58	23	−710	10	10
Alt 2	Alt 1	+ Sky lights	38	−630	60	1	326	5	−1	52	−14	−630	−110	−2
Cumulative Savings (relative to DFE base; negative entries represent increases)														
Alt 1	Base	+ Daylighting	81	−720	210	3	761	12	27	58	23	−710	10	10
Alt 2	Alt 1	+ Sky lights	119	−1350	270	4	1087	16	26	110	9	−1340	−100	8

2 - STORY OFFICE BUILDING - NEW YORK

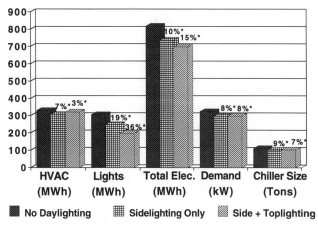

■ No Daylighting　　▦ Sidelighting Only　　▨ Side + Toplighting

* Percentage savings (compared to base case)

SEATTLE

			Site Energy				Utility Costs				Capital Cost ($)	Simple Payback (Years)
			Elect. (MWh)	N. Gas (Therms)	Total (MBtu)	Intensity (kBtu/ft²)	Electric ($)	Gas ($)	Total ($)	Intensity ($/ft²)		
Case	Measures											
Absolute Results												
	Base		757	4900	3070	46	57,800	300	58,100	0.88	na	na
Alt 1	Base	+ Daylighting	689	5680	2920	44	52,590	350	52,940	0.80	7530	na
Alt 2	Alt 1	+ Sky lights	651	6210	2840	43	49,720	380	50,100	0.76	27,675	na
Incremental Savings (relative to previously adopted measures; negative entries represent increases)												
Alt 1	Base	+ Daylighting	68	−780	150	2	5210	−50	5160	0.08	7530	1.5
Alt 2	Alt 1	+ Sky lights	38	−530	80	1	2870	−30	2840	0.04	20,145	7.1
Cumulative Savings (relative to DFE base; negative entries represent increases)												
Alt 1	Base	+ Daylighting	68	−780	150	2	5210	−50	5160	0.08	7530	1.5
Alt 2	Alt 1	+ Sky lights	106	−1310	230	4	8080	−80	8000	0.12	27,675	3.5

			Site Energy				Source Energy		Peak Demand (kW)	Light Elect. (MWh)	HVAC Energy			Peak Cooling (tons)
			Elect. (MWh)	N. Gas (Therms)	Total (MBtu)	Intensity (kBtu/ft²)	Total (MBtu)	Intensity (kBtu/ft²)			Elect. (MWh)	N. Gas (Therms)	Total (MBtu)	
Case	Measures													
Absolute Results														
	Base		757	4900	3070	46	8252	125	295	306	269	4900	1410	81
Alt 1	Base	+ Daylighting	689	5680	2920	44	7630	115	251	252	254	5680	1440	70
Alt 2	Alt 1	+ Sky lights	651	6210	2840	43	7298	110	239	203	266	6210	1530	72
Incremental Savings (relative to previously adopted measures; negative entries represent increases)														
Alt 1	Base	+ Daylighting	68	−780	150	2	622	9	44	54	15	−780	−30	12
Alt 2	Alt 1	+ Sky lights	38	−530	80	1	333	5	12	49	−11	−530	−90	−2
Cumulative Savings (relative to DFE base; negative entries represent increases)														
Alt 1	Base	+ Daylighting	68	−780	150	2	622	9	44	54	15	−780	−30	12
Alt 2	Alt 1	+ Sky lights	106	−1310	230	4	954	14	56	103	3	−1310	−120	9

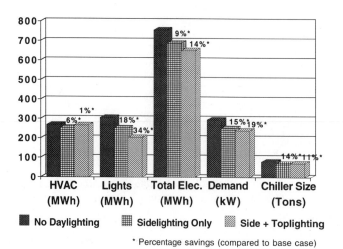

2 - STORY OFFICE BUILDING - SEATTLE

■ No Daylighting   ▦ Sidelighting Only   ▨ Side + Toplighting

* Percentage savings (compared to base case)

Appendix F.4   Light Power Reduction Summary

PERCENT POWER REDUCTION: ATLANTA

For a typical 2-story office building with 15'-0" deep perimeter zones and a top-lit core zone.

Weather Data:	Atlanta (TMY)
% Opening:	37.5% WWR (windows)
	4% of roof area (skylights)
Overhangs:	2'-3" (horizontal)
Lighting Control Type:	Stepped (2 steps)
Lighting Set Point:	50 footcandles
No. of Ref. Points:	One (2'-6" high in the center of zone)

Glass Type: ¼" solar bronze tinted (single pane) (SC = 0.57; VT = 0.47)

NORTH

MONTH	1	2	3	4	5	6	7	8	9	10	11	12	13	14	15	16	17	18	19	20	21	22	23	24	HOURS
JAN	0	0	0	0	0	0	0	0	23	25	42	52	51	46	57	40	31	5	0	0	0	0	0	0	33
FEB	0	0	0	0	0	0	0	0	22	35	44	57	63	63	63	55	39	19	0	0	0	0	0	0	40
MAR	0	0	0	0	0	0	0	29	58	69	86	96	96	96	93	77	75	61	4	0	0	0	0	0	71
APR	0	0	0	0	0	0	11	36	75	81	92	92	95	93	93	89	86	73	28	0	0	0	0	0	78
MAY	0	0	0	0	0	0	37	84	88	98	98	99	99	100	100	100	90	85	66	0	0	0	0	0	87
JUN	0	0	0	0	0	0	37	75	90	96	98	98	94	93	93	93	89	89	73	0	0	0	0	0	85
JUL	0	0	0	0	0	0	23	77	88	85	92	96	100	100	98	93	89	91	61	0	0	0	0	0	85
AUG	0	0	0	0	0	0	14	73	87	87	100	100	100	100	100	98	95	93	48	0	0	0	0	0	86
SEP	0	0	0	0	0	0	0	48	77	83	98	98	98	93	95	86	84	55	0	0	0	0	0	0	78
OCT	0	0	0	0	0	0	0	30	60	60	73	75	69	71	60	53	62	5	0	0	0	0	0	0	53
NOV	0	0	0	0	0	0	0	0	26	37	52	48	56	60	53	45	32	0	0	0	0	0	0	0	36
DEC	0	0	0	0	0	0	0	0	10	34	52	54	51	54	50	36	30	0	0	0	0	0	0	0	33
ANNUAL	0	0	0	0	0	0	10	62	59	66	78	80	81	81	80	72	67	40	10	0	0	0	0	0	64

SOUTH

MONTH	1	2	3	4	5	6	7	8	9	10	11	12	13	14	15	16	17	18	19	20	21	22	23	24	HOURS
JAN	0	0	0	0	0	0	0	0	52	50	69	73	75	77	81	76	62	23	0	0	0	0	0	0	56
FEB	0	0	0	0	0	0	0	0	44	61	61	74	79	81	79	82	74	45	0	0	0	0	0	0	59
MAR	0	0	0	0	0	0	0	45	63	71	86	96	96	96	93	80	77	63	9	0	0	0	0	0	73
APR	0	0	0	0	0	0	6	38	77	81	92	92	95	95	93	89	86	72	25	0	0	0	0	0	78
MAY	0	0	0	0	0	0	26	84	88	98	98	99	99	100	100	100	90	84	40	0	0	0	0	0	87
JUN	0	0	0	0	0	0	25	71	90	96	98	98	94	93	93	93	89	89	43	0	0	0	0	0	85
JUL	0	0	0	0	0	0	6	77	88	85	92	96	100	100	98	93	89	91	32	0	0	0	0	0	84
AUG	0	0	0	0	0	0	2	73	89	87	100	100	100	100	100	98	95	93	37	0	0	0	0	0	86
SEP	0	0	0	0	0	0	0	63	81	83	98	98	98	93	95	86	86	59	0	0	0	0	0	0	80
OCT	0	0	0	0	0	0	0	67	86	92	94	100	100	97	90	93	88	30	0	0	0	0	0	0	80
NOV	0	0	0	0	0	0	0	16	57	74	78	78	87	92	87	84	66	0	0	0	0	0	0	0	62
DEC	0	0	0	0	0	0	0	0	67	71	83	83	77	83	84	70	68	0	0	0	0	0	0	0	61
ANNUAL	0	0	0	0	0	0	5	68	74	79	88	91	92	92	91	87	81	47	8	0	0	0	0	0	74

EAST

MONTH	1	2	3	4	5	6	7	8	9	10	11	12	13	14	15	16	17	18	19	20	21	22	23	24	HOURS
JAN	0	0	0	0	0	0	0	0	52	50	69	73	54	51	59	43	31	2	0	0	0	0	0	0	44
FEB	0	0	0	0	0	0	0	6	46	61	61	74	77	67	66	55	39	19	0	0	0	0	0	0	50
MAR	0	0	0	0	0	0	0	51	63	71	87	96	96	96	93	75	73	41	0	0	0	0	0	0	70
APR	0	0	0	0	0	0	35	38	77	81	92	92	95	95	93	89	86	71	11	0	0	0	0	0	78
MAY	0	0	0	0	0	0	74	86	90	98	98	99	99	100	100	100	90	84	40	0	0	0	0	0	88
JUN	0	0	0	0	0	0	65	89	92	96	98	98	94	93	93	98	89	86	37	0	0	0	0	0	87
JUL	0	0	0	0	0	0	61	85	88	87	94	96	100	100	98	93	87	84	32	0	0	0	0	0	85
AUG	0	0	0	0	0	0	49	77	89	87	100	100	100	100	100	98	95	63	27	0	0	0	0	0	86
SEP	0	0	0	0	0	0	6	65	82	83	98	98	98	93	95	86	79	36	0	0	0	0	0	0	79
OCT	0	0	0	0	0	0	0	72	88	90	98	100	98	90	72	55	45	0	0	0	0	0	0	0	71
NOV	0	0	0	0	0	0	0	28	57	74	78	74	56	60	53	45	32	0	0	0	0	0	0	0	48
DEC	0	0	0	0	0	0	0	0	73	71	83	77	53	54	52	36	32	0	0	0	0	0	0	0	48
ANNUAL	0	0	0	0	0	0	24	75	75	79	88	90	85	83	82	73	65	33	5	0	0	0	0	0	70

WEST

MONTH	1	2	3	4	5	6	7	8	9	10	11	12	13	14	15	16	17	18	19	20	21	22	23	24	HOURS
JAN	0	0	0	0	0	0	0	0	21	25	42	52	53	63	81	76	62	38	0	0	0	0	0	0	44
FEB	0	0	0	0	0	0	0	0	20	33	44	61	69	81	79	82	76	51	0	0	0	0	0	0	51
MAR	0	0	0	0	0	0	0	19	50	65	87	96	96	96	96	80	77	63	30	0	0	0	0	0	72
APR	0	0	0	0	0	0	0	23	73	81	92	92	95	95	93	89	86	78	58	0	0	0	0	0	79
MAY	0	0	0	0	0	0	18	76	90	98	98	99	99	100	100	100	92	85	81	0	0	0	0	0	87
JUN	0	0	0	0	0	0	25	71	89	96	98	98	94	93	93	98	89	89	80	12	0	0	0	0	85
JUL	0	0	0	0	0	0	3	75	88	85	94	96	100	100	98	93	91	93	76	0	0	0	0	0	85
AUG	0	0	0	0	0	0	0	37	87	87	100	100	100	100	100	98	98	98	77	0	0	0	0	0	83
SEP	0	0	0	0	0	0	0	31	77	83	98	98	98	93	95	86	86	79	10	0	0	0	0	0	77
OCT	0	0	0	0	0	0	0	19	42	62	88	96	98	97	90	93	90	56	0	0	0	0	0	0	69
NOV	0	0	0	0	0	0	0	0	26	39	52	50	58	92	84	87	66	9	0	0	0	0	0	0	49
DEC	0	0	0	0	0	0	0	0	12	34	54	60	53	78	84	73	72	0	0	0	0	0	0	0	45
ANNUAL	0	0	0	0	0	0	4	49	57	66	79	83	85	91	91	88	82	54	20	1	0	0	0	0	69

CORE (Top-lit)

MONTH	1	2	3	4	5	6	7	8	9	10	11	12	13	14	15	16	17	18	19	20	21	22	23	24	HOURS
JAN	0	0	0	0	0	0	0	0	0	25	63	71	69	68	69	33	7	0	0	0	0	0	0	0	36
FEB	0	0	0	0	0	0	0	0	0	28	59	72	66	71	76	71	34	0	0	0	0	0	0	0	42
MAR	0	0	0	0	0	0	0	0	29	69	75	92	96	94	89	77	68	25	0	0	0	0	0	0	63
APR	0	0	0	0	0	0	0	17	68	79	90	90	93	93	93	86	84	36	0	0	0	0	0	0	72
MAY	0	0	0	0	0	0	0	42	88	90	98	99	99	100	100	100	90	42	0	0	0	0	0	0	80
JUN	0	0	0	0	0	0	0	31	83	92	98	94	93	93	93	87	67	0	0	0	0	0	0	0	78
JUL	0	0	0	0	0	0	0	36	85	85	92	96	100	100	98	93	84	70	0	0	0	0	0	0	79
AUG	0	0	0	0	0	0	0	23	83	87	100	100	100	100	100	98	95	48	0	0	0	0	0	0	79
SEP	0	0	0	0	0	0	0	0	57	81	86	98	98	93	89	84	66	5	0	0	0	0	0	0	66
OCT	0	0	0	0	0	0	0	0	35	83	92	100	100	97	90	81	38	0	0	0	0	0	0	0	62
NOV	0	0	0	0	0	0	0	0	4	41	72	78	85	89	82	34	0	0	0	0	0	0	0	0	43
DEC	0	0	0	0	0	0	0	0	0	34	59	81	77	76	66	36	0	0	0	0	0	0	0	0	38
ANNUAL	0	0	0	0	0	0	0	21	45	67	82	89	90	89	87	74	55	19	0	0	0	0	0	0	62

PERCENT POWER REDUCTION: CHICAGO

For a typical 2-story office building with 15'-0" deep perimeter zones and a top-lit core zone.

Weather Data:	Chicago (TMY)
% Opening:	37.5% WWR (windows)
	4% of roof area (skylights)
Overhangs:	2'-3" (horizontal)
Lighting Control Type:	Stepped (2 steps)
Lighting Set Point:	50 footcandles
No. of Ref. Points:	One (2'-6" high in the center of zone)

Glass Type: ¼" solar bronze tinted (single pane) (SC = 0.57; VT = 0.47)

NORTH

MONTH	1	2	3	4	5	6	7	8	9	10	11	12	13	14	15	16	17	18	19	20	21	22	23	24	HOURS
JAN	0	0	0	0	0	0	0	0	29	32	40	39	40	40	35	30	0	0	0	0	0	0	0	0	26
FEB	0	0	0	0	0	0	0	11	26	46	50	46	48	46	50	34	18	0	0	0	0	0	0	0	33
MAR	0	0	0	0	0	0	11	39	69	71	84	84	83	79	68	61	52	11	0	0	0	0	0	0	59
APR	0	0	0	0	0	5	48	37	73	90	92	96	94	94	82	73	57	45	0	0	0	0	0	0	72
MAY	0	0	0	0	0	48	74	82	80	92	92	92	92	95	93	73	75	48	8	0	0	0	0	0	79
JUN	0	0	0	0	0	60	68	81	83	92	94	95	97	98	98	86	80	70	30	0	0	0	0	0	83
JUL	0	0	0	0	0	48	82	92	96	96	98	98	98	98	98	95	95	84	31	0	0	0	0	0	89
AUG	0	0	0	0	0	0	55	75	85	98	98	100	100	100	98	86	79	62	0	0	0	0	0	0	83
SEP	0	0	0	0	0	0	40	69	79	85	90	95	96	93	89	77	59	14	0	0	0	0	0	0	74
OCT	0	0	0	0	0	0	2	40	42	56	58	63	69	55	38	31	12	0	0	0	0	0	0	0	41
NOV	0	0	0	0	0	0	0	8	28	39	46	48	51	47	34	13	0	0	0	0	0	0	0	0	28
DEC	0	0	0	0	0	0	0	0	12	23	36	39	34	24	27	0	0	0	0	0	0	0	0	0	18
ANNUAL	0	0	0	0	0	14	32	70	59	69	74	74	75	72	68	56	45	21	2	0	0	0	0	0	57

SOUTH

MONTH	1	2	3	4	5	6	7	8	9	10	11	12	13	14	15	16	17	18	19	20	21	22	23	24	HOURS
JAN	0	0	0	0	0	0	0	4	61	73	75	73	68	70	71	66	13	0	0	0	0	0	0	0	51
FEB	0	0	0	0	0	0	0	40	52	74	76	72	71	70	77	63	52	0	0	0	0	0	0	0	54
MAR	0	0	0	0	0	0	17	58	81	79	90	90	91	81	75	70	61	15	0	0	0	0	0	0	66
APR	0	0	0	0	0	2	53	39	75	90	92	96	94	94	82	77	64	45	0	0	0	0	0	0	73
MAY	0	0	0	0	0	29	73	82	80	92	92	92	92	95	93	73	75	48	0	0	0	0	0	0	79
JUN	0	0	0	0	0	32	68	83	83	92	94	95	97	98	98	86	82	68	8	0	0	0	0	0	83
JUL	0	0	0	0	0	26	87	92	96	96	98	98	98	98	98	95	95	66	11	0	0	0	0	0	88
AUG	0	0	0	0	0	0	64	83	92	98	98	100	100	100	98	88	83	48	0	0	0	0	0	0	85
SEP	0	0	0	0	0	0	60	79	85	85	90	95	98	93	91	86	70	16	0	0	0	0	0	0	78
OCT	0	0	0	0	0	0	15	68	79	77	73	83	84	69	70	58	33	0	0	0	0	0	0	0	61
NOV	0	0	0	0	0	0	0	48	69	78	76	78	80	80	76	50	0	0	0	0	0	0	0	0	53
DEC	0	0	0	0	0	0	0	3	38	50	63	63	61	52	54	36	0	0	0	0	0	0	0	0	38
ANNUAL	0	0	0	0	0	7	37	78	75	82	85	86	86	83	82	71	53	20	0	0	0	0	0	0	68

EAST

MONTH	1	2	3	4	5	6	7	8	9	10	11	12	13	14	15	16	17	18	19	20	21	22	23	24	HOURS
JAN	0	0	0	0	0	0	0	9	59	71	73	69	43	43	35	30	0	0	0	0	0	0	0	0	39
FEB	0	0	0	0	0	0	0	48	52	74	76	72	62	46	50	34	18	0	0	0	0	0	0	0	44
MAR	0	0	0	0	0	0	30	58	81	79	92	90	89	81	75	59	36	4	0	0	0	0	0	0	62
APR	0	0	0	0	0	13	55	39	77	90	92	96	94	94	82	75	57	24	0	0	0	0	0	0	71
MAY	0	0	0	0	0	64	84	82	82	92	92	92	92	95	93	76	73	28	0	0	0	0	0	0	78
JUN	0	0	0	0	0	72	80	83	85	92	94	95	97	98	98	84	77	57	8	0	0	0	0	0	83
JUL	0	0	0	0	0	82	92	92	96	96	98	98	98	98	98	95	93	70	11	0	0	0	0	0	89
AUG	0	0	0	0	0	19	68	87	92	100	98	100	100	100	98	86	65	34	0	0	0	0	0	0	83
SEP	0	0	0	0	0	0	70	79	85	85	90	95	98	93	89	77	38	7	0	0	0	0	0	0	74
OCT	0	0	0	0	0	0	34	68	79	77	73	81	77	62	48	29	7	0	0	0	0	0	0	0	53
NOV	0	0	0	0	0	0	0	50	67	76	76	54	52	47	34	13	0	0	0	0	0	0	0	0	39
DEC	0	0	0	0	0	0	0	9	36	48	59	50	39	24	27	0	0	0	0	0	0	0	0	0	26
ANNUAL	0	0	0	0	0	21	43	78	75	82	85	83	79	73	69	55	39	14	0	0	0	0	0	0	62

WEST

MONTH	1	2	3	4	5	6	7	8	9	10	11	12	13	14	15	16	17	18	19	20	21	22	23	24	HOURS
JAN	0	0	0	0	0	0	0	0	31	34	42	42	66	70	71	68	24	0	0	0	0	0	0	0	39
FEB	0	0	0	0	0	0	0	11	26	48	52	54	71	70	77	66	63	0	0	0	0	0	0	0	46
MAR	0	0	0	0	0	0	5	29	59	73	90	90	89	81	75	70	68	39	0	0	0	0	0	0	65
APR	0	0	0	0	0	0	25	36	71	90	92	96	94	94	82	77	68	53	0	0	0	0	0	0	73
MAY	0	0	0	0	0	24	64	82	80	92	92	92	92	95	93	76	80	63	27	0	0	0	0	0	80
JUN	0	0	0	0	0	32	65	81	83	92	94	95	97	100	98	86	84	77	65	0	0	0	0	0	84
JUL	0	0	0	0	0	24	74	87	94	96	98	98	98	98	98	95	95	93	69	0	0	0	0	0	89
AUG	0	0	0	0	0	0	32	71	81	100	98	100	100	100	98	93	95	76	5	0	0	0	0	0	85
SEP	0	0	0	0	0	0	27	48	73	85	90	95	98	93	91	86	73	42	0	0	0	0	0	0	75
OCT	0	0	0	0	0	0	0	32	42	64	66	77	82	69	70	63	45	0	0	0	0	0	0	0	53
NOV	0	0	0	0	0	0	0	8	28	41	48	52	79	80	73	65	2	0	0	0	0	0	0	0	41
DEC	0	0	0	0	0	0	0	0	15	23	38	40	59	52	54	47	0	0	0	0	0	0	0	0	29
ANNUAL	0	0	0	0	0	7	25	64	58	70	76	77	85	83	82	75	59	29	4	0	0	0	0	0	64

CORE (Top-lit)

MONTH	1	2	3	4	5	6	7	8	9	10	11	12	13	14	15	16	17	18	19	20	21	22	23	24	HOURS
JAN	0	0	0	0	0	0	0	0	0	32	52	65	63	47	33	0	0	0	0	0	0	0	0	0	27
FEB	0	0	0	0	0	0	0	0	15	52	74	72	69	70	63	26	0	0	0	0	0	0	0	0	40
MAR	0	0	0	0	0	0	0	11	61	77	79	86	83	74	73	48	16	0	0	0	0	0	0	0	54
APR	0	0	0	0	0	0	10	32	73	79	92	96	94	91	75	75	32	0	0	0	0	0	0	0	64
MAY	0	0	0	0	0	0	32	82	78	92	92	92	92	95	81	68	65	8	0	0	0	0	0	0	74
JUN	0	0	0	0	0	0	35	79	81	92	94	95	97	98	98	80	77	34	0	0	0	0	0	0	80
JUL	0	0	0	0	0	0	44	83	94	96	98	98	98	98	98	95	91	43	0	0	0	0	0	0	85
AUG	0	0	0	0	0	0	11	60	79	96	98	100	100	100	95	88	58	5	0	0	0	0	0	0	77
SEP	0	0	0	0	0	0	0	35	79	79	85	91	94	93	89	70	20	0	0	0	0	0	0	0	65
OCT	0	0	0	0	0	0	0	17	50	75	73	77	80	67	48	22	0	0	0	0	0	0	0	0	45
NOV	0	0	0	0	0	0	0	0	22	48	71	71	76	55	31	0	0	0	0	0	0	0	0	0	34
DEC	0	0	0	0	0	0	0	0	0	21	32	56	46	22	4	0	0	0	0	0	0	0	0	0	17
ANNUAL	0	0	0	0	0	0	11	57	53	70	78	83	83	76	66	48	30	5	0	0	0	0	0	0	55

PERCENT POWER REDUCTION: DENVER

For a typical 2-story office building with 15'-0" deep perimeter zones and a top-lit core zone.

Weather Data:	Denver (TMY)
% Opening:	37.5% WWR (windows)
	4% of roof area (skylights)
Overhangs:	2'-3" (horizontal)
Lighting Control Type:	Stepped (2 steps)
Lighting Set Point:	50 footcandles
No. of Ref. Points:	One (2'-6" high in the center of zone)

Glass Type: ¼" solar bronze tinted (single pane) (SC = 0.57; VT = 0.47)

NORTH

MONTH	1	2	3	4	5	6	7	8	9	10	11	12	13	14	15	16	17	18	19	20	21	22	23	24	HOURS
JAN	0	0	0	0	0	0	0	2	29	33	15	8	6	7	0	31	0	0	0	0	0	0	0	0	12
FEB	0	0	0	0	0	0	0	40	56	44	48	52	42	15	16	0	23	0	0	0	0	0	0	0	28
MAR	0	0	0	0	0	0	44	73	83	77	69	64	59	44	28	18	57	22	0	0	0	0	0	0	48
APR	0	0	0	0	0	20	82	87	89	94	94	92	74	69	59	37	27	32	0	0	0	0	0	0	63
MAY	0	0	0	0	0	78	90	92	98	98	100	100	95	85	75	55	45	26	19	0	0	0	0	0	77
JUN	0	0	0	0	0	78	88	90	98	98	98	98	100	84	62	59	46	30	30	0	0	0	0	0	77
JUL	0	0	0	0	0	80	90	96	100	100	100	100	94	70	70	54	52	35	21	0	0	0	0	0	77
AUG	0	0	0	0	0	18	87	90	96	98	98	100	82	65	58	36	34	45	0	0	0	0	0	0	70
SEP	0	0	0	0	0	0	78	87	96	92	90	80	57	54	23	14	32	22	0	0	0	0	0	0	58
OCT	0	0	0	0	0	0	23	79	58	58	54	50	33	9	5	0	24	0	0	0	0	0	0	0	33
NOV	0	0	0	0	0	0	0	37	46	48	31	17	12	13	3	8	4	0	0	0	0	0	0	0	17
DEC	0	0	0	0	0	0	0	0	31	31	10	4	2	0	0	5	0	0	0	0	0	0	0	0	8
ANNUAL	0	0	0	0	0	23	49	86	74	73	68	63	55	43	33	27	29	14	2	0	0	0	0	0	48

SOUTH

MONTH	1	2	3	4	5	6	7	8	9	10	11	12	13	14	15	16	17	18	19	20	21	22	23	24	HOURS
JAN	0	0	0	0	0	0	0	36	81	85	89	89	87	91	86	72	27	0	0	0	0	0	0	0	64
FEB	0	0	0	0	0	0	0	65	87	87	87	89	89	88	87	92	55	0	0	0	0	0	0	0	68
MAR	0	0	0	0	0	0	50	89	96	96	96	96	96	96	73	86	86	39	0	0	0	0	0	0	77
APR	0	0	0	0	0	12	83	87	89	94	94	98	98	86	68	57	73	31	0	0	0	0	0	0	73
MAY	0	0	0	0	0	64	90	92	98	98	100	100	100	90	80	62	70	41	2	0	0	0	0	0	81
JUN	0	0	0	0	0	72	88	90	98	98	98	98	100	96	64	59	50	44	0	0	0	0	0	0	79
JUL	0	0	0	0	0	45	92	98	100	100	100	100	100	91	73	57	55	46	0	0	0	0	0	0	80
AUG	0	0	0	0	0	8	87	92	96	98	98	100	100	88	62	53	86	47	0	0	0	0	0	0	80
SEP	0	0	0	0	0	0	87	94	96	100	100	100	99	86	54	77	79	26	0	0	0	0	0	0	80
OCT	0	0	0	0	0	0	46	95	96	96	96	96	96	77	86	86	38	0	0	0	0	0	0	0	75
NOV	0	0	0	0	0	0	6	78	94	100	98	98	97	97	92	63	22	0	0	0	0	0	0	0	69
DEC	0	0	0	0	0	0	0	46	89	90	90	92	94	94	93	75	19	0	0	0	0	0	0	0	66
ANNUAL	0	0	0	0	0	17	53	92	93	95	96	96	96	90	76	70	55	19	0	0	0	0	0	0	74

EAST

MONTH	1	2	3	4	5	6	7	8	9	10	11	12	13	14	15	16	17	18	19	20	21	22	23	24	HOURS
JAN	0	0	0	0	0	0	0	32	81	85	87	71	6	7	5	31	0	0	0	0	0	0	0	0	36
FEB	0	0	0	0	0	0	0	65	82	87	87	69	45	15	18	0	21	0	0	0	0	0	0	0	40
MAR	0	0	0	0	0	0	56	90	96	96	96	81	62	44	30	18	48	2	0	0	0	0	0	0	53
APR	0	0	0	0	0	34	85	88	89	94	94	98	91	71	59	32	16	19	0	0	0	0	0	0	63
MAY	0	0	0	0	0	84	95	96	98	98	100	100	100	85	75	57	45	18	2	0	0	0	0	0	78
JUN	0	0	0	0	10	85	92	92	98	98	98	98	100	84	62	59	37	29	0	0	0	0	0	0	76
JUL	0	0	0	0	4	86	93	98	100	100	100	100	98	73	70	54	47	23	0	0	0	0	0	0	77
AUG	0	0	0	0	0	45	92	94	96	98	98	100	95	65	58	33	14	28	0	0	0	0	0	0	70
SEP	0	0	0	0	0	10	87	94	100	100	100	90	63	57	27	11	13	15	0	0	0	0	0	0	61
OCT	0	0	0	0	0	0	58	95	96	96	92	59	39	9	5	0	7	0	0	0	0	0	0	0	46
NOV	0	0	0	0	0	0	9	82	93	96	91	33	12	13	3	8	2	0	0	0	0	0	0	0	34
DEC	0	0	0	0	0	0	0	48	87	90	90	68	4	0	0	9	0	0	0	0	0	0	0	0	33
ANNUAL	0	0	0	0	1	29	56	93	93	95	95	80	60	44	35	27	21	8	0	0	0	0	0	0	56

WEST

MONTH	1	2	3	4	5	6	7	8	9	10	11	12	13	14	15	16	17	18	19	20	21	22	23	24	HOURS
JAN	0	0	0	0	0	0	0	2	31	34	15	8	30	88	86	79	41	0	0	0	0	0	0	0	35
FEB	0	0	0	0	0	0	0	0	34	54	48	48	52	48	49	92	94	63	4	0	0	0	0	0	48
MAR	0	0	0	0	0	0	0	30	69	81	79	75	67	64	65	84	93	88	69	0	0	0	0	0	68
APR	0	0	0	0	0	9	77	87	89	94	94	94	94	89	93	91	89	55	4	0	0	0	0	0	80
MAY	0	0	0	0	0	56	87	92	98	98	100	100	100	98	100	93	83	50	45	0	0	0	0	0	87
JUN	0	0	0	0	0	72	87	90	98	98	98	98	100	96	93	91	87	72	63	0	0	0	0	0	88
JUL	0	0	0	0	0	46	87	96	100	100	100	100	100	95	93	89	82	87	55	0	0	0	0	0	89
AUG	0	0	0	0	0	7	82	88	96	98	98	100	100	95	98	95	97	76	5	0	0	0	0	0	88
SEP	0	0	0	0	0	0	65	85	94	94	90	87	80	82	91	91	88	63	0	0	0	0	0	0	81
OCT	0	0	0	0	0	0	13	69	62	63	62	52	53	50	84	86	60	3	0	0	0	0	0	0	55
NOV	0	0	0	0	0	0	0	35	48	48	37	22	56	95	95	84	30	0	0	0	0	0	0	0	45
DEC	0	0	0	0	0	0	0	0	32	38	12	4	94	94	91	80	20	0	0	0	0	0	0	0	40
ANNUAL	0	0	0	0	0	16	44	84	74	75	70	65	77	83	92	89	69	33	5	0	0	0	0	0	67

CORE (Top-lit)

MONTH	1	2	3	4	5	6	7	8	9	10	11	12	13	14	15	16	17	18	19	20	21	22	23	24	HOURS
JAN	0	0	0	0	0	0	0	0	17	54	83	89	85	84	48	9	0	0	0	0	0	0	0	0	43
FEB	0	0	0	0	0	0	0	11	52	82	85	87	89	88	84	34	0	0	0	0	0	0	0	0	54
MAR	0	0	0	0	0	0	6	45	94	96	96	96	96	96	93	66	32	0	0	0	0	0	0	0	69
APR	0	0	0	0	0	0	40	86	89	89	94	96	96	98	93	86	36	1	0	0	0	0	0	0	72
MAY	0	0	0	0	0	10	74	88	98	98	100	100	100	100	100	93	55	10	0	0	0	0	0	0	83
JUN	0	0	0	0	0	35	85	90	96	98	98	98	98	96	91	91	75	22	0	0	0	0	0	0	84
JUL	0	0	0	0	0	2	71	98	100	100	100	100	100	98	98	86	78	14	0	0	0	0	0	0	86
AUG	0	0	0	0	0	0	42	92	96	98	98	100	100	100	100	95	57	7	0	0	0	0	0	0	83
SEP	0	0	0	0	0	0	30	83	98	100	100	100	99	100	95	70	16	0	0	0	0	0	0	0	77
OCT	0	0	0	0	0	0	0	45	92	96	96	96	96	91	79	19	0	0	0	0	0	0	0	0	63
NOV	0	0	0	0	0	0	0	5	50	89	91	98	93	84	39	0	0	0	0	0	0	0	0	0	50
DEC	0	0	0	0	0	0	0	0	23	44	83	88	89	69	30	0	0	0	0	0	0	0	0	0	39
ANNUAL	0	0	0	0	0	4	29	81	76	87	94	96	95	92	79	55	30	3	0	0	0	0	0	0	67

PERCENT POWER REDUCTION (BASED ON MAXIMUM ILLUMINATION FOR EACH SPACE): DENVER

For a typical 2-story office building with 15'-0" deep perimeter zones and a top-lit core zone.

Weather Data:	Denver (TMY)	Glass Type:	¹/₄" solar bronze tinted (single pane)
% Opening:	37.5% WWR (windows)		(SC = 0.57; VT = 0.47)
	4% of roof area (skylights)		
Overhangs:	2'-3" (horizontal)		
Lighting Control Type:	Continuous		
No. of Ref. Points:	One (2'-6" high in the center of zone)		
Max. Illum.:	118 footcandles		

NORTH

MONTH	1	2	3	4	5	6	7	8	9	10	11	12	13	14	15	16	17	18	19	20	21	22	23	24	HOURS
JAN	0	0	0	0	0	0	0	8	22	22	20	16	15	13	9	24	9	0	0	0	0	0	0	0	14
FEB	0	0	0	0	0	0	0	26	34	33	32	31	27	20	16	10	20	2	0	0	0	0	0	0	21
MAR	0	0	0	0	0	0	27	44	46	43	41	39	35	30	24	18	34	19	0	0	0	0	0	0	30
APR	0	0	0	0	0	13	60	61	55	52	50	49	46	41	35	28	21	25	2	0	0	0	0	0	38
MAY	0	0	0	0	0	52	73	68	64	63	61	58	57	50	42	35	27	24	16	0	0	0	0	0	49
JUN	0	0	0	0	4	59	77	70	67	64	60	58	54	47	39	34	28	28	22	0	0	0	0	0	49
JUL	0	0	0	0	1	50	78	73	68	62	56	53	48	43	40	33	28	25	19	0	0	0	0	0	47
AUG	0	0	0	0	0	15	66	67	60	55	52	50	46	40	33	27	23	32	5	0	0	0	0	0	43
SEP	0	0	0	0	0	3	50	55	52	49	48	43	37	30	23	18	24	19	0	0	0	0	0	0	35
OCT	0	0	0	0	0	0	18	44	38	37	35	30	24	18	13	9	19	1	0	0	0	0	0	0	24
NOV	0	0	0	0	0	0	2	25	28	27	25	21	18	14	10	14	9	0	0	0	0	0	0	0	15
DEC	0	0	0	0	0	0	0	10	22	22	19	14	12	10	6	17	6	0	0	0	0	0	0	0	12
ANNUAL	0	0	0	0	0	16	38	61	47	44	42	38	35	30	24	22	21	12	2	0	0	0	0	0	31

SOUTH

Max. Illum.:   763 footcandles

MONTH	1	2	3	4	5	6	7	8	9	10	11	12	13	14	15	16	17	18	19	20	21	22	23	24	HOURS
JAN	0	0	0	0	0	0	0	3	21	41	37	31	28	30	29	11	3	0	0	0	0	0	0	0	21
FEB	0	0	0	0	0	0	0	12	28	32	19	19	19	16	18	18	6	0	0	0	0	0	0	0	16
MAR	0	0	0	0	0	0	6	33	38	16	16	17	15	13	9	13	12	4	0	0	0	0	0	0	14
APR	0	0	0	0	0	2	16	25	12	11	10	10	9	7	7	5	9	4	0	0	0	0	0	0	8
MAY	0	0	0	0	0	5	18	17	12	11	11	11	10	8	7	6	7	4	2	0	0	0	0	0	9
JUN	0	0	0	0	0	6	15	12	11	11	11	10	10	8	7	6	5	6	2	0	0	0	0	0	8
JUL	0	0	0	0	0	5	16	18	12	11	10	10	9	7	6	5	5	6	2	0	0	0	0	0	9
AUG	0	0	0	0	0	2	19	30	12	11	10	10	9	7	6	5	10	5	1	0	0	0	0	0	10
SEP	0	0	0	0	0	0	16	44	21	12	11	11	9	7	5	13	9	3	0	0	0	0	0	0	13
OCT	0	0	0	0	0	0	5	58	39	21	22	23	20	14	17	21	4	0	0	0	0	0	0	0	21
NOV	0	0	0	0	0	0	1	18	43	39	25	20	22	26	23	11	2	0	0	0	0	0	0	0	19
DEC	0	0	0	0	0	0	0	5	34	38	41	37	37	37	28	8	2	0	0	0	0	0	0	0	24
ANNUAL	0	0	0	0	0	2	9	28	23	21	19	18	16	15	13	10	6	2	0	0	0	0	0	0	14

EAST

MONTH	1	2	3	4	5	6	7	8	9	10	11	12	13	14	15	16	17	18	19	20	21	22	23	24	HOURS
JAN	0	0	0	0	0	0	0	3	25	32	21	7	2	2	1	4	1	0	0	0	0	0	0	0	9
FEB	0	0	0	0	0	0	0	11	32	28	11	6	4	3	3	2	3	0	0	0	0	0	0	0	9
MAR	0	0	0	0	0	0	7	28	39	23	10	7	6	5	4	3	5	2	0	0	0	0	0	0	10
APR	0	0	0	0	0	4	26	41	22	18	10	9	8	7	6	4	3	3	0	0	0	0	0	0	9
MAY	0	0	0	0	0	0	14	40	34	23	14	12	10	9	8	7	5	4	3	2	0	0	0	0	12
JUN	0	0	0	0	1	21	48	32	26	14	12	10	9	7	6	5	4	3	2	0	0	0	0	0	12
JUL	0	0	0	0	0	18	48	43	29	15	12	9	8	7	6	5	4	3	2	0	0	0	0	0	13
AUG	0	0	0	0	0	5	35	46	29	15	11	9	8	6	5	4	3	4	1	0	0	0	0	0	13
SEP	0	0	0	0	0	1	21	44	31	20	11	8	6	5	4	3	3	2	0	0	0	0	0	0	13
OCT	0	0	0	0	0	0	7	39	44	21	9	5	4	3	2	1	3	0	0	0	0	0	0	0	12
NOV	0	0	0	0	0	0	1	17	33	26	11	4	3	2	2	2	1	0	0	0	0	0	0	0	8
DEC	0	0	0	0	0	0	0	5	27	26	18	7	2	2	1	3	1	0	0	0	0	0	0	0	8
ANNUAL	0	0	0	0	0	5	20	38	30	21	12	8	6	5	4	3	3	1	0	0	0	0	0	0	11

WEST

Max. Illum.:   520 footcandles

MONTH	1	2	3	4	5	6	7	8	9	10	11	12	13	14	15	16	17	18	19	20	21	22	23	24	HOURS
JAN	0	0	0	0	0	0	0	2	5	5	5	4	6	24	39	25	6	0	0	0	0	0	0	0	10
FEB	0	0	0	0	0	0	0	5	7	8	8	7	7	7	24	41	11	1	0	0	0	0	0	0	10
MAR	0	0	0	0	0	0	5	8	10	10	10	9	9	9	17	33	31	9	0	0	0	0	0	0	13
APR	0	0	0	0	0	2	10	11	11	12	12	12	12	11	17	16	33	10	1	0	0	0	0	0	13
MAY	0	0	0	0	0	8	11	12	13	14	14	14	14	13	13	18	24	13	6	0	0	0	0	0	14
JUN	0	0	0	0	1	8	11	12	13	14	14	14	14	13	12	22	22	26	9	0	0	0	0	0	14
JUL	0	0	0	0	0	7	11	12	13	13	13	12	12	12	11	18	19	23	8	0	0	0	0	0	13
AUG	0	0	0	0	0	2	10	11	12	12	12	12	12	11	11	24	33	14	2	0	0	0	0	0	14
SEP	0	0	0	0	0	1	8	10	11	11	11	10	10	10	18	35	31	9	0	0	0	0	0	0	14
OCT	0	0	0	0	0	0	3	9	9	9	8	7	7	7	36	38	10	1	0	0	0	0	0	0	12
NOV	0	0	0	0	0	0	1	5	7	6	6	5	7	27	44	19	5	0	0	0	0	0	0	0	11
DEC	0	0	0	0	0	0	0	2	5	5	4	3	11	39	35	13	4	0	0	0	0	0	0	0	10
ANNUAL	0	0	0	0	0	2	6	11	10	10	10	9	10	15	23	25	19	7	1	0	0	0	0	0	12

CORE (Top-lit)

MONTH	1	2	3	4	5	6	7	8	9	10	11	12	13	14	15	16	17	18	19	20	21	22	23	24	HOURS
JAN	0	0	0	0	0	0	0	3	11	21	30	36	35	29	18	10	3	0	0	0	0	0	0	0	18
FEB	0	0	0	0	0	0	0	9	19	32	42	46	46	40	30	14	6	0	0	0	0	0	0	0	25
MAR	0	0	0	0	0	0	6	18	36	53	63	64	60	51	40	24	14	5	0	0	0	0	0	0	37
APR	0	0	0	0	0	3	16	34	49	61	69	71	68	60	47	32	15	7	1	0	0	0	0	0	44
MAY	0	0	0	0	0	11	24	42	58	70	77	78	72	63	51	36	20	9	4	0	0	0	0	0	51
JUN	0	0	0	0	1	12	26	47	64	77	84	84	79	71	59	44	27	11	4	0	0	0	0	0	57
JUL	0	0	0	0	0	9	24	47	67	81	88	90	85	74	55	39	26	11	4	0	0	0	0	0	59
AUG	0	0	0	0	0	3	18	36	57	70	78	80	76	68	56	39	21	9	1	0	0	0	0	0	52
SEP	0	0	0	0	0	1	13	27	46	61	70	73	70	60	44	26	11	5	0	0	0	0	0	0	44
OCT	0	0	0	0	0	0	4	20	33	48	55	56	52	42	28	11	5	0	0	0	0	0	0	0	31
NOV	0	0	0	0	0	0	1	9	19	30	38	40	37	28	15	6	3	0	0	0	0	0	0	0	20
DEC	0	0	0	0	0	0	0	3	12	21	28	32	31	24	13	6	2	0	0	0	0	0	0	0	15
ANNUAL	0	0	0	0	0	3	11	36	40	52	61	62	60	51	38	24	13	4	0	0	0	0	0	0	38

PERCENT POWER REDUCTION: LOS ANGELES

For a typical 2-story office building with 15'-0" deep perimeter zones and a top-lit core zone.

Weather Data:	Los Angeles (TMY)	Glass Type:	¼" solar bronze tinted (single pane)
% Opening:	37.5% WWR (windows)		(SC = 0.57; VT = 0.47)
	4% of roof area (skylights)		
Overhangs:	2'-3" (horizontal)		
Lighting Control Type:	Stepped (2 steps)		
Lighting Set Point:	50 footcandles		
No. of Ref. Points:	One (2'-6" high in the center of zone)		

NORTH

MONTH	1	2	3	4	5	6	7	8	9	10	11	12	13	14	15	16	17	18	19	20	21	22	23	24	HOURS
JAN	0	0	0	0	0	0	0	0	39	46	52	56	56	52	48	43	7	0	0	0	0	0	0	0	36
FEB	0	0	0	0	0	0	0	37	54	54	61	67	69	70	66	50	42	0	0	0	0	0	0	0	48
MAR	0	0	0	0	0	0	5	71	85	100	100	100	100	100	100	96	91	23	0	0	0	0	0	0	80
APR	0	0	0	0	0	0	53	67	100	100	100	100	100	100	100	98	88	70	0	0	0	0	0	0	86
MAY	0	0	0	0	0	11	40	94	100	100	100	100	100	100	100	98	88	0	0	0	0	0	0	0	90
JUN	0	0	0	0	0	18	45	87	100	100	100	100	100	100	100	100	93	84	26	0	0	0	0	0	90
JUL	0	0	0	0	0	2	64	87	100	98	98	100	100	100	100	100	96	93	19	0	0	0	0	0	90
AUG	0	0	0	0	0	0	56	83	94	100	100	100	100	98	100	100	95	83	0	0	0	0	0	0	89
SEP	0	0	0	0	0	0	17	69	85	100	100	100	100	100	98	96	84	23	0	0	0	0	0	0	83
OCT	0	0	0	0	0	0	3	37	63	73	79	77	74	67	57	69	36	0	0	0	0	0	0	0	55
NOV	0	0	0	0	0	0	0	35	46	46	57	61	59	56	50	45	0	0	0	0	0	0	0	0	38
DEC	0	0	0	0	0	0	0	0	42	48	52	50	53	52	48	41	0	0	0	0	0	0	0	0	35
ANNUAL	0	0	0	0	0	3	24	75	76	81	84	84	85	83	81	79	62	30	1	0	0	0	0	0	69

SOUTH

MONTH	1	2	3	4	5	6	7	8	9	10	11	12	13	14	15	16	17	18	19	20	21	22	23	24	HOURS
JAN	0	0	0	0	0	0	0	48	87	90	92	96	97	91	95	86	45	0	0	0	0	0	0	0	70
FEB	0	0	0	0	0	0	0	82	91	96	100	100	100	100	100	97	83	0	0	0	0	0	0	0	78
MAR	0	0	0	0	0	0	11	79	85	100	100	100	100	100	100	96	93	31	0	0	0	0	0	0	81
APR	0	0	0	0	0	0	53	68	100	100	100	100	100	100	100	98	91	83	0	0	0	0	0	0	87
MAY	0	0	0	0	0	0	40	94	100	100	100	100	100	100	100	100	98	90	0	0	0	0	0	0	91
JUN	0	0	0	0	0	0	47	87	100	100	100	100	100	100	100	100	93	84	0	0	0	0	0	0	90
JUL	0	0	0	0	0	0	64	89	100	98	98	100	100	100	100	100	96	73	0	0	0	0	0	0	89
AUG	0	0	0	0	0	0	56	85	96	100	100	100	100	98	100	100	98	63	0	0	0	0	0	0	88
SEP	0	0	0	0	0	0	22	77	85	100	100	100	100	100	100	98	93	31	0	0	0	0	0	0	85
OCT	0	0	0	0	0	0	17	70	88	96	100	100	100	100	100	95	71	0	0	0	0	0	0	0	80
NOV	0	0	0	0	0	0	0	78	85	89	96	98	98	98	95	90	14	0	0	0	0	0	0	0	68
DEC	0	0	0	0	0	0	0	63	92	90	92	94	96	98	93	89	8	0	0	0	0	0	0	0	68
ANNUAL	0	0	0	0	0	26	83	92	97	98	99	99	99	99	96	74	31	0	0	0	0	0	0	0	81

EAST

MONTH	1	2	3	4	5	6	7	8	9	10	11	12	13	14	15	16	17	18	19	20	21	22	23	24	HOURS
JAN	0	0	0	0	0	0	0	70	85	87	90	63	56	52	48	43	7	0	0	0	0	0	0	0	49
FEB	0	0	0	0	0	0	0	84	91	91	100	100	84	80	68	50	42	0	0	0	0	0	0	0	64
MAR	0	0	0	0	0	0	25	82	94	100	100	100	100	100	100	93	64	5	0	0	0	0	0	0	77
APR	0	0	0	0	0	6	57	97	100	100	100	100	100	100	100	100	98	86	41	0	0	0	0	0	84
MAY	0	0	0	0	0	32	64	100	100	100	100	100	100	100	100	100	95	45	0	0	0	0	0	0	90
JUN	0	0	0	0	0	40	73	87	100	100	100	100	100	100	100	100	91	66	0	0	0	0	0	0	89
JUL	0	0	0	0	0	17	85	100	100	98	98	100	100	100	100	100	93	64	0	0	0	0	0	0	90
AUG	0	0	0	0	0	7	58	89	100	100	100	100	100	98	100	100	90	43	0	0	0	0	0	0	88
SEP	0	0	0	0	0	0	37	79	85	100	100	100	100	100	91	50	11	0	0	0	0	0	0	0	81
OCT	0	0	0	0	0	0	31	78	90	100	100	100	88	81	57	50	24	0	0	0	0	0	0	0	68
NOV	0	0	0	0	0	0	6	78	85	89	96	61	59	58	50	45	0	0	0	0	0	0	0	0	50
DEC	0	0	0	0	0	0	0	74	92	90	92	54	57	52	48	41	0	0	0	0	0	0	0	0	49
ANNUAL	0	0	0	0	0	9	37	89	94	96	98	89	87	85	81	76	54	17	0	0	0	0	0	0	73

WEST

MONTH	1	2	3	4	5	6	7	8	9	10	11	12	13	14	15	16	17	18	19	20	21	22	23	24	HOURS
JAN	0	0	0	0	0	0	0	0	39	46	52	56	57	91	90	88	64	0	0	0	0	0	0	0	51
FEB	0	0	0	0	0	0	0	34	50	59	76	83	100	100	100	97	89	7	0	0	0	0	0	0	67
MAR	0	0	0	0	0	0	3	48	83	100	100	100	100	100	100	100	98	67	0	0	0	0	0	0	84
APR	0	0	0	0	0	0	27	67	100	100	100	100	100	100	100	100	93	86	0	0	0	0	0	0	87
MAY	0	0	0	0	0	0	31	86	100	100	100	100	100	100	100	100	100	95	14	0	0	0	0	0	90
JUN	0	0	0	0	0	0	37	83	100	100	100	100	100	100	100	100	100	93	64	0	0	0	0	0	91
JUL	0	0	0	0	0	0	47	83	100	98	98	100	100	100	100	100	98	96	53	0	0	0	0	0	90
AUG	0	0	0	0	0	0	27	81	98	100	100	100	100	98	100	100	100	93	0	0	0	0	0	0	89
SEP	0	0	0	0	0	0	8	61	85	100	100	100	100	100	100	98	96	60	0	0	0	0	0	0	85
OCT	0	0	0	0	0	0	0	30	60	77	90	92	100	100	100	100	90	0	0	0	0	0	0	0	72
NOV	0	0	0	0	0	0	0	33	46	48	59	61	86	98	97	95	41	0	0	0	0	0	0	0	55
DEC	0	0	0	0	0	0	0	0	42	48	56	52	59	96	93	89	26	0	0	0	0	0	0	0	49
ANNUAL	0	0	0	0	0	0	15	69	76	82	86	87	92	98	98	97	83	41	3	0	0	0	0	0	76

CORE (Top-lit)

MONTH	1	2	3	4	5	6	7	8	9	10	11	12	13	14	15	16	17	18	19	20	21	22	23	24	HOURS
JAN	0	0	0	0	0	0	0	0	33	60	90	94	95	91	74	26	0	0	0	0	0	0	0	0	51
FEB	0	0	0	0	0	0	0	0	46	91	96	100	100	98	95	58	3	0	0	0	0	0	0	0	62
MAR	0	0	0	0	0	0	0	24	85	100	100	100	100	100	100	96	43	0	0	0	0	0	0	0	74
APR	0	0	0	0	0	0	5	63	94	100	100	100	100	100	100	93	54	0	0	0	0	0	0	0	77
MAY	0	0	0	0	0	0	19	72	100	100	100	100	100	100	100	100	92	15	0	0	0	0	0	0	85
JUN	0	0	0	0	0	0	23	71	100	100	100	100	100	100	100	100	91	41	0	0	0	0	0	0	87
JUL	0	0	0	0	0	0	27	85	100	98	98	100	100	100	100	100	93	48	0	0	0	0	0	0	88
AUG	0	0	0	0	0	0	6	69	90	100	100	100	100	98	100	100	81	5	0	0	0	0	0	0	83
SEP	0	0	0	0	0	0	0	44	79	100	100	100	100	100	100	98	32	0	0	0	0	0	0	0	75
OCT	0	0	0	0	0	0	0	22	75	94	100	100	100	100	100	57	0	0	0	0	0	0	0	0	66
NOV	0	0	0	0	0	0	0	0	46	85	93	96	95	93	63	8	0	0	0	0	0	0	0	0	52
DEC	0	0	0	0	0	0	0	0	42	67	88	92	93	94	48	0	0	0	0	0	0	0	0	0	48
ANNUAL	0	0	0	0	0	0	7	59	75	91	97	98	99	98	90	70	42	6	0	0	0	0	0	0	71

PERCENT POWER REDUCTION: NEW YORK

For a typical 2-story office building with 15'-0" deep perimeter zones and a top-lit core zone.

Weather Data:	New York (TMY)	Glass Type:	¼" solar bronze tinted (single pane)
% Opening:	37.5% WWR (windows)		(SC = 0.57; VT = 0.47)
	4% of roof area (skylights)		
Overhangs:	2'-3" (horizontal)		
Lighting Control Type:	Stepped (2 steps)		
Lighting Set Point:	50 footcandles		
No. of Ref. Points:	One (2'-6" high in the center of zone)		

NORTH

MONTH	1	2	3	4	5	6	7	8	9	10	11	12	13	14	15	16	17	18	19	20	21	22	23	24	HOURS
JAN	0	0	0	0	0	0	0	12	21	21	25	25	25	23	24	19	13	0	0	0	0	0	0	0	18
FEB	0	0	0	0	0	0	0	21	24	28	26	31	35	39	32	29	29	12	0	0	0	0	0	0	25
MAR	0	0	0	0	0	0	23	29	29	33	54	67	70	66	39	30	23	20	0	0	0	0	0	0	39
APR	0	0	0	0	0	25	45	58	56	71	73	75	71	73	73	59	57	50	18	0	0	0	0	0	60
MAY	0	0	0	0	0	50	58	73	86	82	90	91	86	89	84	69	74	65	43	0	0	0	0	0	76
JUN	0	0	0	0	20	53	57	58	79	81	85	84	91	91	86	84	61	61	60	16	0	0	0	0	74
JUL	0	0	0	0	13	56	61	73	88	88	87	85	76	82	77	80	75	73	73	15	0	0	0	0	76
AUG	0	0	0	0	0	57	76	83	89	83	92	94	91	91	88	88	84	79	57	0	0	0	0	0	82
SEP	0	0	0	0	0	18	68	75	78	86	85	86	83	86	86	75	70	61	8	0	0	0	0	0	75
OCT	0	0	0	0	0	0	36	64	60	71	81	79	78	78	64	57	63	7	0	0	0	0	0	0	61
NOV	0	0	0	0	0	0	6	23	28	35	54	52	40	45	29	26	17	0	0	0	0	0	0	0	29
DEC	0	0	0	0	0	0	0	14	23	25	25	27	29	28	21	14	7	0	0	0	0	0	0	0	18
ANNUAL	0	0	0	0	3	22	36	68	56	59	65	66	65	66	59	53	48	27	8	3	0	0	0	0	53

SOUTH

MONTH	1	2	3	4	5	6	7	8	9	10	11	12	13	14	15	16	17	18	19	20	21	22	23	24	HOURS
JAN	0	0	0	0	0	0	0	28	54	58	54	54	53	52	55	50	28	0	0	0	0	0	0	0	41
FEB	0	0	0	0	0	0	0	47	55	61	55	59	69	69	69	69	53	19	0	0	0	0	0	0	51
MAR	0	0	0	0	0	0	36	58	58	60	65	85	83	81	59	62	46	39	0	0	0	0	0	0	57
APR	0	0	0	0	0	15	47	71	61	75	79	81	78	82	84	64	70	55	12	0	0	0	0	0	66
MAY	0	0	0	0	0	21	61	73	88	86	90	91	91	92	84	71	74	61	22	0	0	0	0	0	77
JUN	0	0	0	0	9	43	57	58	81	81	85	89	93	91	88	84	61	61	45	7	0	0	0	0	75
JUL	0	0	0	0	5	44	64	73	90	88	87	91	84	82	80	82	75	71	56	7	0	0	0	0	77
AUG	0	0	0	0	0	45	77	85	90	90	94	96	93	93	91	88	88	81	43	0	0	0	0	0	84
SEP	0	0	0	0	0	17	70	79	81	86	88	91	86	88	86	82	75	63	5	0	0	0	0	0	77
OCT	0	0	0	0	0	0	51	79	77	75	90	88	85	88	71	76	74	12	0	0	0	0	0	0	70
NOV	0	0	0	0	0	0	13	68	78	69	80	78	61	75	74	63	36	0	0	0	0	0	0	0	55
DEC	0	0	0	0	0	0	0	40	62	58	58	62	58	57	53	46	20	0	0	0	0	0	0	0	43
ANNUAL	0	0	0	0	1	15	40	73	73	74	77	80	78	79	75	70	59	31	6	1	0	0	0	0	65

EAST

MONTH	1	2	3	4	5	6	7	8	9	10	11	12	13	14	15	16	17	18	19	20	21	22	23	24	HOURS
JAN	0	0	0	0	0	0	0	33	52	54	54	44	42	23	24	19	13	0	0	0	0	0	0	0	30
FEB	0	0	0	0	0	0	0	54	55	59	55	57	52	55	32	29	26	9	0	0	0	0	0	0	39
MAR	0	0	0	0	0	0	46	60	58	62	81	79	75	70	43	30	23	17	0	0	0	0	0	0	49
APR	0	0	0	0	0	40	55	81	69	81	79	79	73	73	70	52	41	26	10	0	0	0	0	0	60
MAY	0	0	0	0	0	61	63	77	88	90	90	91	86	89	84	66	61	53	22	0	0	0	0	0	76
JUN	0	0	0	0	23	60	63	62	81	81	86	84	91	91	86	82	61	57	45	7	0	0	0	0	74
JUL	0	0	0	0	15	69	68	73	92	90	90	89	76	82	77	80	75	66	56	7	0	0	0	0	77
AUG	0	0	0	0	0	61	84	89	94	92	96	94	91	91	88	88	81	70	41	0	0	0	0	0	84
SEP	0	0	0	0	0	21	73	81	82	86	88	88	86	86	86	75	68	48	4	0	0	0	0	0	76
OCT	0	0	0	0	0	0	55	79	75	75	90	85	80	78	64	57	35	6	0	0	0	0	0	0	63
NOV	0	0	0	0	0	0	14	67	71	67	74	59	45	49	32	26	17	0	0	0	0	0	0	0	40
DEC	0	0	0	0	0	0	0	46	58	56	54	52	37	31	21	14	7	0	0	0	0	0	0	0	31
ANNUAL	0	0	0	0	3	26	44	75	73	75	78	75	70	68	59	52	43	22	5	1	0	0	0	0	58

WEST

MONTH	1	2	3	4	5	6	7	8	9	10	11	12	13	14	15	16	17	18	19	20	21	22	23	24	HOURS
JAN	0	0	0	0	0	0	0	12	21	21	25	44	44	51	57	55	32	0	0	0	0	0	0	0	31
FEB	0	0	0	0	0	0	0	21	24	28	33	50	59	67	71	71	69	24	0	0	0	0	0	0	43
MAR	0	0	0	0	0	0	21	29	29	35	71	73	78	81	61	64	55	47	0	0	0	0	0	0	52
APR	0	0	0	0	0	15	22	27	54	71	73	77	75	80	84	68	77	71	26	0	0	0	0	0	65
MAY	0	0	0	0	0	21	45	65	80	82	90	91	91	92	92	74	77	76	54	0	0	0	0	0	76
JUN	0	0	0	0	9	43	53	54	79	81	85	84	91	93	88	84	72	68	67	19	0	0	0	0	75
JUL	0	0	0	0	5	44	60	73	85	88	87	85	78	82	80	84	78	78	81	18	0	0	0	0	76
AUG	0	0	0	0	0	29	66	79	89	83	92	94	91	95	95	91	91	91	61	0	0	0	0	0	83
SEP	0	0	0	0	0	9	62	71	78	86	85	88	86	86	86	84	77	68	9	0	0	0	0	0	76
OCT	0	0	0	0	0	0	24	59	60	71	85	83	80	85	74	81	77	13	0	0	0	0	0	0	66
NOV	0	0	0	0	0	0	5	23	28	46	59	54	46	73	74	69	42	0	0	0	0	0	0	0	43
DEC	0	0	0	0	0	0	0	14	23	25	35	40	53	57	55	53	22	0	0	0	0	0	0	0	32
ANNUAL	0	0	0	0	1	13	30	64	55	60	68	72	73	78	76	73	64	37	10	3	0	0	0	0	60

CORE (Top-lit)

MONTH	1	2	3	4	5	6	7	8	9	10	11	12	13	14	15	16	17	18	19	20	21	22	23	24	HOURS
JAN	0	0	0	0	0	0	0	0	0	21	40	44	42	37	22	0	0	0	0	0	0	0	0	0	19
FEB	0	0	0	0	0	0	0	0	15	30	48	57	59	64	42	21	0	0	0	0	0	0	0	0	30
MAR	0	0	0	0	0	0	0	0	29	56	65	67	68	64	57	37	14	0	0	0	0	0	0	0	41
APR	0	0	0	0	0	0	0	25	59	58	79	81	78	80	66	59	30	0	0	0	0	0	0	0	53
MAY	0	0	0	0	0	0	19	60	75	86	90	91	91	92	84	69	54	21	0	0	0	0	0	0	70
JUN	0	0	0	0	0	17	25	54	79	81	85	84	91	91	88	72	59	30	0	0	0	0	0	0	70
JUL	0	0	0	0	0	0	27	69	88	88	87	85	76	82	80	64	71	34	21	0	0	0	0	0	71
AUG	0	0	0	0	0	0	27	62	83	90	92	94	91	91	91	79	65	34	0	0	0	0	0	0	75
SEP	0	0	0	0	0	0	27	40	78	86	88	88	86	86	86	75	34	17	0	0	0	0	0	0	67
OCT	0	0	0	0	0	0	0	32	60	71	88	85	80	73	64	29	12	0	0	0	0	0	0	0	52
NOV	0	0	0	0	0	0	0	0	24	46	61	65	45	49	29	13	0	0	0	0	0	0	0	0	30
DEC	0	0	0	0	0	0	0	0	6	21	35	40	43	33	14	0	0	0	0	0	0	0	0	0	18
ANNUAL	0	0	0	0	0	1	11	50	50	62	72	73	71	70	61	44	29	7	1	0	0	0	0	0	50

PERCENT POWER REDUCTION: SEATTLE

For a typical 2-story office building with 15'-0" deep perimeter zones and a top-lit core zone.

Weather Data:	Seattle (TMY)	Glass Type:	¼" solar bronze tinted (single pane)
% Opening:	37.5% WWR (windows)		(SC = 0.57; VT = 0.47)
	4% of roof area (skylights)		
Overhangs:	2'-3" (horizontal)		
Lighting Control Type:	Stepped (2 steps)		
Lighting Set Point:	50 footcandles		
No. of Ref. Points:	One (2'-6" high in the center of zone)		

NORTH

MONTH	1	2	3	4	5	6	7	8	9	10	11	12	13	14	15	16	17	18	19	20	21	22	23	24	HOURS
JAN	0	0	0	0	0	0	0	0	0	13	19	31	32	32	23	12	0	0	0	0	0	0	0	0	14
FEB	0	0	0	0	0	0	0	0	9	24	43	48	42	42	34	19	5	0	0	0	0	0	0	0	24
MAR	0	0	0	0	0	0	6	21	40	44	64	73	75	69	73	59	46	16	0	0	0	0	0	0	50
APR	0	0	0	0	0	0	1	37	79	71	87	90	94	92	91	91	77	65	41	6	0	0	0	0	73
MAY	0	0	0	0	0	0	27	44	62	66	82	92	90	95	90	83	70	58	47	40	0	0	0	0	72
JUN	0	0	0	0	0	0	20	43	61	84	92	94	86	87	87	87	84	80	67	55	5	0	0	0	78
JUL	0	0	0	0	0	0	34	48	64	81	90	92	100	100	95	93	89	84	83	66	3	0	0	0	82
AUG	0	0	0	0	0	0	0	39	71	81	88	94	97	97	97	95	86	81	78	27	0	0	0	0	81
SEP	0	0	0	0	0	0	0	17	46	54	71	79	81	82	82	75	70	59	29	0	0	0	0	0	63
OCT	0	0	0	0	0	0	0	0	15	21	44	52	54	60	48	41	27	10	0	0	0	0	0	0	33
NOV	0	0	0	0	0	0	0	0	0	13	26	39	41	44	28	16	10	0	0	0	0	0	0	0	20
DEC	0	0	0	0	0	0	0	0	0	6	13	21	17	21	9	0	0	0	0	0	0	0	0	0	8
ANNUAL	0	0	0	0	0	7	20	53	44	56	65	68	69	65	61	51	41	22	5	1	0	0	0	0	50

SOUTH

MONTH	1	2	3	4	5	6	7	8	9	10	11	12	13	14	15	16	17	18	19	20	21	22	23	24	HOURS
JAN	0	0	0	0	0	0	0	0	19	31	40	48	49	49	45	31	7	0	0	0	0	0	0	0	29
FEB	0	0	0	0	0	0	0	0	32	43	65	67	58	66	63	47	24	0	0	0	0	0	0	0	42
MAR	0	0	0	0	0	0	6	32	48	54	68	77	82	75	80	71	61	29	0	0	0	0	0	0	57
APR	0	0	0	0	0	0	38	80	73	88	92	96	94	91	93	81	72	47	0	0	0	0	0	0	75
MAY	0	0	0	0	0	11	45	62	74	82	92	90	95	90	85	73	61	49	24	0	0	0	0	0	73
JUN	0	0	0	0	0	10	40	61	84	94	96	89	91	91	93	89	82	64	37	0	0	0	0	0	80
JUL	0	0	0	0	0	15	50	66	83	90	94	100	100	98	98	95	89	88	45	0	0	0	0	0	84
AUG	0	0	0	0	0	0	48	81	85	94	100	100	100	100	97	88	95	83	23	0	0	0	0	0	86
SEP	0	0	0	0	0	0	38	54	61	77	85	89	89	88	88	81	72	35	0	0	0	0	0	0	70
OCT	0	0	0	0	0	0	0	44	60	54	65	69	69	61	53	48	29	0	0	0	0	0	0	0	48
NOV	0	0	0	0	0	0	0	2	54	56	57	65	59	54	45	36	0	0	0	0	0	0	0	0	38
DEC	0	0	0	0	0	0	0	0	14	31	35	37	43	44	28	7	0	0	0	0	0	0	0	0	21
ANNUAL	0	0	0	0	0	3	22	60	57	67	74	77	78	76	73	63	50	25	3	0	0	0	0	0	59

EAST

MONTH	1	2	3	4	5	6	7	8	9	10	11	12	13	14	15	16	17	18	19	20	21	22	23	24	HOURS
JAN	0	0	0	0	0	0	0	0	25	31	40	44	36	38	26	12	0	0	0	0	0	0	0	0	23
FEB	0	0	0	0	0	0	0	0	35	43	63	65	52	47	40	19	5	0	0	0	0	0	0	0	33
MAR	0	0	0	0	0	0	13	39	54	54	68	77	75	71	73	59	43	7	0	0	0	0	0	0	52
APR	0	0	0	0	0	4	47	80	75	88	92	96	94	91	91	75	61	28	0	0	0	0	0	0	72
MAY	0	0	0	0	0	40	55	64	76	82	92	90	95	90	83	70	56	42	23	0	0	0	0	0	72
JUN	0	0	0	0	1	33	52	69	86	94	96	91	89	89	87	80	77	54	33	0	0	0	0	0	79
JUL	0	0	0	0	0	55	61	67	83	90	94	100	100	95	93	87	77	63	39	0	0	0	0	0	81
AUG	0	0	0	0	0	15	60	85	85	94	100	100	98	98	95	83	76	58	8	0	0	0	0	0	83
SEP	0	0	0	0	0	0	46	54	63	79	85	87	87	86	75	70	52	16	0	0	0	0	0	0	66
OCT	0	0	0	0	0	0	3	49	60	52	64	61	60	50	43	27	10	0	0	0	0	0	0	0	42
NOV	0	0	0	0	0	0	0	3	48	52	54	56	46	28	18	10	0	0	0	0	0	0	0	0	29
DEC	0	0	0	0	0	0	0	0	14	29	31	31	19	23	9	0	0	0	0	0	0	0	0	0	14
ANNUAL	0	0	0	0	0	12	28	63	59	66	73	74	71	67	62	50	39	16	3	0	0	0	0	0	54

WEST

MONTH	1	2	3	4	5	6	7	8	9	10	11	12	13	14	15	16	17	18	19	20	21	22	23	24	HOURS
JAN	0	0	0	0	0	0	0	0	0	13	19	33	43	47	45	33	7	0	0	0	0	0	0	0	21
FEB	0	0	0	0	0	0	0	0	9	24	45	52	55	56	66	50	35	0	0	0	0	0	0	0	34
MAR	0	0	0	0	0	0	3	16	40	46	64	75	75	75	80	73	66	51	0	0	0	0	0	0	57
APR	0	0	0	0	0	0	22	68	71	87	90	96	94	91	93	81	74	54	22	0	0	0	0	0	75
MAY	0	0	0	0	0	11	37	60	68	82	92	90	95	90	85	73	66	64	61	6	0	0	0	0	73
JUN	0	0	0	0	0	10	33	58	84	92	94	91	91	91	93	93	84	73	68	34	0	0	0	0	81
JUL	0	0	0	0	0	15	32	54	77	88	94	100	100	98	100	98	91	91	79	28	0	0	0	0	83
AUG	0	0	0	0	0	0	24	62	73	88	98	100	98	100	98	90	95	90	67	0	0	0	0	0	83
SEP	0	0	0	0	0	0	10	33	52	71	79	84	89	91	88	88	75	59	5	0	0	0	0	0	68
OCT	0	0	0	0	0	0	0	12	21	44	54	56	65	58	56	51	41	1	0	0	0	0	0	0	40
NOV	0	0	0	0	0	0	0	0	13	26	41	43	54	54	45	42	0	0	0	0	0	0	0	0	28
DEC	0	0	0	0	0	0	0	0	0	6	15	23	30	36	28	12	0	0	0	0	0	0	0	0	13
ANNUAL	0	0	0	0	0	3	14	46	43	56	66	70	74	74	73	66	53	32	10	6	0	0	0	0	55

CORE (Top-lit)

MONTH	1	2	3	4	5	6	7	8	9	10	11	12	13	14	15	16	17	18	19	20	21	22	23	24	HOURS
JAN	0	0	0	0	0	0	0	0	0	2	17	23	29	21	14	0	0	0	0	0	0	0	0	0	9
FEB	0	0	0	0	0	0	0	0	0	19	45	52	51	49	32	8	0	0	0	0	0	0	0	0	23
MAR	0	0	0	0	0	0	0	5	27	54	60	71	75	71	75	52	18	0	0	0	0	0	0	0	45
APR	0	0	0	0	0	0	2	53	69	85	90	96	94	91	88	72	50	11	0	0	0	0	0	0	68
MAY	0	0	0	0	0	0	19	56	72	80	86	86	95	90	83	73	56	21	2	0	0	0	0	0	69
JUN	0	0	0	0	0	0	20	50	79	94	94	91	94	93	93	93	80	39	7	0	0	0	0	0	77
JUL	0	0	0	0	0	0	26	60	77	90	94	100	100	98	100	98	89	55	3	0	0	0	0	0	82
AUG	0	0	0	0	0	0	5	50	79	89	100	100	100	100	98	88	83	35	0	0	0	0	0	0	79
SEP	0	0	0	0	0	0	0	23	57	69	85	82	89	88	86	77	29	0	0	0	0	0	0	0	60
OCT	0	0	0	0	0	0	0	0	21	44	60	66	65	54	36	14	0	0	0	0	0	0	0	0	32
NOV	0	0	0	0	0	0	0	0	0	22	30	43	41	20	13	0	0	0	0	0	0	0	0	0	15
DEC	0	0	0	0	0	0	0	0	0	0	8	15	18	12	0	0	0	0	0	0	0	0	0	0	5
ANNUAL	0	0	0	0	0	0	6	40	41	55	65	68	71	65	61	49	34	9	0	0	0	0	0	0	47

Appendix F.5   Average Illuminance Summary

AVERAGE ILLUMINANCE (FOOTCANDLES):ATLANTA

For a typical 2-story office building with 15'-0" deep perimeter zones and a top-lit core zone.

Weather Data:	Atlanta (TMY)	Glass Type:	¼" solar bronze tinted (single pane)
% Opening:	37.5% WWR (windows)		(SC = 0.57; VT = 0.47)
	4% of roof area (skylights)		
Overhangs:	2'-3" (horizontal)		
Lighting Control Type:	Continuous		
No. of Ref. Points:	One (2'-6" high in the center of zone)		

NORTH

MONTH	1	2	3	4	5	6	7	8	9	10	11	12	13	14	15	16	17	18	19	20	21	22	23	24	HOURS
JAN	0	0	0	0	0	0	0	0	13	19	25	29	29	29	28	24	19	9	0	0	0	0	0	0	20
FEB	0	0	0	0	0	0	0	2	18	24	29	32	32	33	33	31	25	19	1	0	0	0	0	0	24
MAR	0	0	0	0	0	0	0	17	28	33	35	37	37	37	36	35	32	27	8	0	0	0	0	0	30
APR	0	0	0	0	0	0	11	23	32	35	37	37	37	38	37	36	36	32	21	0	0	0	0	0	32
MAY	0	0	0	0	0	1	26	35	37	37	38	39	39	39	39	39	37	36	29	2	0	0	0	0	35
JUN	0	0	0	0	0	1	25	34	36	37	38	37	38	38	37	37	36	35	31	6	0	0	0	0	34
JUL	0	0	0	0	0	0	19	34	35	36	37	38	39	39	39	37	36	36	29	3	0	0	0	0	34
AUG	0	0	0	0	0	0	15	31	35	37	38	39	39	39	39	39	37	37	30	0	0	0	0	0	34
SEP	0	0	0	0	0	0	3	24	32	35	37	38	38	37	37	36	35	26	6	0	0	0	0	0	32
OCT	0	0	0	0	0	0	0	18	29	32	37	38	38	37	35	33	32	13	0	0	0	0	0	0	29
NOV	0	0	0	0	0	0	0	7	19	23	27	30	31	31	28	27	20	3	0	0	0	0	0	0	21
DEC	0	0	0	0	0	0	0	1	14	20	26	29	28	28	25	21	15	2	0	0	0	0	0	0	19
ANNUAL	0	0	0	0	0	0	8	28	28	31	34	35	35	35	35	33	30	20	7	1	0	0	0	0	29

SOUTH

MONTH	1	2	3	4	5	6	7	8	9	10	11	12	13	14	15	16	17	18	19	20	21	22	23	24	HOURS
JAN	0	0	0	0	0	0	0	0	29	41	48	49	49	51	51	48	44	18	0	0	0	0	0	0	38
FEB	0	0	0	0	0	0	0	4	31	41	45	50	51	53	52	53	48	30	0	0	0	0	0	0	40
MAR	0	0	0	0	0	0	0	24	45	49	52	58	58	59	57	54	51	43	10	0	0	0	0	0	47
APR	0	0	0	0	0	0	10	26	48	54	57	57	58	60	58	59	56	48	19	0	0	0	0	0	50
MAY	0	0	0	0	0	0	19	48	58	60	59	63	65	65	63	63	58	53	24	1	0	0	0	0	54
JUN	0	0	0	0	0	1	17	43	51	60	59	62	62	61	60	59	55	48	25	4	0	0	0	0	52
JUL	0	0	0	0	0	0	12	44	52	57	55	58	60	62	59	55	55	50	23	2	0	0	0	0	51
AUG	0	0	0	0	0	0	11	37	53	55	59	64	63	66	62	65	61	51	27	0	0	0	0	0	53
SEP	0	0	0	0	0	0	3	30	50	53	57	61	61	60	58	58	54	34	6	0	0	0	0	0	48
OCT	0	0	0	0	0	0	0	34	53	60	63	64	65	64	62	62	60	23	0	0	0	0	0	0	51
NOV	0	0	0	0	0	0	0	13	42	47	52	51	57	60	56	55	46	5	0	0	0	0	0	0	42
DEC	0	0	0	0	0	0	0	2	44	50	54	55	53	55	54	49	43	3	0	0	0	0	0	0	41
ANNUAL	0	0	0	0	0	0	6	37	47	52	55	57	59	60	58	57	52	30	7	1	0	0	0	0	48

EAST

MONTH	1	2	3	4	5	6	7	8	9	10	11	12	13	14	15	16	17	18	19	20	21	22	23	24	HOURS
JAN	0	0	0	0	0	0	0	1	29	32	37	40	36	31	29	24	20	8	0	0	0	0	0	0	26
FEB	0	0	0	0	0	0	0	6	29	34	37	41	41	37	36	34	25	16	0	0	0	0	0	0	29
MAR	0	0	0	0	0	0	0	28	36	40	42	45	46	46	43	39	33	24	6	0	0	0	0	0	35
APR	0	0	0	0	0	0	21	28	41	43	45	46	46	47	47	43	40	31	15	0	0	0	0	0	39
MAY	0	0	0	0	0	1	39	44	46	47	47	48	48	49	49	47	42	36	22	1	0	0	0	0	43
JUN	0	0	0	0	0	2	34	44	46	47	48	47	48	47	47	47	41	37	23	4	0	0	0	0	43
JUL	0	0	0	0	0	0	35	43	44	45	45	47	48	48	48	45	41	35	20	2	0	0	0	0	41
AUG	0	0	0	0	0	0	29	41	44	44	48	48	49	49	49	46	39	32	22	0	0	0	0	0	41
SEP	0	0	0	0	0	0	6	35	41	43	46	46	47	46	43	40	34	21	4	0	0	0	0	0	39
OCT	0	0	0	0	0	0	0	37	43	46	48	48	44	41	36	34	26	11	0	0	0	0	0	0	36
NOV	0	0	0	0	0	0	0	18	33	38	41	40	34	32	28	25	18	3	0	0	0	0	0	0	26
DEC	0	0	0	0	0	0	0	2	37	39	42	43	32	29	26	22	15	1	0	0	0	0	0	0	26
ANNUAL	0	0	0	0	0	0	14	39	39	41	43	45	43	42	41	37	32	18	5	1	0	0	0	0	36

WEST

MONTH	1	2	3	4	5	6	7	8	9	10	11	12	13	14	15	16	17	18	19	20	21	22	23	24	HOURS
JAN	0	0	0	0	0	0	0	0	13	20	26	30	32	40	41	39	34	22	0	0	0	0	0	0	26
FEB	0	0	0	0	0	0	0	2	17	24	31	36	37	41	41	43	39	27	1	0	0	0	0	0	29
MAR	0	0	0	0	0	0	0	15	27	34	39	44	46	46	45	43	41	35	18	0	0	0	0	0	36
APR	0	0	0	0	0	0	8	21	35	40	44	46	46	48	47	45	44	41	34	0	0	0	0	0	40
MAY	0	0	0	0	0	0	18	33	41	46	47	48	48	49	48	48	47	45	41	3	0	0	0	0	41
JUN	0	0	0	0	0	1	17	33	40	46	48	48	48	47	47	46	46	45	41	11	0	0	0	0	41
JUL	0	0	0	0	0	0	12	32	39	42	45	47	48	48	48	46	46	46	40	6	0	0	0	0	41
AUG	0	0	0	0	0	0	10	25	34	41	46	48	48	49	49	48	48	48	41	0	0	0	0	0	40
SEP	0	0	0	0	0	0	2	19	32	39	43	46	47	48	46	45	44	41	11	0	0	0	0	0	37
OCT	0	0	0	0	0	0	0	15	27	36	40	43	46	48	47	47	46	33	0	0	0	0	0	0	36
NOV	0	0	0	0	0	0	0	6	18	25	29	31	36	46	43	43	36	8	0	0	0	0	0	0	27
DEC	0	0	0	0	0	0	0	1	14	21	28	30	31	43	42	39	37	4	0	0	0	0	0	0	25
ANNUAL	0	0	0	0	0	0	6	25	28	34	39	41	43	46	46	44	43	29	11	1	0	0	0	0	35

CORE (Top-lit)

MONTH	1	2	3	4	5	6	7	8	9	10	11	12	13	14	15	16	17	18	19	20	21	22	23	24	HOURS
JAN	0	0	0	0	0	0	0	0	9	20	33	36	38	37	36	29	16	4	0	0	0	0	0	0	23
FEB	0	0	0	0	0	0	0	1	12	25	33	39	38	39	39	36	25	10	0	0	0	0	0	0	26
MAR	0	0	0	0	0	0	0	9	24	36	40	44	44	44	43	40	36	18	3	0	0	0	0	0	33
APR	0	0	0	0	0	0	4	18	36	40	42	43	44	44	44	42	41	26	8	0	0	0	0	0	36
MAY	0	0	0	0	0	0	8	30	42	44	45	45	46	46	46	46	44	34	12	1	0	0	0	0	39
JUN	0	0	0	0	0	0	8	28	41	44	45	44	44	44	44	44	42	38	16	2	0	0	0	0	38
JUL	0	0	0	0	0	0	6	27	41	42	44	44	46	46	45	43	42	39	15	1	0	0	0	0	38
AUG	0	0	0	0	0	0	5	20	40	43	46	46	46	46	46	45	44	31	12	0	0	0	0	0	38
SEP	0	0	0	0	0	0	1	14	34	40	44	45	45	44	43	42	37	16	2	0	0	0	0	0	34
OCT	0	0	0	0	0	0	0	9	27	41	44	46	46	45	44	42	24	5	0	0	0	0	0	0	32
NOV	0	0	0	0	0	0	0	3	15	30	37	40	42	43	40	28	13	1	0	0	0	0	0	0	25
DEC	0	0	0	0	0	0	0	1	10	22	36	39	40	38	36	23	10	1	0	0	0	0	0	0	23
ANNUAL	0	0	0	0	0	0	3	21	28	36	41	42	43	43	42	38	31	16	3	0	0	0	0	0	33

AVERAGE ILLUMINANCE (FOOTCANDLES): CHICAGO

For a typical 2-story office building with 15'-0" deep perimeter zones and a top-lit core zone.

Weather Data:	Chicago (TMY)	Glass Type:	¼" solar bronze tinted (single pane)
% Opening:	37.5% WWR (windows)		(SC = 0.57; VT = 0.47)
	4% of roof area (skylights)		
Overhangs:	2'-3" (horizontal)		
Lighting Control Type:	Continuous		
No. of Ref. Points:	One (2'-6" high in the center of zone)		

NORTH

MONTH	1	2	3	4	5	6	7	8	9	10	11	12	13	14	15	16	17	18	19	20	21	22	23	24	HOURS
JAN	0	0	0	0	0	0	0	3	15	20	22	24	24	24	21	17	5	0	0	0	0	0	0	0	16
FEB	0	0	0	0	0	0	0	13	21	27	31	31	31	30	28	24	16	1	0	0	0	0	0	0	21
MAR	0	0	0	0	0	0	12	26	32	34	33	33	33	32	32	29	26	12	0	0	0	0	0	0	27
APR	0	0	0	0	0	6	24	22	32	34	35	35	35	34	33	32	27	21	1	0	0	0	0	0	29
MAY	0	0	0	0	1	24	31	33	33	34	34	34	35	34	33	31	31	24	10	0	0	0	0	0	31
JUN	0	0	0	0	4	26	29	32	33	34	34	35	35	35	35	33	32	29	24	0	0	0	0	0	31
JUL	0	0	0	0	2	28	32	34	35	34	35	35	35	35	35	34	32	23	0	0	0	0	0	0	32
AUG	0	0	0	0	0	8	26	31	33	35	35	35	35	35	35	33	33	27	2	0	0	0	0	0	31
SEP	0	0	0	0	0	2	23	29	32	33	33	34	35	34	34	32	27	13	0	0	0	0	0	0	29
OCT	0	0	0	0	0	0	8	23	26	29	30	33	32	30	27	22	12	0	0	0	0	0	0	0	23
NOV	0	0	0	0	0	0	1	11	19	23	25	25	26	24	21	12	2	0	0	0	0	0	0	0	16
DEC	0	0	0	0	0	0	0	3	12	17	20	22	22	20	17	9	0	0	0	0	0	0	0	0	13
ANNUAL	0	0	0	0	1	8	16	29	27	30	31	31	31	31	29	26	21	11	2	0	0	0	0	0	25

SOUTH

MONTH	1	2	3	4	5	6	7	8	9	10	11	12	13	14	15	16	17	18	19	20	21	22	23	24	HOURS
JAN	0	0	0	0	0	0	0	7	42	49	49	49	48	48	48	46	11	0	0	0	0	0	0	0	35
FEB	0	0	0	0	0	0	0	28	41	49	52	51	50	49	51	46	32	2	0	0	0	0	0	0	38
MAR	0	0	0	0	0	0	15	43	51	53	53	54	54	53	51	47	45	14	0	0	0	0	0	0	43
APR	0	0	0	0	0	5	32	32	49	53	55	56	55	54	53	50	44	24	0	0	0	0	0	0	45
MAY	0	0	0	0	1	20	44	53	54	52	55	57	57	56	53	48	46	25	7	0	0	0	0	0	48
JUN	0	0	0	0	3	20	43	50	56	54	60	60	62	61	57	54	50	33	15	0	0	0	0	0	51
JUL	0	0	0	0	1	19	46	54	60	56	63	65	65	61	60	63	57	39	14	0	0	0	0	0	55
AUG	0	0	0	0	0	7	33	48	53	62	63	65	64	65	61	57	54	33	1	0	0	0	0	0	53
SEP	0	0	0	0	0	2	29	49	53	57	58	59	63	62	56	54	44	14	0	0	0	0	0	0	49
OCT	0	0	0	0	0	0	13	44	51	51	50	55	54	48	46	39	20	0	0	0	0	0	0	0	40
NOV	0	0	0	0	0	0	1	29	48	49	49	50	52	51	49	33	3	0	0	0	0	0	0	0	35
DEC	0	0	0	0	0	0	0	6	29	37	41	43	41	39	40	23	0	0	0	0	0	0	0	0	27
ANNUAL	0	0	0	0	0	6	22	48	49	52	54	55	55	54	52	47	34	12	1	0	0	0	0	0	44

EAST

MONTH	1	2	3	4	5	6	7	8	9	10	11	12	13	14	15	16	17	18	19	20	21	22	23	24	HOURS
JAN	0	0	0	0	0	0	0	8	34	38	39	37	26	24	21	18	5	0	0	0	0	0	0	0	22
FEB	0	0	0	0	0	0	0	26	33	39	42	40	34	32	29	23	14	1	0	0	0	0	0	0	26
MAR	0	0	0	0	0	0	19	36	42	43	43	44	40	39	36	30	22	9	0	0	0	0	0	0	32
APR	0	0	0	0	0	11	33	27	41	44	43	46	45	43	40	36	29	16	1	0	0	0	0	0	35
MAY	0	0	0	0	2	34	43	43	43	45	44	45	46	46	43	36	34	23	6	0	0	0	0	0	39
JUN	0	0	0	0	7	37	41	43	44	46	46	47	48	47	47	41	35	28	15	0	0	0	0	0	41
JUL	0	0	0	0	3	42	46	46	48	48	48	48	48	48	47	44	38	30	15	0	0	0	0	0	43
AUG	0	0	0	0	0	17	37	43	46	48	48	48	48	48	44	39	33	21	1	0	0	0	0	0	41
SEP	0	0	0	0	0	4	37	41	43	43	45	45	46	43	39	34	23	10	0	0	0	0	0	0	36
OCT	0	0	0	0	0	0	20	37	41	41	39	39	36	32	27	21	10	0	0	0	0	0	0	0	29
NOV	0	0	0	0	0	0	1	29	36	39	39	32	29	26	21	15	1	0	0	0	0	0	0	0	22
DEC	0	0	0	0	0	0	0	6	24	29	33	29	22	20	16	10	0	0	0	0	0	0	0	0	17
ANNUAL	0	0	0	0	1	12	23	41	40	42	43	41	39	37	34	29	20	9	1	0	0	0	0	0	32

WEST

MONTH	1	2	3	4	5	6	7	8	9	10	11	12	13	14	15	16	17	18	19	20	21	22	23	24	HOURS
JAN	0	0	0	0	0	0	0	3	15	22	25	25	35	37	36	36	15	0	0	0	0	0	0	0	22
FEB	0	0	0	0	0	0	0	11	20	28	34	34	40	39	40	36	32	3	0	0	0	0	0	0	27
MAR	0	0	0	0	0	0	10	22	32	38	39	41	44	42	41	38	36	22	0	0	0	0	0	0	34
APR	0	0	0	0	0	4	21	22	35	41	45	45	46	44	43	42	36	30	1	0	0	0	0	0	36
MAY	0	0	0	0	1	19	31	38	41	43	45	46	46	46	44	41	41	34	18	0	0	0	0	0	39
JUN	0	0	0	0	2	19	30	36	41	44	46	46	48	48	48	44	43	41	35	0	0	0	0	0	41
JUL	0	0	0	0	1	19	32	38	43	47	47	48	48	48	48	48	48	46	38	0	0	0	0	0	43
AUG	0	0	0	0	0	6	21	31	39	45	48	48	48	49	48	46	46	40	4	0	0	0	0	0	41
SEP	0	0	0	0	0	1	17	27	35	39	43	46	47	47	46	43	39	23	0	0	0	0	0	0	37
OCT	0	0	0	0	0	0	7	20	28	34	34	38	41	39	36	34	26	0	0	0	0	0	0	0	29
NOV	0	0	0	0	0	0	1	11	20	25	27	28	40	40	39	35	4	0	0	0	0	0	0	0	22
DEC	0	0	0	0	0	0	0	2	12	18	21	23	32	31	32	25	0	0	0	0	0	0	0	0	17
ANNUAL	0	0	0	0	0	6	14	31	30	35	38	39	43	42	42	39	31	16	3	0	0	0	0	0	32

CORE (Top-lit)

MONTH	1	2	3	4	5	6	7	8	9	10	11	12	13	14	15	16	17	18	19	20	21	22	23	24	HOURS
JAN	0	0	0	0	0	0	0	1	12	23	33	34	33	31	23	13	2	0	0	0	0	0	0	0	18
FEB	0	0	0	0	0	0	0	7	19	33	38	38	38	36	35	21	10	1	0	0	0	0	0	0	24
MAR	0	0	0	0	0	0	5	19	34	40	42	42	42	40	38	33	18	5	0	0	0	0	0	0	30
APR	0	0	0	0	0	3	16	24	38	42	42	44	43	42	40	38	29	11	0	0	0	0	0	0	33
MAY	0	0	0	0	1	10	27	39	40	42	42	42	43	44	42	38	33	16	3	0	0	0	0	0	36
JUN	0	0	0	0	1	12	29	39	42	42	43	44	44	45	44	41	38	23	8	0	0	0	0	0	38
JUL	0	0	0	0	1	9	29	41	44	44	45	45	45	45	44	44	44	25	7	0	0	0	0	0	40
AUG	0	0	0	0	0	3	18	34	40	45	45	46	46	46	45	43	35	16	1	0	0	0	0	0	38
SEP	0	0	0	0	0	1	11	29	39	41	42	43	44	44	42	37	20	5	0	0	0	0	0	0	34
OCT	0	0	0	0	0	0	3	18	33	37	37	40	40	36	31	19	7	0	0	0	0	0	0	0	27
NOV	0	0	0	0	0	0	0	8	20	32	36	36	38	34	23	10	1	0	0	0	0	0	0	0	21
DEC	0	0	0	0	0	0	0	1	10	18	26	30	28	23	15	7	0	0	0	0	0	0	0	0	14
ANNUAL	0	0	0	0	0	3	12	33	31	36	39	40	40	38	35	29	20	7	1	0	0	0	0	0	30

AVERAGE ILLUMINANCE (FOOTCANDLES): DENVER

For a typical 2-story office building with 15'-0" deep perimeter zones and a top-lit core zone.

Weather Data:	Denver (TMY)	Glass Type:	¼" solar bronze tinted (single pane)
% Opening:	37.5% WWR (windows)		(SC = 0.57; VT = 0.47)
	4% of roof area (skylights)		
Overhangs:	2'-3" (horizontal)		
Lighting Control Type:	Continuous		
No. of Ref. Points:	One (2'-6" high in the center of zone)		

NORTH

MONTH	1	2	3	4	5	6	7	8	9	10	11	12	13	14	15	16	17	18	19	20	21	22	23	24	HOURS
JAN	0	0	0	0	0	0	0	8	19	21	20	19	18	15	11	20	9	0	0	0	0	0	0	0	14
FEB	0	0	0	0	0	0	0	21	27	30	30	30	26	22	17	11	20	2	0	0	0	0	0	0	20
MAR	0	0	0	0	0	0	20	31	34	34	34	34	32	28	24	19	28	19	0	0	0	0	0	0	26
APR	0	0	0	0	0	12	31	33	33	34	35	35	35	35	32	27	25	22	3	0	0	0	0	0	29
MAY	0	0	0	0	0	30	34	34	35	35	35	35	35	35	34	31	28	22	17	0	0	0	0	0	31
JUN	0	0	0	0	4	31	33	34	35	35	35	35	35	35	34	32	28	26	23	0	0	0	0	0	31
JUL	0	0	0	0	2	30	33	35	35	35	35	35	35	35	35	31	28	27	20	0	0	0	0	0	31
AUG	0	0	0	0	0	15	33	34	34	35	35	35	35	35	32	27	27	27	5	0	0	0	0	0	31
SEP	0	0	0	0	0	4	32	34	35	35	35	35	34	31	24	19	25	20	0	0	0	0	0	0	28
OCT	0	0	0	0	0	0	16	34	32	33	33	30	26	20	15	12	19	1	0	0	0	0	0	0	23
NOV	0	0	0	0	0	0	3	22	24	26	25	22	19	16	10	12	10	0	0	0	0	0	0	0	15
DEC	0	0	0	0	0	0	0	9	19	21	19	16	15	12	8	17	6	0	0	0	0	0	0	0	12
ANNUAL	0	0	0	0	1	10	20	33	30	31	31	30	29	27	23	22	21	12	2	0	0	0	0	0	24

SOUTH

MONTH	1	2	3	4	5	6	7	8	9	10	11	12	13	14	15	16	17	18	19	20	21	22	23	24	HOURS
JAN	0	0	0	0	0	0	0	22	104	114	114	120	118	116	114	64	20	0	0	0	0	0	0	0	80
FEB	0	0	0	0	0	0	0	46	102	114	110	116	116	110	110	114	34	2	0	0	0	0	0	0	84
MAR	0	0	0	0	0	0	30	88	126	114	118	112	108	92	76	86	66	24	0	0	0	0	0	0	84
APR	0	0	0	0	0	10	62	90	82	78	68	76	70	54	52	46	60	24	2	0	0	0	0	0	56
MAY	0	0	0	0	0	30	72	82	78	68	66	70	68	52	46	42	40	22	12	0	0	0	0	0	56
JUN	0	0	0	0	2	28	64	70	74	64	66	66	60	50	40	42	34	30	14	0	0	0	0	0	52
JUL	0	0	0	0	0	26	68	94	82	68	62	68	60	50	38	40	32	24	14	0	0	0	0	0	54
AUG	0	0	0	0	0	12	74	102	88	78	68	78	72	52	48	48	60	30	4	0	0	0	0	0	64
SEP	0	0	0	0	0	4	62	112	106	94	98	102	96	74	62	74	52	22	0	0	0	0	0	0	80
OCT	0	0	0	0	0	0	26	124	128	126	128	124	120	108	106	98	30	2	0	0	0	0	0	0	96
NOV	0	0	0	0	0	0	4	72	122	126	122	126	126	120	112	58	16	0	0	0	0	0	0	0	84
DEC	0	0	0	0	0	0	0	28	112	122	126	126	130	130	126	52	12	0	0	0	0	0	0	0	84
ANNUAL	0	0	0	0	0	10	38	94	100	96	96	100	96	84	76	64	38	12	2	0	0	0	0	0	72

EAST

MONTH	1	2	3	4	5	6	7	8	9	10	11	12	13	14	15	16	17	18	19	20	21	22	23	24	HOURS
JAN	0	0	0	0	0	0	0	20	51	53	54	47	17	16	10	21	9	0	0	0	0	0	0	0	26
FEB	0	0	0	0	0	0	0	41	54	56	54	50	28	23	18	11	19	2	0	0	0	0	0	0	29
MAR	0	0	0	0	0	0	37	57	61	61	61	56	36	31	23	16	24	15	0	0	0	0	0	0	36
APR	0	0	0	0	0	23	54	55	57	58	59	55	45	40	33	25	16	20	2	0	0	0	0	0	39
MAY	0	0	0	0	0	54	60	59	59	61	61	59	54	48	39	31	22	19	11	0	0	0	0	0	46
JUN	0	0	0	0	7	55	59	59	60	61	61	59	53	46	38	30	23	15	14	0	0	0	0	0	46
JUL	0	0	0	0	3	55	59	61	63	62	62	59	50	43	39	31	24	15	14	0	0	0	0	0	46
AUG	0	0	0	0	0	30	59	59	59	61	61	58	47	41	32	25	18	24	4	0	0	0	0	0	43
SEP	0	0	0	0	0	7	57	60	61	62	61	53	39	32	24	17	17	15	0	0	0	0	0	0	40
OCT	0	0	0	0	0	0	35	60	59	59	59	41	27	22	14	9	17	1	0	0	0	0	0	0	33
NOV	0	0	0	0	0	0	6	52	59	59	58	32	20	15	11	13	9	0	0	0	0	0	0	0	26
DEC	0	0	0	0	0	0	0	30	54	58	58	41	15	12	8	17	6	0	0	0	0	0	0	0	25
ANNUAL	0	0	0	0	1	19	36	59	59	59	59	50	36	31	24	21	17	9	1	0	0	0	0	0	36

WEST

MONTH	1	2	3	4	5	6	7	8	9	10	11	12	13	14	15	16	17	18	19	20	21	22	23	24	HOURS
JAN	0	0	0	0	0	0	0	7	19	22	20	19	32	38	37	35	25	0	0	0	0	0	0	0	22
FEB	0	0	0	0	0	0	0	19	29	31	32	31	35	37	40	40	30	5	0	0	0	0	0	0	28
MAR	0	0	0	0	0	0	17	30	37	38	38	38	39	39	41	40	38	32	0	0	0	0	0	0	34
APR	0	0	0	0	0	9	31	37	39	40	41	41	41	41	41	40	38	28	4	0	0	0	0	0	35
MAY	0	0	0	0	0	28	38	39	41	41	42	42	42	42	42	41	37	28	24	0	0	0	0	0	38
JUN	0	0	0	0	2	29	37	40	41	41	41	41	41	41	40	40	38	34	32	0	0	0	0	0	38
JUL	0	0	0	0	1	25	37	41	42	42	42	42	42	42	41	41	39	39	37	30	0	0	0	0	38
AUG	0	0	0	0	0	10	34	40	40	41	41	42	42	42	42	41	41	37	10	0	0	0	0	0	38
SEP	0	0	0	0	0	2	28	37	40	41	41	41	41	41	41	39	38	30	0	0	0	0	0	0	37
OCT	0	0	0	0	0	0	13	32	34	35	35	32	37	38	39	38	32	2	0	0	0	0	0	0	31
NOV	0	0	0	0	0	0	2	20	25	26	25	22	39	40	40	37	20	0	0	0	0	0	0	0	24
DEC	0	0	0	0	0	0	0	9	20	22	20	17	40	40	40	37	16	0	0	0	0	0	0	0	22
ANNUAL	0	0	0	0	0	8	20	37	34	35	35	34	40	40	40	39	33	16	3	0	0	0	0	0	32

CORE (Top-lit)

MONTH	1	2	3	4	5	6	7	8	9	10	11	12	13	14	15	16	17	18	19	20	21	22	23	24	HOURS
JAN	0	0	0	0	0	0	0	5	19	36	47	50	49	47	30	17	5	0	0	0	0	0	0	0	27
FEB	0	0	0	0	0	0	0	15	32	47	50	50	51	51	47	25	11	1	0	0	0	0	0	0	33
MAR	0	0	0	0	0	0	10	30	53	54	54	54	54	54	53	42	24	8	0	0	0	0	0	0	41
APR	0	0	0	0	0	5	26	50	51	52	53	54	54	54	54	50	26	12	1	0	0	0	0	0	42
MAY	0	0	0	0	0	18	41	51	54	55	56	56	56	56	54	50	34	15	6	0	0	0	0	0	47
JUN	0	0	0	0	1	21	45	52	54	54	55	55	55	54	52	50	44	18	7	0	0	0	0	0	48
JUL	0	0	0	0	0	16	42	54	54	56	56	56	56	56	53	49	42	18	7	0	0	0	0	0	48
AUG	0	0	0	0	0	5	30	52	54	54	55	56	56	56	56	53	35	14	2	0	0	0	0	0	47
SEP	0	0	0	0	0	1	22	46	54	55	56	56	55	55	54	42	18	8	0	0	0	0	0	0	44
OCT	0	0	0	0	0	0	7	34	51	54	54	54	54	51	45	19	10	1	0	0	0	0	0	0	38
NOV	0	0	0	0	0	0	2	16	33	49	53	54	53	46	26	11	5	0	0	0	0	0	0	0	30
DEC	0	0	0	0	0	0	0	6	21	35	47	50	50	41	22	10	3	0	0	0	0	0	0	0	26
ANNUAL	0	0	0	0	0	6	19	47	45	50	53	54	54	51	46	35	22	6	1	0	0	0	0	0	39

AVERAGE ILLUMINANCE (FOOTCANDLES): LOS ANGELES

For a typical 2-story office building with 15'-0" deep perimeter zones and a top-lit core zone.

Weather Data:	Los Angeles (TMY)	Glass Type: ¼" solar bronze tinted (single pane)
% Opening:	37.5% WWR (windows)	(SC = 0.57; VT = 0.47)
	4% of roof area (skylights)	
Overhangs:	2'-3" (horizontal)	
Lighting Control Type:	Continuous	
No. of Ref. Points:	One (2'-6" high in the center of zone)	

NORTH

MONTH	1	2	3	4	5	6	7	8	9	10	11	12	13	14	15	16	17	18	19	20	21	22	23	24	HOURS
JAN	0	0	0	0	0	0	0	11	20	23	25	26	26	25	22	20	12	0	0	0	0	0	0	0	18
FEB	0	0	0	0	0	0	0	18	28	31	35	35	35	35	32	28	23	3	0	0	0	0	0	0	25
MAR	0	0	0	0	0	0	8	29	34	37	39	39	39	39	38	37	36	15	0	0	0	0	0	0	31
APR	0	0	0	0	0	3	24	29	37	39	39	39	39	39	39	37	35	29	0	0	0	0	0	0	33
MAY	0	0	0	0	0	10	24	35	38	39	39	39	39	39	39	39	37	35	6	0	0	0	0	0	35
JUN	0	0	0	0	0	13	26	34	37	39	39	39	39	39	39	38	36	35	17	0	0	0	0	0	35
JUL	0	0	0	0	0	7	29	35	37	38	38	39	39	39	39	39	37	36	14	0	0	0	0	0	35
AUG	0	0	0	0	0	3	25	33	36	39	39	39	39	38	39	38	37	32	1	0	0	0	0	0	34
SEP	0	0	0	0	0	1	13	28	35	38	39	39	39	39	38	37	35	15	0	0	0	0	0	0	33
OCT	0	0	0	0	0	0	8	22	29	34	37	37	37	36	32	32	20	0	0	0	0	0	0	0	28
NOV	0	0	0	0	0	0	2	18	23	26	28	30	29	28	25	20	8	0	0	0	0	0	0	0	19
DEC	0	0	0	0	0	0	0	11	19	22	25	26	26	25	21	17	5	0	0	0	0	0	0	0	17
ANNUAL	0	0	0	0	0	3	13	31	31	34	35	35	35	35	34	32	27	13	1	0	0	0	0	0	29

SOUTH

MONTH	1	2	3	4	5	6	7	8	9	10	11	12	13	14	15	16	17	18	19	20	21	22	23	24	HOURS
JAN	0	0	0	0	0	0	0	27	74	77	78	79	79	79	79	75	30	0	0	0	0	0	0	0	59
FEB	0	0	0	0	0	0	0	43	79	79	82	82	79	83	81	82	57	4	0	0	0	0	0	0	64
MAR	0	0	0	0	0	0	9	52	68	66	74	74	70	77	77	79	74	20	0	0	0	0	0	0	61
APR	0	0	0	0	0	3	26	44	55	60	57	59	60	59	65	60	66	31	0	0	0	0	0	0	51
MAY	0	0	0	0	0	7	26	46	59	59	59	64	62	60	62	57	56	33	4	0	0	0	0	0	52
JUN	0	0	0	0	0	9	29	39	51	56	59	64	61	57	56	52	53	34	10	0	0	0	0	0	49
JUL	0	0	0	0	0	5	29	51	49	53	55	57	59	56	55	55	60	40	9	0	0	0	0	0	49
AUG	0	0	0	0	0	3	27	53	55	59	56	60	59	56	61	60	64	34	0	0	0	0	0	0	52
SEP	0	0	0	0	0	0	14	51	57	68	68	64	65	72	70	78	60	18	0	0	0	0	0	0	59
OCT	0	0	0	0	0	0	12	47	66	68	78	82	85	83	85	85	38	0	0	0	0	0	0	0	62
NOV	0	0	0	0	0	0	3	49	73	75	75	77	79	79	81	73	16	0	0	0	0	0	0	0	56
DEC	0	0	0	0	0	0	0	34	77	79	79	79	82	85	82	70	10	0	0	0	0	0	0	0	59
ANNUAL	0	0	0	0	0	3	14	48	64	66	68	70	70	70	72	69	49	14	0	0	0	0	0	0	56

EAST

MONTH	1	2	3	4	5	6	7	8	9	10	11	12	13	14	15	16	17	18	19	20	21	22	23	24	HOURS
JAN	0	0	0	0	0	0	0	34	43	43	44	39	28	26	23	21	12	0	0	0	0	0	0	0	26
FEB	0	0	0	0	0	0	0	42	46	46	47	46	38	37	34	27	20	2	0	0	0	0	0	0	32
MAR	0	0	0	0	0	0	15	41	44	46	48	48	47	45	41	36	29	12	0	0	0	0	0	0	36
APR	0	0	0	0	0	5	32	39	46	48	48	49	49	48	44	39	32	20	0	0	0	0	0	0	39
MAY	0	0	0	0	0	18	32	47	48	48	49	49	49	49	48	43	36	25	4	0	0	0	0	0	42
JUN	0	0	0	0	0	24	36	44	46	48	49	49	49	49	47	42	34	29	11	0	0	0	0	0	42
JUL	0	0	0	0	0	14	41	45	47	47	48	49	49	49	46	41	35	28	9	0	0	0	0	0	41
AUG	0	0	0	0	0	6	32	43	47	48	49	48	49	48	46	40	33	20	1	0	0	0	0	0	41
SEP	0	0	0	0	0	1	22	40	43	48	49	49	48	45	41	34	28	11	0	0	0	0	0	0	39
OCT	0	0	0	0	0	0	19	36	44	46	48	44	40	37	34	28	17	0	0	0	0	0	0	0	33
NOV	0	0	0	0	0	0	5	41	42	43	43	34	30	29	25	20	7	0	0	0	0	0	0	0	25
DEC	0	0	0	0	0	0	0	38	46	45	46	34	28	27	21	18	5	0	0	0	0	0	0	0	25
ANNUAL	0	0	0	0	0	6	20	43	45	46	48	45	42	41	38	32	24	10	1	0	0	0	0	0	35

WEST

MONTH	1	2	3	4	5	6	7	8	9	10	11	12	13	14	15	16	17	18	19	20	21	22	23	24	HOURS
JAN	0	0	0	0	0	0	0	11	20	23	26	27	38	49	49	48	34	0	0	0	0	0	0	0	27
FEB	0	0	0	0	0	0	0	16	27	32	37	39	46	52	53	51	48	7	0	0	0	0	0	0	34
MAR	0	0	0	0	0	0	6	25	34	39	45	48	52	54	54	52	53	36	0	0	0	0	0	0	41
APR	0	0	0	0	0	2	18	27	37	46	49	51	54	53	53	51	51	48	0	0	0	0	0	0	44
MAY	0	0	0	0	0	6	21	34	46	50	52	55	55	55	55	55	53	52	11	0	0	0	0	0	46
JUN	0	0	0	0	0	9	23	34	44	49	53	54	54	54	53	52	51	50	33	0	0	0	0	0	46
JUL	0	0	0	0	0	5	23	34	40	46	50	53	54	54	54	55	53	52	29	0	0	0	0	0	45
AUG	0	0	0	0	0	2	18	29	40	44	49	53	54	52	54	54	54	51	2	0	0	0	0	0	44
SEP	0	0	0	0	0	0	10	25	34	42	47	49	54	55	55	53	53	33	0	0	0	0	0	0	42
OCT	0	0	0	0	0	0	7	20	28	35	41	41	52	54	55	55	48	0	0	0	0	0	0	0	37
NOV	0	0	0	0	0	0	2	16	22	27	30	31	48	51	52	49	23	0	0	0	0	0	0	0	29
DEC	0	0	0	0	0	0	0	11	20	23	27	27	41	51	51	48	14	0	0	0	0	0	0	0	27
ANNUAL	0	0	0	0	0	2	11	29	33	38	42	44	50	53	53	52	44	23	2	0	0	0	0	0	39

CORE (Top-lit)

MONTH	1	2	3	4	5	6	7	8	9	10	11	12	13	14	15	16	17	18	19	20	21	22	23	24	HOURS
JAN	0	0	0	0	0	0	0	6	22	40	51	52	53	51	42	22	7	0	0	0	0	0	0	0	30
FEB	0	0	0	0	0	0	0	12	31	51	54	55	54	54	54	38	17	2	0	0	0	0	0	0	37
MAR	0	0	0	0	0	0	5	22	46	54	56	56	56	56	56	53	28	7	0	0	0	0	0	0	42
APR	0	0	0	0	0	2	16	37	51	56	56	56	56	56	56	54	38	15	0	0	0	0	0	0	45
MAY	0	0	0	0	0	4	22	43	55	56	55	56	56	56	56	56	48	20	2	0	0	0	0	0	48
JUN	0	0	0	0	0	6	23	43	54	56	56	56	56	56	56	55	51	25	6	0	0	0	0	0	49
JUL	0	0	0	0	0	3	22	46	54	55	55	56	56	56	56	56	53	26	6	0	0	0	0	0	49
AUG	0	0	0	0	0	2	16	37	53	56	56	56	56	55	56	55	45	18	0	0	0	0	0	0	47
SEP	0	0	0	0	0	0	8	28	49	55	56	56	56	56	56	53	26	6	0	0	0	0	0	0	44
OCT	0	0	0	0	0	0	5	21	42	53	55	56	56	56	54	34	11	0	0	0	0	0	0	0	38
NOV	0	0	0	0	0	0	1	13	31	49	52	54	54	53	41	19	4	0	0	0	0	0	0	0	32
DEC	0	0	0	0	0	0	0	7	22	40	50	53	53	52	34	16	2	0	0	0	0	0	0	0	30
ANNUAL	0	0	0	0	0	2	10	36	42	52	54	55	55	54	51	42	28	8	0	0	0	0	0	0	41

AVERAGE ILLUMINANCE (FOOTCANDLES): NEW YORK

For a typical 2-story office building with 15'-0" deep perimeter zones and a top-lit core zone.

Weather Data:	New York (TMY)
% Opening:	37.5% WWR (windows)
	4% of roof area (skylights)
Overhangs:	2'-3" (horizontal)
Lighting Control Type:	Continuous
No. of Ref. Points:	One (2'-6" high in the center of zone)

Glass Type: ¼" solar bronze tinted (single pane)
(SC = 0.57; VT = 0.47)

NORTH

MONTH	1	2	3	4	5	6	7	8	9	10	11	12	13	14	15	16	17	18	19	20	21	22	23	24	HOURS
JAN	0	0	0	0	0	0	0	9	15	20	21	23	22	21	20	14	10	0	0	0	0	0	0	0	15
FEB	0	0	0	0	0	0	0	17	18	21	24	27	28	25	23	19	15	7	0	0	0	0	0	0	19
MAR	0	0	0	0	0	0	18	21	23	27	32	33	33	31	27	23	20	18	0	0	0	0	0	0	24
APR	0	0	0	0	0	16	21	29	31	33	36	36	36	35	34	33	31	25	10	0	0	0	0	0	30
MAY	0	0	0	0	0	26	31	36	37	38	41	42	40	40	38	36	36	33	24	0	0	0	0	0	36
JUN	0	0	0	0	10	28	32	34	37	39	41	42	42	41	40	38	34	33	31	8	0	0	0	0	36
JUL	0	0	0	0	7	30	33	38	40	41	42	41	40	40	39	37	38	35	35	8	0	0	0	0	37
AUG	0	0	0	0	0	29	36	39	39	40	42	43	43	42	42	38	40	38	28	0	0	0	0	0	38
SEP	0	0	0	0	0	9	33	37	38	39	39	40	40	41	40	38	36	29	4	0	0	0	0	0	36
OCT	0	0	0	0	0	0	19	31	33	36	38	36	36	36	32	30	28	5	0	0	0	0	0	0	29
NOV	0	0	0	0	0	0	5	18	21	26	28	27	26	26	22	20	13	0	0	0	0	0	0	0	19
DEC	0	0	0	0	0	0	0	12	16	21	23	25	23	21	18	13	7	0	0	0	0	0	0	0	15
ANNUAL	0	0	0	0	1	12	19	34	29	32	34	34	34	33	31	29	25	15	5	1	0	0	0	0	28

SOUTH

MONTH	1	2	3	4	5	6	7	8	9	10	11	12	13	14	15	16	17	18	19	20	21	22	23	24	HOURS
JAN	0	0	0	0	0	0	0	21	44	46	49	49	48	46	49	38	21	0	0	0	0	0	0	0	36
FEB	0	0	0	0	0	0	0	35	46	53	49	55	60	58	54	55	31	12	0	0	0	0	0	0	43
MAR	0	0	0	0	0	0	21	38	49	53	56	60	60	59	52	48	41	23	0	0	0	0	0	0	45
APR	0	0	0	0	0	13	28	43	46	47	52	55	53	52	49	46	24	8	0	0	0	0	0	0	44
MAY	0	0	0	0	0	21	32	49	56	52	59	64	61	60	56	54	49	33	17	0	0	0	0	0	51
JUN	0	0	0	0	7	22	38	46	52	58	58	61	66	61	59	55	46	35	26	6	0	0	0	0	52
JUL	0	0	0	0	5	23	39	55	62	62	63	61	58	55	55	54	55	41	29	6	0	0	0	0	54
AUG	0	0	0	0	0	28	45	58	63	61	67	70	68	67	64	60	60	47	26	0	0	0	0	0	59
SEP	0	0	0	0	0	9	41	63	64	66	63	68	66	66	64	66	59	35	3	0	0	0	0	0	59
OCT	0	0	0	0	0	0	37	60	63	66	69	67	63	66	62	61	51	7	0	0	0	0	0	0	55
NOV	0	0	0	0	0	0	8	45	58	58	63	63	54	61	60	54	28	0	0	0	0	0	0	0	45
DEC	0	0	0	0	0	0	0	31	46	51	51	52	53	52	48	39	14	0	0	0	0	0	0	0	37
ANNUAL	0	0	0	0	1	9	24	54	54	56	59	60	59	59	56	53	41	17	3	1	0	0	0	0	48

EAST

MONTH	1	2	3	4	5	6	7	8	9	10	11	12	13	14	15	16	17	18	19	20	21	22	23	24	HOURS
JAN	0	0	0	0	0	0	0	21	37	38	41	35	25	23	19	14	9	0	0	0	0	0	0	0	23
FEB	0	0	0	0	0	0	0	33	39	42	41	41	31	28	22	19	14	6	0	0	0	0	0	0	26
MAR	0	0	0	0	0	0	29	41	42	45	47	43	35	32	29	22	16	14	0	0	0	0	0	0	30
APR	0	0	0	0	0	25	36	48	47	46	47	44	40	39	34	33	25	18	7	0	0	0	0	0	35
MAY	0	0	0	0	0	40	44	51	54	53	54	52	49	47	43	37	31	23	17	0	0	0	0	0	43
JUN	0	0	0	0	14	40	44	46	50	50	52	52	53	51	49	43	34	30	26	5	0	0	0	0	44
JUL	0	0	0	0	10	44	45	51	56	56	55	50	48	47	44	42	42	34	31	5	0	0	0	0	46
AUG	0	0	0	0	0	41	53	56	57	56	57	55	53	51	49	43	41	32	23	0	0	0	0	0	48
SEP	0	0	0	0	0	14	48	51	55	54	53	53	50	49	48	42	36	23	3	0	0	0	0	0	45
OCT	0	0	0	0	0	0	36	51	51	52	54	49	41	40	33	28	23	4	0	0	0	0	0	0	38
NOV	0	0	0	0	0	0	9	42	48	46	47	35	30	27	22	19	12	0	0	0	0	0	0	0	26
DEC	0	0	0	0	0	0	0	30	40	40	41	32	25	22	18	14	6	0	0	0	0	0	0	0	22
ANNUAL	0	0	0	0	2	17	29	50	48	49	49	45	40	38	34	30	24	12	4	1	0	0	0	0	35

WEST

MONTH	1	2	3	4	5	6	7	8	9	10	11	12	13	14	15	16	17	18	19	20	21	22	23	24	HOURS
JAN	0	0	0	0	0	0	0	9	16	21	23	26	32	36	40	33	21	0	0	0	0	0	0	0	22
FEB	0	0	0	0	0	0	0	15	17	23	25	31	37	45	47	48	41	16	0	0	0	0	0	0	29
MAR	0	0	0	0	0	0	14	17	23	28	32	35	42	47	45	44	36	29	0	0	0	0	0	0	32
APR	0	0	0	0	0	11	15	21	28	33	37	41	43	48	50	48	49	44	16	0	0	0	0	0	38
MAY	0	0	0	0	0	20	23	33	39	43	47	51	51	54	55	51	52	50	36	0	0	0	0	0	43
JUN	0	0	0	0	7	23	29	37	41	46	50	52	55	55	55	52	50	46	43	12	0	0	0	0	46
JUL	0	0	0	0	5	23	30	40	49	50	51	50	49	50	49	50	53	50	50	12	0	0	0	0	46
AUG	0	0	0	0	0	24	33	41	46	49	53	56	55	57	57	55	59	57	40	0	0	0	0	0	49
SEP	0	0	0	0	0	7	26	36	44	46	47	52	52	54	53	55	50	43	5	0	0	0	0	0	45
OCT	0	0	0	0	0	0	19	28	35	39	41	42	49	53	50	52	50	8	0	0	0	0	0	0	38
NOV	0	0	0	0	0	0	4	16	23	27	31	30	38	49	50	43	27	0	0	0	0	0	0	0	28
DEC	0	0	0	0	0	0	0	13	17	21	23	26	37	41	37	33	15	0	0	0	0	0	0	0	23
ANNUAL	0	0	0	0	1	9	16	34	32	36	39	41	45	49	49	47	41	23	6	2	0	0	0	0	36

CORE (Top-lit)

MONTH	1	2	3	4	5	6	7	8	9	10	11	12	13	14	15	16	17	18	19	20	21	22	23	24	HOURS
JAN	0	0	0	0	0	0	0	5	12	20	25	26	25	24	20	11	5	0	0	0	0	0	0	0	15
FEB	0	0	0	0	0	0	0	8	15	26	28	30	31	31	28	19	10	3	0	0	0	0	0	0	20
MAR	0	0	0	0	0	0	6	13	25	30	32	33	33	32	30	25	14	7	0	0	0	0	0	0	23
APR	0	0	0	0	0	5	11	24	30	32	34	34	34	35	33	31	24	12	3	0	0	0	0	0	27
MAY	0	0	0	0	0	9	19	32	34	36	36	37	37	37	36	33	31	19	8	0	0	0	0	0	31
JUN	0	0	0	0	3	14	24	29	33	35	36	36	37	37	36	34	30	24	13	3	0	0	0	0	31
JUL	0	0	0	0	2	14	25	32	36	36	37	37	36	35	34	33	33	28	17	3	0	0	0	0	32
AUG	0	0	0	0	0	11	24	32	36	36	37	38	37	37	37	35	34	25	12	0	0	0	0	0	33
SEP	0	0	0	0	0	3	18	31	34	35	35	36	36	36	34	34	29	15	1	0	0	0	0	0	31
OCT	0	0	0	0	0	0	9	23	31	34	36	35	35	34	31	27	17	2	0	0	0	0	0	0	26
NOV	0	0	0	0	0	0	2	13	21	27	31	32	29	29	25	15	6	0	0	0	0	0	0	0	19
DEC	0	0	0	0	0	0	0	7	14	22	25	26	26	24	17	10	3	0	0	0	0	0	0	0	15
ANNUAL	0	0	0	0	1	5	12	29	27	31	32	34	33	32	30	26	20	8	2	1	0	0	0	0	25

AVERAGE ILLUMINANCE (FOOTCANDLES): SEATTLE

For a typical 2-story office building with 15'-0" deep perimeter zones and a top-lit core zone.

Weather Data: Seattle (TMY)

% Opening: 37.5% WWR (windows)

4% of roof area (skylights)

Overhangs: 2'-3" (horizontal)

Lighting Control Type: Continuous

No. of Ref. Points: One (2'-6" high in the center of zone)

Glass Type: 1/4" solar bronze tinted (single pane)
(SC = 0.57; VT = 0.47)

NORTH

MONTH	1	2	3	4	5	6	7	8	9	10	11	12	13	14	15	16	17	18	19	20	21	22	23	24	HOURS
JAN	0	0	0	0	0	0	0	0	6	14	20	23	23	23	18	11	3	0	0	0	0	0	0	0	13
FEB	0	0	0	0	0	0	0	2	13	20	25	27	27	27	18	11	1	0	0	0	0	0	0	0	17
MAR	0	0	0	0	0	0	6	16	22	26	30	32	33	31	31	28	23	15	0	0	0	0	0	0	24
APR	0	0	0	0	0	4	19	31	32	33	34	35	35	34	34	33	29	23	8	0	0	0	0	0	29
MAY	0	0	0	0	0	15	24	29	31	33	34	34	35	34	32	30	28	25	22	4	0	0	0	0	29
JUN	0	0	0	0	2	14	23	29	33	35	35	34	34	35	35	34	32	30	26	11	0	0	0	0	31
JUL	0	0	0	0	1	18	24	28	32	33	35	35	35	35	35	35	34	33	29	9	0	0	0	0	32
AUG	0	0	0	0	0	7	23	30	33	34	35	35	35	35	35	34	33	31	19	1	0	0	0	0	31
SEP	0	0	0	0	0	0	12	23	27	31	33	33	34	34	32	31	27	17	2	0	0	0	0	0	28
OCT	0	0	0	0	0	0	2	13	18	24	27	28	29	27	23	18	12	1	0	0	0	0	0	0	19
NOV	0	0	0	0	0	0	0	2	12	19	23	24	23	21	17	10	1	0	0	0	0	0	0	0	14
DEC	0	0	0	0	0	0	0	0	4	10	15	17	15	15	11	4	0	0	0	0	0	0	0	0	8
ANNUAL	0	0	0	0	0	5	11	25	22	26	29	30	30	29	27	24	20	12	4	2	0	0	0	0	23

SOUTH

MONTH	1	2	3	4	5	6	7	8	9	10	11	12	13	14	15	16	17	18	19	20	21	22	23	24	HOURS
JAN	0	0	0	0	0	0	0	0	13	22	28	30	31	31	29	21	6	0	0	0	0	0	0	0	19
FEB	0	0	0	0	0	0	0	3	22	27	36	37	36	36	36	30	20	1	0	0	0	0	0	0	25
MAR	0	0	0	0	0	0	6	22	29	32	37	41	42	41	41	39	33	21	0	0	0	0	0	0	32
APR	0	0	0	0	0	3	23	41	41	43	45	46	47	44	45	42	37	27	6	0	0	0	0	0	38
MAY	0	0	0	0	0	13	29	35	39	43	44	45	46	45	43	39	34	29	20	2	0	0	0	0	38
JUN	0	0	0	0	1	11	25	34	41	46	46	46	46	46	46	44	41	37	21	7	0	0	0	0	41
JUL	0	0	0	0	1	13	29	35	41	45	47	48	48	48	48	46	44	25	6	0	0	0	0	0	42
AUG	0	0	0	0	0	5	25	38	42	45	48	48	48	48	48	44	44	40	16	1	0	0	0	0	41
SEP	0	0	0	0	0	0	15	30	34	40	43	44	46	45	45	44	38	23	1	0	0	0	0	0	37
OCT	0	0	0	0	0	0	3	24	31	32	36	38	38	35	33	28	20	1	0	0	0	0	0	0	27
NOV	0	0	0	0	0	0	0	4	28	32	34	36	33	33	29	22	1	0	0	0	0	0	0	0	22
DEC	0	0	0	0	0	0	0	0	10	20	24	25	25	26	18	8	0	0	0	0	0	0	0	0	14
ANNUAL	0	0	0	0	0	4	13	32	31	36	39	40	41	40	39	34	27	15	3	1	0	0	0	0	32

EAST

MONTH	1	2	3	4	5	6	7	8	9	10	11	12	13	14	15	16	17	18	19	20	21	22	23	24	HOURS
JAN	0	0	0	0	0	0	0	0	15	21	27	27	24	24	19	10	3	0	0	0	0	0	0	0	16
FEB	0	0	0	0	0	0	0	4	23	27	33	34	30	30	25	19	10	1	0	0	0	0	0	0	21
MAR	0	0	0	0	0	0	9	23	29	32	36	38	38	36	36	30	23	13	0	0	0	0	0	0	28
APR	0	0	0	0	0	7	26	39	39	41	42	44	44	42	41	36	30	20	5	0	0	0	0	0	34
MAY	0	0	0	0	0	22	31	34	38	41	42	42	43	42	40	36	31	25	18	3	0	0	0	0	36
JUN	0	0	0	0	3	20	29	36	40	44	44	43	42	43	41	38	36	30	22	7	0	0	0	0	38
JUL	0	0	0	0	1	28	32	36	40	42	44	46	45	45	44	42	38	33	23	6	0	0	0	0	39
AUG	0	0	0	0	0	13	31	40	42	44	45	44	44	44	39	35	29	12	1	0	0	0	0	0	38
SEP	0	0	0	0	0	1	23	30	34	38	41	42	42	40	36	33	25	13	1	0	0	0	0	0	33
OCT	0	0	0	0	0	0	4	28	30	31	33	34	33	30	25	19	11	1	0	0	0	0	0	0	24
NOV	0	0	0	0	0	0	0	6	29	29	31	29	27	23	18	10	1	0	0	0	0	0	0	0	18
DEC	0	0	0	0	0	0	0	0	10	18	21	21	16	16	11	4	0	0	0	0	0	0	0	0	10
ANNUAL	0	0	0	0	1	8	16	33	31	34	36	37	36	34	32	27	21	10	3	1	0	0	0	0	28

WEST

MONTH	1	2	3	4	5	6	7	8	9	10	11	12	13	14	15	16	17	18	19	20	21	22	23	24	HOURS
JAN	0	0	0	0	0	0	0	0	6	14	20	24	26	30	29	21	7	0	0	0	0	0	0	0	16
FEB	0	0	0	0	0	0	0	1	12	19	27	30	32	36	35	31	23	1	0	0	0	0	0	0	22
MAR	0	0	0	0	0	0	4	15	23	27	35	40	42	42	42	40	37	28	0	0	0	0	0	0	31
APR	0	0	0	0	0	2	17	36	37	42	45	47	48	45	46	43	39	33	15	0	0	0	0	0	39
MAY	0	0	0	0	0	12	24	32	37	41	44	45	46	46	45	40	37	36	34	7	0	0	0	0	37
JUN	0	0	0	0	1	12	21	32	40	45	46	46	46	48	48	48	44	41	37	22	0	0	0	0	41
JUL	0	0	0	0	1	12	21	30	37	42	47	49	50	50	50	49	48	46	42	19	0	0	0	0	42
AUG	0	0	0	0	0	4	18	32	37	42	48	48	50	49	49	47	48	46	36	1	0	0	0	0	41
SEP	0	0	0	0	0	0	9	22	28	35	40	42	46	47	46	45	40	32	4	0	0	0	0	0	35
OCT	0	0	0	0	0	0	1	12	19	27	30	32	37	35	33	30	24	2	0	0	0	0	0	0	24
NOV	0	0	0	0	0	0	0	2	12	19	24	26	30	32	30	24	1	0	0	0	0	0	0	0	17
DEC	0	0	0	0	0	0	0	0	4	11	14	17	20	24	18	9	0	0	0	0	0	0	0	0	11
ANNUAL	0	0	0	0	0	4	10	26	24	31	35	37	40	40	40	36	30	18	6	4	0	0	0	0	30

CORE (Top-lit)

MONTH	1	2	3	4	5	6	7	8	9	10	11	12	13	14	15	16	17	18	19	20	21	22	23	24	HOURS
JAN	0	0	0	0	0	0	0	0	4	12	19	23	25	22	16	8	1	0	0	0	0	0	0	0	12
FEB	0	0	0	0	0	0	0	1	9	19	28	32	33	31	26	16	7	1	0	0	0	0	0	0	18
MAR	0	0	0	0	0	0	2	10	21	29	34	38	39	37	38	33	19	7	0	0	0	0	0	0	27
APR	0	0	0	0	0	1	11	34	38	41	43	44	44	42	43	39	31	16	3	0	0	0	0	0	34
MAY	0	0	0	0	0	7	20	32	38	40	42	43	44	42	40	37	31	21	10	1	0	0	0	0	35
JUN	0	0	0	0	1	8	19	32	40	44	44	43	43	44	44	44	40	31	16	4	0	0	0	0	38
JUL	0	0	0	0	0	8	20	33	39	42	44	46	46	46	46	46	43	36	16	3	0	0	0	0	39
AUG	0	0	0	0	0	3	14	32	41	44	46	46	46	46	46	43	40	25	7	0	0	0	0	0	38
SEP	0	0	0	0	0	0	6	20	31	36	40	41	42	42	41	39	24	8	1	0	0	0	0	0	32
OCT	0	0	0	0	0	0	1	10	19	28	33	34	35	31	25	16	7	1	0	0	0	0	0	0	21
NOV	0	0	0	0	0	0	0	1	10	20	25	29	27	23	16	7	0	0	0	0	0	0	0	0	14
DEC	0	0	0	0	0	0	0	0	3	8	14	16	16	14	9	3	0	0	0	0	0	0	0	0	8
ANNUAL	0	0	0	0	0	2	8	26	25	31	34	36	36	35	33	28	21	9	1	1	0	0	0	0	27

Appendix G

Post Occupancy Visual Comfort Evaluation Form
Questionnaire for Daylighted Spaces (Uncontrolled Cases)

Space I.D. and respondent _____

Date _____ Time _____

Weather conditions (clear, partly cloudy, or cloudy) _____

Number of persons occupying the space _____

Location of respondent's work area (check one):

    _____ center of room and along wall

    _____ along wall opposite window

    _____ along side wall

    _____ along wall at window

Please **circle** the appropriate responses describing the conditions in your office at the **present time:**

    Electric light sensor: On/Off

    Position of miniblinds: fully raised/partially raised/completely lowered

    Angle of partially raised or lowered miniblinds: closed up/45-degree angled up/90-degree open/45-degree angled down/closed down

    Position of door: open/closed

The following questions ask you to provide perceptual responses to lighting levels for a variety of everyday tasks you carry out in your office: **desk work, computer work, filing tasks,** and **social meetings.** For each task, please answer the full set of questions and provide comments as you like. Brief definitions of several lighting terms have been included at the end of the questionnaire should you have any questions regarding terminology. **Thanks for your help!**

1. Your impressions of the space at this time:

very unpleasant	O	O	O	O	O	very pleasant
not enough light to work	O	O	O	O	O	too much light to work
room too dark	O	O	O	O	O	room too light

Take a little time to adapt to each of the following five tasks **before** responding to the questions about lighting in these areas:

2.   Desk work–writing and paperwork at main desk area:

   A.   Is the lighting adequate?

   totally inadequate   ○   ○   ○   ○   ○   completely adequate

   B.   Are there reflections on your work surface?

   many ○   ○   ○   ○   ○   none

   C.   And are they annoying?

   very annoying ○   ○   ○   ○   ○   not at all

   D.   Is the brightness of this work area in relation to the rest of the room

   too bright?   ○   ○   ○   ○   ○   too dark?

3.   Desk work–reading papers or a book at main desk area:

   A.   Is the lighting adequate?

   totally inadequate   ○   ○   ○   ○   ○   completely adequate

   B.   Are there reflections on your work surface?

   many ○   ○   ○   ○   ○   none

   C.   And are they annoying?

   very annoying ○   ○   ○   ○   ○   not at all

   D.   Is the brightness of this work in relation to the rest of the room

   too bright?   ○   ○   ○   ○   ○   too dark?

4.   Computer work–data entry looking at desk top near computer:

   A.   Is the lighting adequate?

   totally inadequate   ○   ○   ○   ○   ○   completely adequate

   B.   Are there reflections on your work surface?

   many ○   ○   ○   ○   ○   none

   C.   And are they annoying?

   very annoying ○   ○   ○   ○   ○   not at all

   D.   Is the brightness of this work in relation to the rest of the room

   too bright?   ○   ○   ○   ○   ○   too dark?

5. Computer work–data editing looking at the computer screen:

   A. Is the lighting adequate?

   totally inadequate   ○   ○   ○   ○   ○   completely adequate

   B. Are there reflections on your work surface?

   many   ○   ○   ○   ○   ○   none

   C. And are they annoying?

   very annoying   ○   ○   ○   ○   ○   not at all

   D. Is the brightness of this work in relation to the rest of the room

   too bright?   ○   ○   ○   ○   ○   too dark?

6. Filing:

   A. Is the lighting adequate?

   totally inadequate   ○   ○   ○   ○   ○   completely adequate

   B. Are there reflections on your work surface?

   many   ○   ○   ○   ○   ○   none

   C. And are they annoying?

   very annoying   ○   ○   ○   ○   ○   not at all

   D. Is the brightness of this work in relation to the rest of the room

   too bright?   ○   ○   ○   ○   ○   too dark?

7. Is there anything in the room which is very bright and, if so, what is it?

   Is this

   very distracting?   ○   ○   ○   ○   ○   not distracting?

8. Is there glare from the windows?

   intolerable glare   ○   ○   ○   ○   ○   no glare

9. Is there a brightness contrast between the room and what you see through the window?

   great contrast   ○   ○   ○   ○   ○   no contrast

10. Is the amount of view through the window

   inadequate?   ○   ○   ○   ○   ○   adequate?

11. Is the quality of the view through the window

   unpleasant?   ○   ○   ○   ○   ○   pleasant?

Please **take the place** of someone who would be sitting in your office to visit or work; where are you located?

_____ opposite the window

_____ facing the wall

_____ facing both window and wall at an angle

12. Facing the direction where you would normally sit to meet with someone, is the view comfortable in terms of glare?

uncomfortable   ○   ○   ○   ○   ○   comfortable

13. From this position are the two areas of your office indicated below decidedly dark or bright?

wall perpendicular to window

too dark   ○   ○   ○   ○   ○   too bright

wall opposite window

too dark   ○   ○   ○   ○   ○   too bright

Do you have any **comments** on the quality of light in your office at this time?

Thanks for your cooperation!

GLOSSARY

Absorptance. The ratio of the luminous flux absorbed by the body to the flux it receives.

Absorption. Transformation of radiant energy to a different form of energy by the intervention of matter.

Altitude. The angular distance of the sun measured upward from the horizon on that vertical plane that passes through the sun. It is measured positively from horizon to zenith from 0 to 90 degrees.

Ambient lighting. Lighting throughout an area that produces general illumination.

Angle of incidence. The angle between a ray of light falling on a surface and a line normal (perpendicular) to the surface. The angle of incidence for specific conditions can be obtained with the use of the LOF Sun Angle Calculator. To calculate angle of incidence on a vertical window (ai), find solar altitude (at) and window azimuth orientation from sun (az).

Azimuth. The azimuth of the sun is the angle between the vertical plane containing sun and the plane of the horizon.

Ballast. A device used with a fluorescent lamp to obtain the necessary circuit conditions for starting and operating.

Blinding glare. Glare so intense that for an appreciable time no object can be seen.

Brightness. The subjective attribute of any light sensation giving rise to the perception of luminous intensity—a subjective sensation. (The preferable term for photometric, or measurable, quantity is *luminance*.)

Candela. The unit of luminous intensity. The magnitude of the candela is such that the lumi-nance of a full radiator at the temperature of solidification of platinum is 60 candelas/cm^2.

Candela per square meter. A unit of luminance recommended by the CIE.

Clear sky. A sky that has less than 30% cloud cover.

Clerestory. That part of a building rising clear of the roof or other parts whose walls contain windows for lighting of interiors.

Cloudy sky. A sky having more than 70% cloud cover.

Coefficient of utilization (cu). The ratio of the luminous flux (lumens) for a light source (luminaire, window, skylight, etc.) received on the work plane to the lumens emitted by the light source.

Daylight. The light from the sun and sky.

Daylight saturation. The condition where the interior daylight illuminance level equals or exceeds the specified design illuminance level and the lighting control system thus provides maximum lighting energy savings. At saturation, any further increase in daylight illuminance will not produce additional lighting energy savings.

Diffuse. A device used to alter the spatial distribution of the luminous flux from a source and depending essentially on the phenomenon of diffusion.

Diffuse reflection. Diffusion by reflection in which, on the macroscopic scale, there is no direct reflection.

Diffuse transmission. Transmission in which light is scattered in many directions and, on the macroscopic scale, independent of the laws of refraction.

Diffuse transmittance. The ratio of the luminous flux diffusely transmitted in all directions (other than that of direct transmission) to the total incident flux.

Diffusion. Alteration of the spatial distribution of a beam of light, which, after reflection at a surface or passage through a medium, travels on in numerous directions.

Direct glare. Glare due to a luminous object situated in the same or nearly the same direction as the object viewed.

Direct reflectance. The ratio of the luminous flux, reflected in accordance with the laws of regular reflection, to the total incident flux.

Direct (regular or specular) reflection. Reflection in accordance with the laws of optical reflection (e.g., in a mirror).

Direct transmittance. The ratio of the luminous flux transmitted in accordance with the laws of direct transmission to the total incident flux.

Disability glare. Excessive contrast, especially to the extent that visibility of one part of the field is obscured by the attempt by the eye to adapt to the brightness of the other part.

Discomfort glare. Glare that causes discomfort without necessarily impairing the vision of objects.

Effective aperture (EA). A measure of the light transmitting ability of a fenestration system. Effective aperture is the product of the skylight-to-floor ratio (SFR) and the visible transmittance (VT). EA values range from 0 to 1.0 and are typically less than 0.1 for most practical skylight systems.

Emission. Release of radiant energy.

Equivalent room. A theoretical room whose dimensions are adjusted to compensate for the effects of special conditions in an actual room. A room with an overhanging window shading device has some of the same coefficients of utilization as a larger room without such overhang.

Fenestration. Any opening or arrangement of openings for the admission of daylight or air.

Footcandle. The illumination on a surface 1 square foot in area on which there is a uniformly distributed flux of 1 lumen:

$$1 \text{ fc} = 10.76 \text{ lux} = 10.76 \text{ lumens/m}^2$$

Footlambert. A unit of luminance equal to the uniform luminance of a perfectly diffusing surface emitting or reflecting light at the rate of 1 lumen per square foot; or the average luminance of any surface emitting or reflecting light at that rate.

Glare. The effect of luminance or luminance differences within the visual field sufficiently high to cause annoyance, discomfort, or loss in visual performance. *Direct glare* is glare resulting from high-luminance or insufficiently shielded light sources in the field of view, or reflecting areas of high luminance and large area. *Reflected glare* is glare resulting from reflections of high-luminance sources by surfaces in the field of view.

Illuminance (illumination). The density of luminous flux (light) incident on a surface.

Illumination. Light falling on a surface.

Illumination at a point of a surface. The quotient of the luminous flux incident on an infinitesimal element of surface containing the point under consideration by the area of that element.

Indirect glare. Glare due to a luminous object situated in a direction other than that of the object viewed.

Latitude. The geographical latitude of a point is the angle measured in the plane of the local meridian between the equator and a line perpendicular to the surface of the earth through the point in question.

Light. For the purpose of illuminating engineering, light is radiant energy evaluated according to its capacity to produce visual sensation. *Skylight* is visible radiation from the sun redirected by the atmosphere. *Sunlight* is direct visible radiation from the sun.

Lighting power density (LPD). A measure of the amount of electric lighting installed in a building. Expressed as the number of watts of lighting power required for the luminaires and lamps installed in a building, divided by the gross number of square feet in the building (watts per square foot).

Light-loss factor. The ratio of the light transmission or utilization after a designated period of time to the initial light transmission or utilization. This is a measure of deterioration because of accumulation of dust or dirt.

Light wells. Light wells are extensively used to bring light through the roof structure and help control light distribution. Local solar geometry (altitude and azimuth of the sun change hourly and seasonally), surface reflectance of the well (influenced by structural material and paint color), and wall slope are basic considerations.

Longitude. The angular distance measure along the earth's equator from the meridian through Greenwich, England, to the local meridian through the point in question. Longitude is measured either east or west from Greenwich through 180 degrees or 12 hours.

Lumen. The unit of luminous flux. It is equal to the flux through a unit of solid angle (steradian) from a uniform point source of one candela; or the flux on a unit surface all points of which are at a unit distance from a uniform point of one candela.

Luminaire. A complete lighting unit consisting of a lamp, or lamps, together with parts designed to distribute the light, to position and protect the lamps, and to connect the lamps to the power supply.

Luminance (photometric brightness). The luminous intensity of any surface in a given direction per unit or projected area of the surface as viewed from that direction.

Luminous efficacy (LE). A measure of the luminous efficiency of a radiant flux, expressed in lumens per watt. For daylighting, this is the ratio of visible flux incident on a surface divided by the radiant flux on that surface. For electric sources, it is the ratio of the total luminous flux emitted divided by the total lamp or luminaire power input.

Luminous flux. The quantity characteristic of radiant flux which expresses its capacity to produce a luminous sensation evaluated according to the values of relative luminous efficiency. Unless otherwise indicated, the luminous flux in question relates to photopic vision and is connected with the radian flux in accordance with the formula adopted in 1948 by the CIE (International Lighting Vocabulary tabulates the relative luminous efficiency of radiation in terms of this agreed formula.)

Lux. The International System (SI) unit of illumination. It is the illumination on a surface 1 square meter in area on which there is a uniformly distributed flux of 1 lumen.

Mean spherical intensity. The average value of the luminous intensity of a source in all directions. Note: It is also the quotient of the total luminous flux by the total solid angle, 4π steradians.

Mixed reflection. The simultaneous occurrence of regular reflection and of diffuse reflection.

Optical density. The logarithm to the base 10 of the reciprocal of the transmission factor.

Overcast sky. Sky completely covered by clouds, with no sun visible.

Perfect diffuser. An ideal uniform diffuser with zero absorption factor. (Note: Practical uniform diffusers always have an absorption factor greater than zero.)

Perfect diffusion. Ideal diffusion in which the whole of the incident light is redistributed uniformly in all possible directions in such a way that the luminance is the same in all directions. (Note: A surface possessing this property is sometimes called "perfectly matte.")

Point source. Source of radiant energy of dimensions negligible compared with the distance between source and receptor.

Profile angle. The projection of the true solar altitude angle on a vertical plane perpendicular to a wall.

Quantity of light. The product of luminous flux and the time during which it is maintained. (Note: The lumen-hour and lumen-second are the quantities of light equal to 1 lumen radiated or received for 1 hour and 1 second, respectively.)

Radiation. Energy in the form of electromagnetic waves or particles.

Reflectance. The ratio of light reflected by a body to the incident light; the total reflection factor of a layer of material of such thickness that there is no change of reflection factor with increase in thickness.

Reflected glare. Glare produced by specular reflections of luminous objects, especially reflections appearing on or near the object viewed.

Reflection. Backward reflection of radiation by a surface without change of frequency of the monochromatic components of which the radiation is composed.

Shading. Use of fixed or movable shading devices can help block, diffuse, or redirect incoming light to control unwanted heat gains and glare.

Shading coefficient (SC). The dimensionless ratio of the total solar heat gain from a particular glazing system to that for one sheet of clear 3 mm (⅛ in.) double-strength glass. The solar heat gain is the sum of the transmitted solar energy plus that portion of the absorbed solar energy that flows inward.

Site energy. Energy consumed at the building site.

Skylight efficacy. Another design parameter, determined by dividing the product of visible transmittance (VT) and well factor (WF) by the shading coefficient, SC (the fraction of solar heat that enters through the skylight glazing).

Skylight-to-floor ratio (SFR). The ratio of skylight opening area to gross daylit floor area.

Solar altitude. The vertical angular distance of the sun in the sky above the horizon.

Solar azimuth. The horizontal angular distance between the vertical plane containing the sun and true south.

Source energy. Total energy consumed including transmission losses and power source.

(Total) transmission factor of a body (total transmittance). The ratio of the luminous flux transmitted by the body to that which it receives. In mixed transmission, the (total) transmission factor is the sum of two components, the direct transmission factor and the diffuse transmission factor.

Transmission. Passage of radiation through a medium without change of frequency of the monochromatic components of which the radiation is composed.

Transmittance. The ratio of the light transmitted by the material to the incident light. *Regular* or *direct transmittance* is that in which the transmitted light is not diffused. In such transmission, the direction of a transmitted beam of light has a definite geometrical relationship to corresponding incident beam. *Diffuse transmittance* of a material is the ratio of the diffusely transmitted light to the incident light.

Uniform diffuse reflection. Diffusion by reflection such that the luminance is the same in all directions.

Uniform diffuser. A diffuser for which the luminance is the same in all directions regardless of the direction of incidence of the light.

Uniform ground. The average brightness of the ground, including all the various reflectances of different ground materials.

Uniform point source. A point source that emits radiation uniformly in all directions.

U-value. A measure of a material's heat transfer capabilities when placed between two spaces of different temperatures, typically given in Btu/hr = ft^2 = °F. The U-value is the inverse of the R-value, which measures the material's resistance to heat transfer.

Veiling reflection. Regular reflections superimposed on diffuse reflections from an object that partially or totally obscures the details to be seen by reducing the contrast. This is sometimes called reflected glare.

Visible radiation or radiant energy. Any radiation capable of causing a visual sensation directly. The wavelength range of such radiation can be considered for practical purposes to lie between 380 and 780 nm.

Well factor (WF). The ratio of the amount of visible light leaving a skylight well to the amount of visible light entering the skylight.

Well index (WI). A parameter used to determine the light well efficiency. Well index is a measure of the geometric shape of the well, and is calculated as follows:

$$\text{Well index} = \frac{\text{Well height (well length + well width)}}{2 \times \text{well length} \times \text{well width}}$$

A light well with proportions of a cube always has a well index of 1.0.

SYMBOLS

DG:	Double glazing
EA:	Effective aperture
fc:	Footcandle
kWh:	Kilowatt-hour
LE:	Luminous efficacy
lm:	Lumen
lm/W:	Lumens per watt
LPD:	Lighting power density
R:	Reflectance
SC:	Shading coefficient
SE:	Skylight efficacy
SFR:	Skylight-to-floor ratio
SG:	Single glazing
VDT:	Visual display terminal
WF:	Well factor
WI:	Well index
W/ft^2:	Watts per square foot

ANNOTATED BIBLIOGRAPHY

AIA/ACSA Council on Architectural Research, *Energy Tools: New Products for Architects,* National Energy Laboratories, Washington, D.C., 1992.

The U.S. Department of Energy operates four laboratories that conduct research on energy-efficient building applications. This document describes each laboratory's activities plus products that were developed to assist building design professionals. These products include handbooks, design manuals, and computer software.

American Institute of Architects, *Architect's Handbook of Energy Practice: Daylighting,* American Institute of Architects, Washington, D.C., 1992.

This handbook is part of a series of monographs published by the AIA on energy-conscious design. It is meant to provide architects with the basic concepts of daylighting. The text is supported with case studies of famous buildings that utilize daylighting.

Ander, Gregg D., *The Integration of Architectural Art and Load-Reducing Fenestration: Daylighting Case Studies,* Thermal Performance of the Exterior Envelopes of Buildings IV, ASHRAE, Atlanta, pp. 108–125.

This article contains six case studies of buildings that utilize daylighting to reduce energy consumption. The daylighting strategies were described and results of DOE-2 computer models given. Significant savings were shown for each project when compared with a base case building.

Ander, Gregg D., and Wilcox, Joe S., *Fenestration Modeling Techniques,* Research and Design 85 Proceedings, March 1985, American Institute of Architects, Washington, D.C., pp. 83–88.

This paper discusses a methodology for analyzing complex fenestration systems and room geometries. This procedure can be used in conjunction with an hourly simulation program to determine the impacts of lighting, mechanical, and peak loads.

Bennett, David J., and Ewadi, David A., Solar Optics: Light as Energy; Energy as Light, *Underground Space,* 4(6):349–354.

This paper reviews the high-technology ideas of beaming light and images to underground spaces. They are state-of-the-art concepts and how they will be tested in a design application being developed for the Civil/Mineral Engineering building at the University of Minnesota.

Bennett, Robert, *Sun Angles for Design,* Robert Bennett, Bala Cynwyd, Pa., 1978.

This book contains sun path diagrams in two-degree increments from 0 to 60 degrees north latitude. It includes examples of how to use these diagrams to determine shadow patterns, prepare solar site analyses and evaluate the effectiveness of shading devices.

Bevington, Rick, and Rosenfeld, Arthur H., Energy for Buildings and Homes, *Scientific American,* September 1990, pp. 77–86.

This article presents and supports an argument that energy conservation in buildings could result in a savings of 50%. The article also describes many of the new technologies available and how they will affect energy usage. The impacts on cost, environment, and thermal comfort are covered in detail.

Boles, Daralice D., Modernism in the City, *Progressive Architecture,* July 1987, pp. 72–79.

The article focuses on the design strategies of the Institut du Monde Arabe (Arab World Institute) in Paris, by French architect Jean Nouvel.

It is a building that combines architecture and technology into a unique sun control device. Some attention is paid to daylighting because it had a strong influence on the design. The building's most notable features are the sun-controlling apertures along the south facade. The architect was successful in creating a sun control device that makes a strong architectural statement consistent with the design concept.

Bryan, Harvey, Standard 90.1P—Daylighting: Energy Conservation, *Architectural Record,* June 1988, p. 156.

Standard 90 and 90.1P were prepared by ASHRAE and the Department of Energy and serve as the model energy conservation code for the United States. Standard 90.1P is a much more flexible revision of Standard 90. The article is concerned primarily with describing the various compliance methods as they relate to daylighting.

Bryan, Harvey J., Simplified Procedure for Calculating the Effects of Daylight from Clear Skies, *Journal of IES,* April 1980, pp. 142–151.

This may be the most important work in the last decade. Using the Daylight Factor method, Bryan has reworked the method recommended by the CIE for use with clear sky conditions. This has been the major hindrance to the use of the Daylight Factor method in the United States, because the Daylight Factor method was developed using overcast or uniform sky conditions. The paper outlines the theory and procedure, the latter being incomplete at the time of this writing.

Bryan, Harvey, and Clear, Robert. *A Procedure for Calculating Interior Daylight Illumination with a Programmable Hand Calculator,* Fifth National Passive Solar Conference, October 1980, pp. 1192–1196.

A procedure is described for calculating interior daylight illumination using an inexpensive programmable hand calculator. The proposed procedure calculates illumination at any point within a room utilizing sky luminance distribution functions that are consistent with the CIE overcast and clear sky functions. This procedure separates the light reaching the point being considered into three components. Two examples are presented to demonstrate the proposed procedure and indicate the speed with which the calculations may be performed.

Building Research Station (BRS), Estimating Daylighting in Buildings: Parts 1 and 2, *Building Research Station Digest,* 42:1–7, January 1977.

Here the Daylight Factor method of analysis is outlined from the source (BRS). This is an excellent condensation of the very basic principles first presented in Hopkinson's *Daylighting.*

Burt Hill Kosar Rittleman Associates, *Thermal and Optical Performance Characteristics of Reflective Light Shelves in Buildings,* Washington, D.C.

This is a study performed with funding provided by the Department of Energy to examine the effectiveness of light shelves for increasing levels of daylight within buildings. The reports concluded that light shelves increase light quality through better distribution but are ineffective at increasing light quantity deep within a space. This conclusion is based on the fact that to increase lighting levels, the light shelves would have to reflect 19% to 24% of the light that hits them. Materials currently being used for reflecting surfaces do not meet these criteria.

Burt Hill Kosar Rittleman Associates, Constructing a Daylighting Model, *Architectural Technology,* Fall 1983, pp. 50–51.

Written by associates in an architectural firm, this article outlines how to use scale models during the schematic and design development phases of a project. Many good tips on construction and photographic techniques were given.

Burt Hill Kosar Rittleman Associates, Stepping Through Daylighting, *Architectural Technology,* Fall 1983, pp. 36–49.

This article is a step-by-step guide to incorporating daylighting into the different phases of the architectural design process. Each phase is outlined independently, and the means for evaluating the design against a base case are given.

Campbell, Robert, Daylighting: Research and Design, *AIA Journal,* June 1983, pp. 63–65.

The author reviewed the 1983 International Conference on Daylighting in Phoenix. Design and research were the two fundamental issues discussed at the conference. The author concluded that the two needed to be more integrated to achieve more successful results.

Dean, Andrea Oppenheimer, Commodity, Firmness, Delight—and Energy, *Architecture,* April 1985, pp. 63–65.

This is an overview of the current attitudes about energy in the architectural profession. Advances in computer and building technologies, along with a heightened ecological awareness by those entering the profession, are fueling a resurgence in energy conservation through building design. Soon buildings might be judged on the basis of energy conservation along with their aesthetic and functional features.

De Nevi, Donald, Master of Natural Light: Frank Lloyd Wright, *AIA Journal,* September 1979, pp. 63–65.

Early in his career Frank Lloyd Wright realized that glass would become a major building material because it would let different types of light (diffused, reflected, refracted) enter a space. Wright believed that light elevates the human spirit to a higher order. He used ribbon windows, clerestories, corner windows, trellises, overhangs, translucent roofs, skylights, and atriums. Each of these has a different effect on lighting. Wright went to great extremes to integrate electric light near the source of natural light.

Eacret, Keg M., *Beamed Daylighting: Historical Review, Current Testing and Analysis and Design Options,* Fifth National Passive Solar Conference Proceedings, October 1980, pp. 1174–1178.

This paper discusses the results of testing of various beamed daylighting prototypes, the findings of a review of patent documents in the field, and some options for design using beamed daylighting techniques.

Evans, Benjamin H., *Daylight in Architecture,* McGraw-Hill, New York, 1971.

This design-oriented book is intended as a primer. It is strong on basic concepts and model testings and is a good place to start for those entering the field.

Evans, Benjamin H., Basics of Daylighting, *Architecture,* February 1981, pp. 78–85.

The article condenses much of what the author wrote in his book *Daylight in Architecture.* None of the items mentioned can ensure that a building will be well designed; however, when architects combine the natural and built environment through daylighting, the results are generally a more beautiful, stimulating, and humanistic architecture.

Evans, Benjamin H., and Nowak, Matthew, Effects of Direct Sunlight on Building Interiors and Subsequent Skylight Studies, *Illuminating Engineering,* 54:715–721, 1969.

This article discusses an interesting procedure using a dome sky in conjunction with a separated sun machine for the purpose of superimposing results to obtain daylighting predictions.

Hass, Eileen, *Natural Lighting: How to Use Daylight,* SolarVision Publications, Churchill-Harrisville, N.H., 1982.

This book offers an overview of the basic concepts and applications of daylighting. It contains input from many of the foremost experts in this field and has interesting sections on analysis methods, daylighting codes, and availability of daylight in urban areas.

Hattrup, M.P., *Daylighting Practices of the Architectural Industry* (baseline results of a national survey), Pacific Northwest Laboratory, Richland, Wash.

This report was prepared for the U.S. Department of Energy by the Batelle Memorial Institute and the Pacific Northwest Laboratory. "This survey was conducted to develop a more accurate profile of architects' knowledge, perceptions, and use of daylighting in commercial building design." The profile was required to determine how much D.O.E.-sponsored research has been incorporated into daily practice.

Heerwagen, Judith H., Windowscapes: The Role of Nature in the View from the Window, *Proceedings I, 1986 International Daylighting Conference,* pp. 352–355.

The author recently conducted research at the University of Washington on "Decor in Windowed and Windowless Offices." People who were in offices that had a view of nature through a window had much less in the way of decor. People in windowless offices tried to compensate for the lack of view by creating a surrogate view. View combined with good daylighting design should provide a more hospitable work environment.

Heerwagen, Judith, and Heerwagen, Dean, Energy and Psychology: Designing for a State of Mind, *AIA Journal,* Spring–Summer 1984, pp. 35–37.

The main point of this article is that once we have a better understanding of the relationship between the built environment and its occupants, we can create the illusion of a better environment. Theoretically, the actual comfort level could be lower than the perceived comfort level. This would be extremely effective for energy conservation measures.

Heschong, Lisa, An Interview with William Lam, *Solar Age,* August 1980, pp. 30, 33.

William Lam has been a lighting design and building systems consultant for the past 19 years. This article presents several interesting views on daylighting design and resultant environments.

Hopkinson, R.G., Petherbridge, P., and Longmore, J., *Daylighting,* University College, London, 1966.

This text is an excellent resource for daylighting research and design methods, including sections on sky luminance, daylight photometry, models, and artificial skies. It is dated in that it does not include more current IES methods. It contains good bibliographical references at the conclusion of each chapter.

Illuminating Engineering Society of North America, *Recommended Practice of Daylighting,* IES, New York, 1979.

This publication is a very good source for daylighting information. The appendix goes through typical examples of the IES method. Charts and tables required for this procedure are included.

Jewell, J.E., Selkowitz, S., and Verderber, R., Solid-State Ballasts Prove to be Energy Savers, *Lighting Design and Application,* January 1980, pp. 36–42.

This article presents the results of a research project testing solid-state ballasts for fluorescent lighting versus the typically used core-coil ballast. Graphs and tables are used to clarify the conclusions indicating that solid-state ballasts outperform the commonly used core-coil ballasts.

Johnson, Janith E., *Facility Program for a Participatory Environment Responsive Educational Facility,* Master's Thesis, California State Polytechnic University, Pomona, 1987.

This is a programming portion of a master's thesis completed by a graduate student of architecture at the California State Polytechnic University in Pomona. The program is for an educational facility at the San Bernardino Valley College. The program reviews the various energy conservation strategies to be used along with outlining the space requirements. There is also a brief site analysis that includes the climatic conditions.

Johnson, Janith E., Ander, Gregg D., and Addison, Marlin, *Daylighting Design Analysis: SCAQMD Headquarters Facility, Diamond Bar, California,* Southern California Edison, Rosemead, Calif., 1989.

This report makes recommendations on ways of conserving energy through the use of daylighting on the proposed South Coast Air Quality Management District (SCAQMD) Headquarters facility. The conclusions contained within the report are based on the results of daylighting studies conducted on physical and computer (DOE2)–generated models. The report concludes that the building be designed with the combination of a drop ceiling with 4-ft overhangs and 4-ft light shelves.

Johnson, Timothy E., *Low-E Glazing Design Guide,* Butterworth Architecture, Stoneham, Mass., 1991.

This text is complete with detailed descriptions of the physical principles by which low-e glazing works, the different types of low-e glazing, how low-e glazing is manufactured, and different design applications for low-e glazing (warm daylighting and cool daylighting). Also included are some very helpful rule of thumb calculations such as those for room depth for daylighting applications (p. 86) and for determining aperture size (p. 88).

Kaleidoscope, *AIA Journal,* September 1979, pp. 77–85.

This is a series of brief case studies of some recent building projects that employ the use of daylighting as a major architectural element. The projects reviewed include Jorn Utzon's church in Bagsvaerd, Denmark; Walter Gropius' last project in the Rosenthal Glass Factory in Amberg, Bavaria; the Mount Vernon College Chapel in Washington, D.C. by Hartman-Cox; Canadian architect Arthur Erickson's Museum of Anthropology for the University of British Columbia; the Louisiana Museum of Modern Art outside of Copenhagen by Vilhelm

Wohlert and Jorgen Bo; the library at the Institute for Advanced Studies in Princeton by Harrison and Abramovitz; a translucent roof for a Bullock's Department Store in San Jose, Calif.; the Auraria Higher Education Center by Helmut Jahn in Denver; and Paul Rudolph's Christian Science Student Center in Urbana, Ill.

Kluck, Martin, *Shadow Angle Charts for a North-South Profile,* Fifth National Passive Solar Conference, October 1980, pp. 1188–1191.

A method and charts are presented to help visualize and determine shadow angles in the plane of a north-south cross section through a building.

Knowles, Ralph, Sun's Rythm as Generator of Form: Student Models, *AIA Journal,* June 1979, pp. 58–69.

Ralph Knowles, a professor of architecture at Auburn University and the University of Southern California, conducted research on how to make forms that respond to gravity and the sun's daily and seasonal rhythms. Five geometric forms were selected to act as three-dimensional graphs. Results are shown in a series of photographs. The pictures show what could be an aesthetic based off natural conditions.

Lam, William M.C., *Perception and Lighting as Formgivers for Architecture,* McGraw-Hill, New York, 1977.

The psychology of visual perception is a primary thesis in this text. Professional experience is the resource for much of what the author conveys. Many case studies are presented with photographs in the last half of the book.

Lam, William M.C., *Sunlighting as Formgiver for Architecture,* Van Nostrand Reinhold, New York, 1986.

Sunlighting is the use of direct beam radiation to illuminate interior spaces. Design strategies are thoroughly covered and supported with case studies. The book ends with some examples of how to use physical models as qualitative design tools.

Libby Owens Ford Company, *How to Predict Interior Daylight Illumination,* LOF, Toledo, Ohio, 1976.

The lumen or IES method of calculating interior daylighting illumination levels is explained in this publication. This method has become the industry standard. Nine examples are worked out that are useful in clarifying the procedures.

Linn, Charles, Calculating Daylighting for Successful Retail Design, *Architectural Lighting,* January 1987.

The main body of the article describes the energy conservation design process that was used in Salzer's Video Store in Ventura, California. Much of this information is in the architect's own words. A smaller companion article describes the DOE-2 computer energy analysis done by Southern California Edison.

Lord, David, Power Applied to Purpose: Towards a Synthesis of Climate, Energy, and Comfort, *Journal of Architectural Education,* Spring–Summer 1984, pp. 38–42.

There are many examples throughout history in which thermal comfort was achieved without the use of mechanical equipment (comfort in a relative sense, how effective these buildings were is not known). The study of architecture includes a survey of historical accomplishments. Many modern-day masterpieces were derived from architecture from the past. Wright, Le Corbusier, Kahn, and Aalto all used historic precedent. They were also successful in merging art with science to create some "well-tempered environments." It is through the combination of these two diametrically opposed methods of design that well-tempered environments will be achieved.

McCluney, Ross, A Daylighting Checklist, *Solar Age,* April 1985, p. 84.

This one-page outline contains 15 factors to consider when one is using daylighting. It contains good references of other articles that delve into some of the factors in more detail, such as roof monitor design and calculator programs for skylight. The article was taken from the "Notebook" section of *Solar Age* magazine. The author is a principal research scientist at the Florida Solar Energy Center.

McCluney, Ross, and Zdepski, M. Stephen, *Proceedings I, 1986 International Daylighting Conference.* ASHRAE, Atlanta.

This is a bound collection of articles, paper, and abstracts for the 1986 International Daylighting Conference divided into three sections with 17 subsections. At the time of its printing, it represented the most up-to-date publication on the subject of daylighting.

McGuiness, Stien, and Reynolds, John, *Mechanical and Electrical Equipment for Build-*

ings, eighth edition, John Wiley & Sons, New York, 1986.

This textbook on environmental equipment and systems for buildings includes sections on HVAC, plumbing, vertical transportation, and electrical power distribution.

Matthews, Scott, Proving the Benefits of Daylighting, *Architectural Record,* August 1981, pp. 46–51.

The article describes buildings in which daylighting was used as an energy-conserving strategy. Three buildings were mentioned: the Gregory Bateson Building in Sacramento, Calif.; the Philippine Government Service Insurance Building in Manila; and the Department of Interior Building in Provo, Utah.

Matthews, Scott, and Calthorpe, Peter, Daylight as Central Determinant of Design, *AIA Journal,* September 1979, pp. 86–92.

Much of the article is dedicated to describing the daylighting features of the Tennessee Valley Authority Chattanooga Office Building. The most unique feature is the atrium space with its louvered control system. The rest of the article describes the various analyses used and explains their results.

Meyers, Marshall, Masters of Light: Louis Kahn, *AIA Journal,* September 1979, pp. 60–62.

In the article, attention was given to the design of the reflector positioned below the skylight. Kahn wanted people to be able to see through the skylight while reflecting light onto the ceilings. Kahn was well aware of the psychological aspects of the view, connection to the outdoors, and orientation that comes with the use of daylighting. The design of the reflector was challenging; it needed to be transparent while protecting the art from direct sunlight.

Moore, Fuller, *Concepts and Practice of Architectural Daylighting,* Van Nostrand Reinhold, New York, 1986.

This good text on the fundamentals of daylighting is well supported with graphics. Simpler and more direct to use than other texts on the subject, it covers all of the major issues pertaining to daylighting and includes a glossary and seven appendices to supplement the material given.

Moore, Fuller, Daylighting: Six Aalto Libraries, *AIA Journal,* June 1983, pp. 58–69.

This is a good short article into the aesthetics of daylighting. Aalto used daylight for its aesthetic values. The manner by which he used it resulted in a very unique and humane architecture.

Moore, James, Daylight in Manhattan, *Solar Age ,* December–June 1981, pp. 32–36.

New York City's first zoning regulation in 1916 recognized the importance of light reaching the street and lower floors of buildings. The regulation established a series of set backs and sky planes to control building form and allow sunlight to reach the ground. The set of regulations became the model for many other cities in the United States and Europe. In 1980 the city recognized the need to update the zoning to once again provide sunlight at street level. The best example that they could find was the original New York City Zoning Regulation of 1916. They revised this regulation and also developed a "Daylight Map."

Navvab, Mojiaba, Daylighting Control Techniques, *Architectural Lighting,* October 1988, pp. 44–46.

This article describes daylighting control techniques from a unique perspective. Control techniques are divided into three groups: exterior, glazing, and interior. The pros and cons of each is briefly given. Also discussed is a new control concept, the dynamic envelope.

Navvab, Mojiaba, and Selkowitz, Stephen, *Daylighting Data for Atrium Design,* paper presented at the Ninth National Passive Solar Conference, August 1984.

A research report supported by the U.S. Department of Energy, this paper focuses on the architectural design characteristics that affect the admittance of solar gain and daylight in atriums. Testing was done on a series of physical models in a sky simulator located at the Lawrence Berkeley Laboratories. Results are given in terms of geometric factors and sky conditions. The report concludes that many factors are involved in daylighting design and that the presence of an atrium is not sufficient to guarantee adequate amounts of light within buildings.

Ne'eman, Eliyahu, A Comprehensive Approach to the Integration of Daylight and Electric Light in Buildings, *Energy and Buildings,* June 1984, pp. 97–108.

For daylighting to be energy and cost efficient, it must be integrated with the space that it will serve. Of the many factors that the designer must consider, human performance is the most important. Energy management is essential for cost savings. Daylighting performance is also evaluated according to its effect on the heating and cooling loads. The selection of a daylighting strategy should be based on the overall performance and the cost benefits.

Olgyay, Aladar, and Olgyay, Victor, *Solar Control and Shading Devices,* Princeton University Press, Princeton, N.J., 1976.

This classic text on designing shading devices begins with a historical overview of indigenous responses to shading and ends by outlining a detailed analysis and design process. Photographs of many different shading devices are used to support the authors' claims.

A Perspective on Daylighting Design, *Architectural Record,* Mid-August 1981, pp. 44–45.

Many design tools are available to assist architects in daylighting design. They range from sophisticated main frame computer programs to hand-held calculators to three-dimensional models made out of cardboard. The benefits of daylighting beyond the energy conservation aspects were reiterated in this article. They include view, connection to the outdoors, and health.

Peters, Richard P., Masters of Light: Alvar Aalto, *AIA Journal,* September 1979, pp. 53–55.

Alvar Aalto was truly a master when it came to light and architecture. Windows, light scoops, and clerestories were used as major design elements. He used these design elements to control daylighting. Artificial lighting, as well as daylighting, was viewed as an integral part of his building design. His buildings were so well done that the article concludes by saying that "Aalto's architecture is light."

Phillips, D., *Lighting in Architectural Design,* McGraw-Hill, New York, 1969.

This book covers lighting from a design point of view. Principles and criteria useful in establishing design goals are discussed, as well as natural and electrical strategies. Computational techniques are also covered but are dated.

Place, Wayne, and Howard, Thomas C., *Daylighting Multistory Office Buildings,* North Carolina Alternative Energy Corporation, 1990.

This simple, easy to follow book offers designers a set of design guidelines for daylighting multistory office buildings. These guidelines include building massing (orientation), light shelves, mirrored systems, tracking systems, interior surfaces, and lighting controls.

Pritchard, M.D.W., *Environmental Physics: Lighting,* American Elsevier Publishing Company, New York, 1969.

Basic fundamentals are thoroughly reviewed. Metric units are used throughout, which may be confusing for those accustomed to English units.

Robbins, Claude L., *Daylighting: Design and Analysis,* Van Nostrand Reinhold Company, New York, 1986.

This is a valuable two-part handbook that explores the fundamentals of daylighting. The first part presents the principal sources, control devices, and analysis methods used in daylighting. The second part contains reference material needed to supplement the design methodologies given.

Rosenfeld, Arthur H., and Selkowitz, Stephen E., Beam Daylighting: An Alternative Illuminating Technique, *Energy and Building,* January 1977.

This article is concerned with the energy savings and peak power reductions associated with the maximum utilization of natural light. The general characteristics of diffused daylighting are discussed in terms of a standard office plan. An innovative technique of daylighting using direct beam radiation from the sun is treated in some detail.

Ross and Baruzzina, Inc., *Lighting and Thermal Operations: Energy Conservation Principles Applied to Office Lighting,* Federal Energy Administration, Washington, D.C., 1975, ir NTIS PB-244, No. 154.

This report gives a detailed investigation of relationships between office lighting (specifically levels and orientation with respect to task) and visual task performance. Its conclusions are strong arguments for reduced light levels and more careful lighting design.

Ruck, Nancy C., Editor, *Building Design and Human Performance,* Van Nostrand Reinhold Company, New York, 1989.

Contributing experts explore the interrelationship between the thermal, visual, and acoustic element of buildings and the occupants within. It includes major sections on daylighting and glazing materials.

Selkowitz, Steven E., *Influence of Windows on Building Energy Use,* paper presented at the Windows in Building Design and Maintenance Conference, Gothenburg, Sweden, June 1984.

The article focuses on heat loss, heat gain, and daylighting. The article concludes that cost is assumed to be the driving factor behind the more conservative design approaches, which have a faster return on investment. The text is supported with some good graphs and diagrams in addition to a list of conclusions at the end of the article.

Selkowitz, Stephen E., Effective Daylighting in Buildings—Revisited, *Lighting Design and Applications,* March 1986, pp. 34–47.

"Buildings are not designed to save energy; they are built to convert energy and other physical resources to produce a useful output and to provide a pleasant and healthy environment for human activities." Although the main emphasis of this article is on daylighting, the author reminds us that there are other important issues involved in building design.

Selkowitz, Stephen, and Johnson, Richard, The Daylighting Solution, *Solar Age,* August 1980, pp. 14–20.

This article reviews the electricity consumed for lighting by residential and office buildings. It looks at the economics involved in saving electricity by reducing lighting loads, and it goes into the control of daylight.

Sobin, Harris, Master of Natural Light: Le Corbusier, *AIA Journal,* September 1979, pp. 56–59.

Le Corbusier believed that "the facade would fulfill its true destiny, it is the provider of light." With this in mind, he created a typology of windows to provide adequate light within a space. Unfortunately, the "window walls" failed because of severe overheating during the summer months. However, Le Corbusier traveled to Africa and became fascinated with the vernacular solutions to his problem. He utilized shade, ventilation, and mass in his new architectural language. Le Corbusier used daylighting to accent, intensify, or delineate space.

State of California, Office of General Services, *Cookbook for Energy-Efficient Classroom Design,* Sacramento, Calif., 1984.

Thirty-five recipes for making classrooms more energy-efficient are outlined in this book. The format, which is geared to a nontechnical audience, is simple and easy to follow. The purpose of the book is to explain to school district officials different strategies that are known to be both energy efficient and cost effective.

Stein, Richard G., Observations on Energy Use in Buildings, *Journal of Architectural Education,* February 1977, pp. 36–41.

This article outlines studies that determined where energy is used in buildings and areas in which substantial amounts of energy could be saved. This is a good article to reference for energy use data. Texts and charts support the need for daylighting applications. Of particular interest was the fact that office building lighting systems provide more than 100 footcandles, whereas prefluorescent and English standards show that 30 footcandles are sufficient. This reinforces the theory that lighting levels in the United States are unnecessarily high.

Sweitzer, G., Arasteh, D., and Selkowitz, S., Effects of Low-Emissivity Glazing on Energy Use Patterns in Nonresidential Daylighted Buildings, Low-E Coatings (ASHRAE Symposium on Fenestration Performance, 1987) *ASHRAE Transactions* vol. 93 (part I), 1987.

This paper shows the results of test data on window performance in two climates: Madison, Wisconsin and Lake Charles, Louisiana. The focus on testing was to improve occupant comfort through better fenestration design. The increased R-value of the glazing provides significant savings in cold climates (e.g., Madison, Wisconsin) and is also beneficial in hot climates.

Technology Pursues, Catches, Daylight, *Architectural Record,* Mid-August 1981, pp. 58–59.

This is a brief case study into the design of the Lockheed Missile and Space Company, Building 157, in Sunnyvale, Calif. This building uses a daylighting energy conservation design strategy. Much of the design is standard practice (orientation, model testing, etc.). Two unique features are 12-ft deep lightshelves (which also act as electrical raceways and house air conditioning ducts) and the "litetrium." DOE2.1 computer energy analysis runs predict energy savings of approximately 50%.

Terraced Pods Invite Daylight and Breezes, *Architectural Record,* Mid-August 1981, pp. 53–58.

This is a case study of the Government Service Insurance System Headquarters Building in Manila, by Jorge Y. Ramos. This building has many interesting design features that respond to the natural surroundings. The upper level steps back to facilitate the daylighting aspects of the design. The building is "notched" to break up the mass and direct cooling breezes. The article is well documented with graphics and photographs. This building can serve as a very good prototype for a daylight building in a hot, humid climate.

Terman, M., The Photic Environment and Physiological Time-Keeping Light, *Proceedings I, 1986 International Daylighting Conference,* p. 356.

Human physiology evolved to synchronize with the daily solar cycle. Light exposure in the evening inhibits the production of melotonin. Melotonin is a hormone that helps induce sleep. It responds to different light intensities by varying the amount of photoreceptive substance in the retina. Studies have shown that their melotonin production runs free, causing fatigue to occur at varying times of the day. Other studies have shown that without adequate light exposure, humans are vulnerable to insomnia and depression.

Turner, D.P., *Windows and Environment,* Pilkington Environmental Advisory Service, Architectural Press, London, 1971.

This book offers excellent qualitative treatment of daylighting in the first section and excellent technical treatment in the second part.

Vezey, E.E., and Evans, B.H., The Study of Natural Illumination by Means of Models Under Artificial Sky, *Illuminating Engineering* 50:3667–3674, 1955.

This article includes a very brief description of the dome sky at the Texas Engineering Experiment Station (19 ft in diameter), and informative explanations of procedures regarding models, instrumentation, and model testing.

Villecco, Marguerite, Natural Light, *AIA Journal,* September 1979, pp. 49–51.

All buildings can benefit from the energy savings and psychological advantages of daylighting; however, daylighting is best suited for buildings with intense daytime use such as schools and office buildings. Daylighting is one of many energy conservation issues that require buildings to be designed to integrate with the environment. The location and form of buildings have become the focus for energy-conscious design instead of mechanical systems. Archi-

tects need to become aware of the delicate balance between the two to design buildings that are energy efficient.

Villecco, M., Selkowitz, S., and Griffith, J.W., Strategies of Daylight Design, *AIA Journal,* September 1979, pp. 68–77, 104, 108, 110, 112.

This is a comprehensive article into daylighting design. It is divided into five parts; introduction, controls, integration, analysis, and codes. Each part focuses on an important aspect of the daylighting design process. The article is a good introduction to principles and concepts due to its scope and accuracy. Emphasis is on the qualitative aspects of design instead of the quantitative.

Villecco, Marguerite, Natural Light, *AIA Journal,* September 1979, pp. 49–51.

Daylighting is an energy conservation strategy that requires buildings to be designed to integrate with the environment. "The location and form of buildings have become the focus for energy-conscious design instead of mechanical and electrical system efficiency." Architects need to become aware of the delicate balance between buildings and their environment for them to be energy efficient.

Villecco, Marguerite, Selkowitz, Stephen, and Griffith, J.W., Strategies of Daylight Design, *AIA Journal,* September 1979, pp. 1–7.

This is an excellent short presentation of daylighting strategies with simple, effective graphics. Some simplified analytical case studies showing illumination levels of various designs are also included. This article is a must for the daylighting newcomer.

Visher, Jacqueline C., Psychology of Daylighting, *Architecture,* 1987, pp. 109–112.

As more people become interested in daylighting, more questions about its benefits are being raised. The general consensus is that daylighting has many therapeutic benefits. Exactly what the benefits are is where research is needed.

Vonier, Thomas, Details, Details, *Progressive Architecture,* April 1984, pp. 94–97.

This article briefly outlines the concepts behind some passive energy conservation design strategies. Ventilation, atriums, light shelves, beam daylighting, and skylights were covered. Each topic includes a case study example and details of how it was integrated into the design of an actual building.

Watson, Donald, Three Perspectives on Energy, *Architectural Record,* January 1979, pp. 125–128.

This is an excellent essay on the historical, technical, and social implications of energy conservation. The architectural and technical capacities are available to design buildings that save substantial amounts of energy; what is not available is an attitude that permits this. Social and cultural values must also change if we are to be successful in achieving this goal. Watson outlines three steps that must be taken to implement energy-conscious design standards. One is simple and available; the others require change on a social and cultural level. These changes focus on the qualitative rather than the quantitative aspects of architectural design.

Watson, Donald, The Energy Within the Space Within, *Progressive Architecture,* July 1982, pp. 97–102.

Atriums can be more than just large public spaces with trees and fountains; they can also be used for passive heating, passive cooling, and daylighting applications. Each of these conservation strategies is outlined and includes a set of design goals and guidelines. A useful dot chart shows which strategies work best in the different cities throughout the United States.

Wilson, Forrest, Daylight and the Human Eye, *Architecture,* June 1987, p. 112.

Architects and interior designers have long had concerns that artificial lighting deprives humans of the full spectrum of light distribution. This article contends that human visual perception did not evolve under conditions of the full spectrum. Most light enters the eye only after reflecting off of other objects. Only by staring at a light source or being inside a completely white or gray room would a person be exposed to the full spectrum.

Where Does the Energy Really Go? *Architectural Record,* January 1981, pp. 108–111.

This is a Department of Energy study to determine exactly where energy is being consumed in high-rise buildings. The article describes proposed research on the 26-story Park Plaza Building in Trenton, N.J. It also offers a description of the controls and compliance methodology.

Woodbury, Sally, Governing Energy, *Progressive Architecture,* April 1984, pp. 86–91.

This is a general review of some of the recently completed state office buildings in California. This article briefly describes the master planning, design, and technology that went into these buildings. The four buildings reviewed are the Employment Development Department, the Energy Department, Water Resources, and San Jose State Office buildings. Good sectional and isometric drawings illustrate energy conservation design strategies.

INDEX